TOURISM POLICY AND INTERNATIONAL TOURISM

IN OECD MEMBER COUNTRIES

EVOLUTION OF TOURISM
IN OECD MEMBER COUNTRIES IN 1984

**REPORT ADOPTED IN JULY 1985
BY THE OECD TOURISM COMMITTEE**

ORGANISATION FOR ECONOMIC CO-OPERATION AND DEVELOPMENT

Pursuant to article 1 of the Convention signed in Paris on 14th December, 1960, and which came into force on 30th September, 1961, the Organisation for Economic Co-operation and Development (OECD) shall promote policies designed:

- to achieve the highest sustainable economic growth and employment and a rising standard of living in Member countries, while maintaining financial stability, and thus to contribute to the development of the world economy;
- to contribute to sound economic expansion in Member as well as non-member countries in the process of economic development; and
- to contribute to the expansion of world trade on a multilateral, non-discriminatory basis in accordance with international obligations.

The Signatories of the Convention on the OECD are Austria, Belgium, Canada, Denmark, France, the Federal Republic of Germany, Greece, Iceland, Ireland, Italy, Luxembourg, the Netherlands, Norway, Portugal, Spain, Sweden, Switzerland, Turkey, the United Kingdom and the United States. The following countries acceded subsequently to this Convention (the dates are those on which the instruments of accession were deposited): Japan (28th April, 1964), Finland (28th January, 1969), Australia (7th June, 1971) and New Zealand (29th May, 1973).

The Socialist Federal Republic of Yugoslavia takes part in certain work of the OECD (agreement of 28th October, 1961).

Publié en français sous le titre :

POLITIQUE DU TOURISME ET TOURISME INTERNATIONAL
DANS LES PAYS MEMBRES DE L'OCDE

Photo Cover: Moraine Lake, Valley of the Ten Peaks, Alberta, Canada. (Tourism Canada).

TABLE OF CONTENTS

INTRODUCTION

A. MAIN FEATURES OF 1984

INTERNATIONAL TOURISM IN THE OECD: RECOVERY IS BEING CONSOLIDATED

From the beginning of the decade, international tourism demand in the Member countries of the OECD was in a state of instability. However, towards the end of 1983 there were signs which suggested that a recovery was on the way during the forthcoming year. In 1984 all indicators have shown that this revival is being consolidated. Although this was not true for everyone, this revival enabled a large number of countries to make up for the losses they recorded in 1983 although they could not match the rates of growth that were experienced during the seventies.

Overall, the main trends which the 1984 results for the OECD Member countries as a whole seem to reveal, by comparison with the previous year, are as follows (see also the Table later in this Section):

- Arrivals at frontiers: + 3 per cent (against 0 per cent in 1983)
- Nights spent in the various means of accommodation: + 4 per cent (against + 1 per cent)
- Receipts in real terms: + 7 per cent (against + 2 per cent)
- Receipts and expenditure in current dollars: $70 billion (in both cases).

At the same time a number of detailed trends can also be seen, notably the sustained growth in international tourist flows toward the countries of the Pacific region; a substantial improvement of the situation in the countries of the Mediterranean basin; a contraction in the use of supplementary accommodation by foreign tourists in most of the countries which have the information; a continuing rise in the number of tourists from the United States in all Member countries; and an upward rebound for French tourists (who restricted their foreign travel in the previous year).

Furthermore, the "destination pattern" (that is to say the distribution of tourist flows between different desti-
nations and the split between international and domestic demand) was affected by a number of variables. For example the extent that the economic revival in Europe trailed behind that of the United States once again encouraged foreign travel by North American tourists and supported the evolution of intra-regional and national movements in Europe. Similarly, the variations in exchange rates and the changes in tourist prices and air fares (particularly the North Atlantic routes) reinforced the vigorous competition which had already developed between the various destinations.

In this context, the agents and providers of services, including transport operators, had to take measures to attract clients whose favours were more and more sought after. These efforts were associated with a rationalisation of the commercial practices often associated with those of official agencies responsible for promoting their country as a tourist destination. As far as government authorities were concerned, a number of countries re-examined their policies for developing and controlling the supply of facilities, particularly in those sectors where they were actively engaged.

In this context the Tourism Committee of the OECD has been particularly concerned with the follow-up to the work which it started in 1982 concerning "Obstacles to International Tourism". It will be recalled that a report on the subject as it affected the OECD Area was adopted for general distribution in 1983 and that the main elements of the report, including the conclusions and recommendations agreed by the Committee for its further work, were included as Chapter V of the Annual Report published in 1984.

As a result of these recommendations, the Tourism Committee worked out a draft Decision and Recommendation of the OECD Council on International Tourism Policy. This draft, which was adopted by the

Trend of International Tourism in the OECD area
(per cent change over previous year)

	Arrivals at frontiers[1]		Nights spent in means of accommodation[2]		Receipts in national currency		Receipts in real terms[3]	
	% 83/82	% 84/83	% 83/82	% 84/83	% 83/82	% 84/83	% 83/82	% 84/83
Austria	0.4	0.1	-2.8	-0.8	-0.7	6.6	-3.7	0.9
Belgium[4]			4.5		21.4	10.6	13.5	3.7
Denmark			3.3	-4.4	9.8	12.0	2.4	5.4
Finland			1.8	2.5	-0.8	6.2	-9.0	-0.8
France	1.6		4.2	7.8	19.7	20.6	9.2	12.4
Germany	-1.8			9.9	6.4	11.9	3.4	9.1
Greece	-5.1	15.6	-7.6	17.2	1.9	42.2	-14.1	20.9
Iceland	6.9	9.9			117.2	59.4	19.7	23.5
Ireland	0.1	1.0	8.6	2.9	9.9	13.3	0.2	4.4
Italy	-3.6	5.5	-3.5	-2.1	21.7	10.0	5.8	-0.8
Luxembourg[4]			9.5	10.0	21.4	10.6	13.5	3.7
Netherlands			-2.7		1.9	16.7	-1.1	13.5
Norway	1.4		2.2	7.3	3.9	7.9	-1.2	-0.5
Portugal	17.4	10.9	0.6	5.0	33.4	50.9	6.3	16.7
Spain	-1.8	4.0	3.7	10.9	25.7	26.0	11.9	13.2
Sweden			18.3	3.9	28.0	8.9	15.9	0.8
Switzerland	0.0	3.0	-2.1	-2.8	7.6	12.5	4.8	9.3
Turkey	16.8	30.3	50.2		51.3	120.2	17.0	46.5
United Kingdom	7.4	9.7	6.3	6.8	15.2	14.2	9.4	8.6
EUROPE[5]	-0.2	2.9	1.2	4.1			5.5	7.9
Canada	2.5	7.4	-4.1		6.1	15.1	0.3	10.7
United States		-4.0			-7.9	0.2	-11.2	-2.9
NORTH AMERICA[5]	2.5	7.4					-9.3	-0.5
Australia[1]	-1.1	7.6			9.3	18.0	-0.3	10.6
New Zealand	7.2	12.7			17.9	54.4	8.5	45.2
Japan	9.8	7.2			3.7	17.9	2.0	15.5
AUSTRALASIA-JAPAN[5]	6.1	8.0					1.5	16.4
OECD[5]	0.0	3.2	1.2	4.1			2.2	6.5
Yugoslavia	4.6	5.3	-0.6	19.6	67.0	123.3	18.9	45.7

1. Arrivals of tourists or visitors. Data estimated for Australia.
2. Nights spent in all means of accommodation except in Finland, France(Ile-de-France) and Norway, where nights spent concern hotels and similar establishments.
3. After correcting for the effects of inflation in each country. For the regional and OECD totals, the receipts of the individual countries are weighted in proportion to their share in the total expressed in dollars.
4. Receipts apply to both Belgium and Luxembourg.
5. Overall trends for countries with data available from 1982 to 1984.

Committee at its 49th Session during July 1985, will be submitted to the Council during the autumn. Furthermore, the Committee, working jointly with the Committee on Capital Movements and Invisible Transactions, undertook the updating of the tourism elements in the Code of Liberalisation of Current Invisible Operations. A report making proposals for extending the obligations accepted by Member countries on such matters as the minimum amounts of money and the means of payment that residents may use for settling their expenditure on travel and foreign tourism, will also be submitted to the Council in the autumn of 1985. Together, these proposals will make a significant contribution to the liberalisation of international tourism

which constitutes one of the most important industries in the service sector.

During the same Session in July 1985, the Tourism Committee also noted, with considerable concern, recent incidents in international terrorism involving airlines and other tourism sectors. As the main customer of international air transport, travel and tourism is particularly vulnerable to this. The Committee expressed the hope that the measures taken, within the spheres of their respective competence, by national authorities and the appropriate international organisations would enable them to combat this scourge, while taking care to disturb as little as possible the normal operation of international tourism.

* *
*

During 1984, the volume of the international tourism flows, expressed in terms of the *number of foreign tourists arriving at the frontiers* of the 14 Member

countries for which data is available increased by 3 per cent compared to zero growth in the previous year. This was most pronounced in the Member countries of the

Pacific region which recorded a rise of 8 per cent. In Europe, after the stagnation of earlier years, there were 3 per cent more arrivals and in North America, the pronounced falls in 1982 and 1983 were followed by a flattening-out in 1984 caused principally by the increased flow of American tourists to Canada (+ 7 per cent). Apart from the United States (– 4 per cent) all Member countries who have the information reported a growth in arrivals at frontiers in 1984. This was particularly true for the countries of the Mediterranean basin where Turkey had a rise of 30 per cent, Portugal, 11 per cent and the unfavourable trend of 1983 was reversed in Greece (+ 16 per cent against – 5 per cent), Italy (+ 6 per cent against – 4 per cent) and Spain (+ 4 per cent against – 2 per cent).

Similarly, in the eleven European countries providing information on the number of *nights spent by foreign tourists in hotels and similar establishments,* the modest increase of 1 per cent recorded in 1983 became stronger in 1984 and reached 5 per cent. On one hand, only Italy suffered a decline (of – 1 per cent) and the most vigorous progressions were reported in Spain and Portugal (both + 12 per cent) and Sweden (+ 8 per cent). Furthermore, after two years of decline, both Switzerland and Austria had a modest increase (of + 2 per cent and + 1 per cent).

For *all means of accommodation* a similar 4 per cent rise in the number of nights spent by foreign tourists, took place for the total of the ten European countries with data for 1984. The strongest growth took place in Spain (+ 11 per cent), Luxembourg (+ 10 per cent) and Greece (+ 17 per cent). The improvement in Greece more than outweighed the decline of the two previous years (– 8 per cent and – 2 per cent). If these figures are compared with the figures for hotels and similar establishments for the nine countries with data for both, there was a clear retreat in the use of supplementary means of accommodation in seven of them, with the fall being most significant in Portugal, Denmark, Sweden and Switzerland. Only in Luxembourg and Yugoslavia was a contrary trend observed.

An examination of the breakdown of the flow of tourists from the four most important tourist generating countries, expressed in terms of *arrivals at frontiers* (of 13 Member countries) brings out the following trends:
– A sustained increase in the number of tourists from the United States in all Member countries with a 13 per cent increase in the Pacific region and 14 per cent in Europe;
– A revival in the French market, whose tourists going abroad rose by 2 per cent after a 5 per cent reduction in 1983; and
– An accelerated growth in tourists from Germany and the United Kingdom (+ 5 per cent against + 2 per cent in both cases).

A similar analysis of the flows from these four markets in terms of *nights spent abroad* for the twelve European Member countries who have appropriate information suggests:
– An overall rise in the number of nights spent by tourists from the United States (+ 16 per cent);
– An increase in British and French tourists, of + 12 per cent and + 10 per cent respectively; and
– A three per cent decline for German tourists, with a major impact on the three countries where they predominate, Austria, Denmark and Switzerland.

The total volume of receipts *in national currency in current terms* went up in all Member countries save the United States which recorded zero growth. In both Austria and Finland, their increase (of 6 per cent in both cases) marked a return to growth after a 1 per cent fall in 1983.

In *real terms,* having eliminated the effects of inflation and changes in exchange rates against the dollar, the receipts for OECD countries as a whole expanded at an increasing rate in 1984, by 7 per cent compared to 2 per cent in the previous year. This was due essentially to the growth in Europe which made up four-fifths of the total for the OECD area. In the Pacific region (which contributed 3 per cent to the total) the growth was as high as 17 per cent whereas in North America, the uninterrupted decline over the last three years showed signs of decelerating with a fall of only 1 per cent compared to – 9 per cent in 1983. The countries where the growth was most marked were Turkey (+ 47 per cent), New Zealand (+ 45 per cent), Iceland (+ 24 per cent) and Greece (+ 20 per cent).

Since 1982 there has been approximate equilibrium in the "tourism balance" of Member countries *(in current dollar terms)* and this continued. Between 1982 and 1984, this equality was attributable to the increased volume of expenditure by the countries of North America and the Pacific region (which rose from $22.1 to $26.8 billion), whereas that of the European Member countries went down from $47.7 to $43.5 billion over the same period. In 1984 both receipts and expenditure reached a figure of $70 billion for the OECD as a whole and made up about 4 per cent of the international payments of the area.

In the international air transport sector the provisional information provided by IATA gave their first positive operating results since 1979. Worldwide, 832 million passengers were transported on the domestic and international flights of the airlines of Member states of ICAO, 4.5 per cent more than in the previous year. At a time when some uncertainty still persists concerning the economic viability of certain operations in international air transport, 1984 was a year of self-examination both for the industry and for the governmental and non-governmental organisations associated with it. Recent experience has enabled them to lay the foundations for new policies in a sector which is vital for the

7

development of international tourism. The objective of these changes is to adapt the present system towards a greater flexibility which can produce increased economic efficiency while still taking into account the interests of the tourist as a consumer.

B. PROSPECTS FOR DEVELOPMENT IN CERTAIN MEMBER COUNTRIES

Quantitative data on the prospects for tourism in the OECD area as a whole are not at present available. However, the encouraging signs of continued moderate growth over the next few years can be drawn from the contributions of a number of Member countries which are set out in the following paragraphs.

Australia.   1985 offers good prospects for continued growth of international tourism to Australia. International arrivals are expected to continue to increase in 1985 and a major portion of this increase should be derived from the Americas and Japan following enhanced promotional efforts in these markets. The strong interest in Australia being demonstrated by major operators and airlines in the United Kingdom and Europe indicates that Australia's market position will be improved in this region.

The 20 per cent devaluation of the New Zealand dollar could affect the number of New Zealand international travellers. Given Australia's strong competitive position in New Zealand, Australia would be hoping to improve its market share.

Tourism is expected to have a significant role in continuing and enhancing the recovery of the Australian economy throughout 1985. Its effect will be particularly felt in relation to employment and foreign exchange.

Austria.   On the occasion of the 1984 Austrian Conference on Tourism, the Ministry of Trade asked the Austrian Economic Research Institute to prepare a study of the current situation of tourism in Austria and the outlook up to the year 2000.

The aim was first to identify the basic conditions governing future development of both international and Austria tourism, demographic, economic and education trends, changes in working conditions and the working week, technical aspects, etc.

Starting from this fundamental evaluation, trends and openings for Austria tourism were to be identified. Existing and foreseeable limits to supply, for example natural environment resources and the structure of capital investment, were to be taken into account here.

The main findings and forecasts can be summed up as follows:

- The slowdown in growth and the resulting deterioration in the overall economic situation over the past decade have been reflected in slacker tourism demand, more marked in Austria than elsewhere in Western Europe. The increase in the number of nights foreigners spent in Austrian hotels, which had been some 8 per cent per year between 1960 and 1973, fell to an average of about 1 per cent over the past ten years.
- In Western Europe, demand developed both before and after the pronounced slowdown in growth in 1973, and more markedly than the economy as a whole or private consumer demand. In Austria, however, development reversed in 1973, so that tourism demand fell behind general economic growth. This means that there was a loss of market share, particularly in the summer, and mainly with regard to the German market.
- Winter-season trends were better, both quantitively and qualitatively.

The outlook for the future development of tourism is as follows:

- The number of nights spent by foreigners is likely to increase in Western Europe up to the year 2000 by some 2¾ per cent per year, whereas economic growth will be about 2 per cent. The number of nights foreigners will spend in Austria will probably increase by 2 per cent per year.
- Up to the year 2000, Austria's real income from international tourism will increase by 2½ per cent per annum, and will thus slightly exceed the growth in the number of nights. During the same period, the number of nights spent by nationals will probably increase by 1¾ per cent per year, a little less than the long-term growth of the economy and the growth in the number of nights spent by foreigners.
- The increase in average incomes will be accompanied by an increase in the amount of free time and a subsequent reduction in the number of hours worked. Paid holidays have already begun to lengthen in several European countries. The increase chiefly affects minimum holiday periods, so it is, above all, younger people who will benefit.
- The various types of working leave granted for training or retraining purposes will come to be increasingly important.
- There will also be an increasing tendency for all income groups to take several holidays each year, for shorter periods.

- According to current forecasts, demographic growth in European countries will fall until 2000. There will be a larger percentage of elderly people in the population. This change in age-group structure will no doubt alter overall behaviour with regard to holidays and travel.

Canada. Results for 1984 show an increase over 1983 in the number of both United States and overseas visitors to Canada. This increase is encouraging in view of the decreasing trend in overseas travel to Canada since 1981. There have also been fewer Canadians travelling in the United States. The problem was the large increase in the number of Canadians travelling in overseas countries. These opposing travel trends will result in a stabilizing travel balance-of-payments deficit for 1984 at the 1983 level in real terms.

Assuming that the Canadian consumers will remain confident although somewhat uncertain about the economy, that personal income in Canada will assume a moderate growth rate, that inflation will remain low in Canada and that the Canadian dollar will stabilize vis-à-vis other currencies, travel between Canada and the United States is not expected to change significantly in 1985 from the 1984 level. There may be a slight increase in United States travel to Canada and in Canadian travel to the United States, but these changes will be minimal, less than 1 per cent for United States to Canada and 2 per cent for Canadian travel to the United States.

Travel to Canada from overseas countries will increase at a rate somewhat slower than that realised in 1984, around 4 per cent. Canadian travel to these countries will continue to increase although at a reduced rate, around 3 per cent compared with 14.8 per cent in 1984.

Overall, Canada's international travel balance-of-payments deficit will worsen and surpass the C$2.6 billion mark, consequent upon an increase in receipts of 6.5 per cent and in payments of 11.6 per cent. Canada's travel receipts from the United States and overseas countries are expected to increase by 13.8 per cent and 6.3 per cent respectively while payments would rise by 12.2 per cent and 12.8 per cent respectively.

France. A number of working groups have been set up within the Administration, which include non-governmental participants with experience in forecasting studies. In parallel with these, the *Conseil Supérieur de Tourisme* has been instructed by the Minister to undertake a work programme of forecasting and forward evaluation. The outcome of these studies will be brought together for comparison during 1986.

Ireland. *Bord Failte's* short to medium term plans are based on the revenue growth rates for Irish export tourism. From 1985 to 1989, their annual increases are expected to be respectively 6.5 per cent in 1985, 4 per cent in 1986 and 3 per cent each year from 1987 to 1989.

A continuing strong surge in receipts in 1985 is expected, mainly arising from an increase in United States visitors. Despite an anticipated weakening of the dollar in 1985, European destinations will remain competitive and attractively priced for United States tourists in 1986. A further increase in American visitors is anticipated.

The main assumptions made in relation to these growth rates are that:

i) International economic recovery will continue for the next two years but will show signs of faltering in 1987. Growth will ease off in 1988. Unemployment will remain at high levels particularly in Europe during the five-year period;

ii) Inflation will remain at about 4 per cent to 5 per cent per annum;

iii) The dollar will fall in 1985 and will stay at about 80 per cent of its current level for the duration of the period. The Deutschmark will continue to appreciate within the EMS;

iv) No major changes in holiday entitlement will occur. Such innovations for coping with the unemployment problem as job sharing or a shorter working week, will not be on a wide scale and will not impact accordingly to any extent on holiday taking;

v) The level of international terrorism and violence will remain at present levels. No deterioration in the international political climate will occur;

vi) No protectionist measures will be introduced by any major tourist generating country;

vii) Notwithstanding these individual items, it is assumed that no major international shock of an economic, political or other nature will occur in the next five years which will adversely affect tourism.

Italy. The economic recovery noted in 1984, the slowdown in inflation (expected to be 7 per cent in 1985 as against 10 per cent in 1984), the rise in the value of the dollar and the agreement reached on the industrial relations front are all factors which should have a positive effect on the 1985 tourist season in Italy and should reverse the trend towards zero growth observed in the last three years.

The intense efforts to promote tourism from both non-European and European countries should attract tourists from Canada, the United States and Japan, bearing in mind that two major symposia will be held in 1985, i.e. the ASTA Symposium to be attended by over 8 000 travel agents and tour operators from the United States and the ABTA Symposium with some 2 000 British travel agents. The first is to take place in Rome in November 1985 and the second in Sorrento late in October. In addition, 1985 has been declared the "International Year of Youth" as well as the "Year of the Etruscans" and the "European Year of Music".

Italy has supported numerous initiatives to promote the development of international tourism in collaboration with other interested government bodies.

Lastly, the use of the mass media has enabled the Valtellina – the scene of the world skiing championships – to increase the interest of a large section of young people for sporting tourism.

Current trends show marked interest in a variety of new fields, including, in addition to cultural tourism, tourism linked to congresses, agriculture, thermal cures, etc. This being so, more diversification and specialisation of demand is to be expected in line with the natural resources offered by the various international "tourism centres".

A common strategy at Community level must not overlook these trends if it is to avoid aggravating competition between countries in the Mediterranean area.

Netherlands. A report, produced by the Netherlands Institute for Recreation and Tourism, has made the following predictions on 1985 demand levels:

- A standstill in total demand with the number of holidays taken by nationals steady at 12.7 million;
- A tendency to make more trips within the country rather than abroad rising from 48.7 per cent of all trips in 1984 to 49.4 per cent in 1985;
- An increase in the number of short stays, particularly during the winter, in rented cottages or bungalows as well as in second homes or caravans on more or less permanent sites;
- A decline in the popularity of camping holidays; and
- A rising trend in foreign tourism to the Netherlands.

Norway. To help in the development of a forecasting analysis of the tourist trade, the Institute of Transport Economics has elaborated a model for policy and sensitivity calculations concerning hotel accommodation and its use. The model is based on the trends over recent years. Taking 1982 as a basic year and forecasting through to 1990, the main elements and hypotheses were as follows:

- The Regional Development Fund and its loans, loan guarantees and support for new construction: – 50 per cent on present levels;
- Tendencies to reduce and reorganise hotel capacity: no change;
- Average prices for accommodation: + 0.9 per cent per annum over average inflation;
- Government support for marketing abroad: + 30 per cent;
- Gross National Product (GNP) in the most important foreign tourist markets: + 1.4 per cent per annum;
- GNP in Norway: + 1.9 per cent per annum;

- Air fares to and from Norway: – 0.8 per cent per annum;
- Real prices of petrol in Norway: no change; and
- The development of consumer prices in Norway and abroad: the same when measured in dollar terms.

The conclusions of the model were:

- Demand for hotel accommodation by foreigners will increase by 3.8 per cent per annum, for supplementary accommodation by 2 per cent per annum and in total by 2.9 per cent per annum;
- Expenditure per bed-night is expected to increase by 1 per cent;
- Income will increase by 3.9 per cent per annum;
- Of the elements examined, the support for new construction and support for marketing abroad were found to be the most significant.

The premises for change put into the model may seem rather drastic. In conclusion these calculations point in the direction of an annual average increase in the tourist income of 3 per cent. In the first few years the increase may be somewhat below this value, but from 1986 onwards, it is likely to be more vigorous than the prediction.

The Institute of Transport Economics has also examined the holiday surveys and the number of Norwegians spending their holidays abroad. Compared with the 1970s, the future increase does not seem to be so marked, which suggests that the development of holidays abroad has reached a certain level of saturation. To 1990, the annual increase in summer holiday trips abroad is estimated to reach 2.8 per cent, while for other seasons, the average is estimated to be 3 per cent. Allowing for the increase in the Norwegian population, this would give a 1990 value of 130.6 (1980 = 100).

A similar use of the model covers tourist expenditure abroad, including business travel and frontier trade, based on a 2.3 per cent per annum increase in the rate of private consumption, equivalent to between 1.5 and 2 per cent. This contributes to an increase of 1 per cent in the total cost per trip that each tourist undertakes over the period 1982-1990. On these and the foregoing hypotheses, Norwegian expenditure on tourism abroad is expected to increase by 4.2 per cent per annum until 1990.

Portugal. Portugal is price-competitive, and given the optimistic outlook for the development of international tourism, could increase its share of the market.

The escudo is likely to remain weak against the dollar, the currency most used by tourists, and this too may increase the likelihood of a satisfactory year for tourism in 1985 at a time when Portugal's external competitiveness seems especially strong.

On the basis of the 1984 data, the forecasts for the period 1985-87 are as follows:

	1984 (thousands)	1985 (thousands)	1987 (thousands)	Percentage change 1985/84	Average annual change 1987/84
Arrivals of foreign visitors at frontiers	9 811.0	10 760.0	13 270.0	+9.7	+10.2
Arrivals of tourists	4 118.6	4 593.0	5 911.2	+11.5	+12.8
Nights spent by foreign tourists in all accommodation	36 685.0	40 350.0	48 961.0	+10.0	+10.1
Nights spent by foreign tourists in hotels*a*	9 041.0*	9 820.0	11 560.0	+8.6	+8.5

* Estimate
a) Not including villages and tourist flats.

These forecasts were based on analyses of past developments, taking into account the relationship between historical data, their trends, and comparisons with other statistical series relevant to the development of tourism.

The forecasts for 1985 show a higher percentage of tourists among the total number of foreign visitors arriving at frontiers (43 per cent, compared with 42 per cent in 1984 and 1983), together with a slight reduction in the average length of stay, as has been the case in recent years. The direct consequence of this trend is a slower rate of growth in the volume of nights spent in all accommodation (+ 10 per cent) compared with that of tourists arriving at frontiers (+ 11.5 per cent).

This favourable forecast for the 1985 tourist year was endorsed by the opinions expressed by hotel managers and travel agencies in the business survey carried out by the General Directorate for Tourism in October 1984.

Switzerland. The outlook for the development of foreign tourism is considered to lie between slight growth of about 2 per cent and a decline of about 4 per cent. With regard to domestic tourism, slight growth is expected, after two years of standstill.

Europe. According to the European Travel Commission, United States visitors to Europe in 1985 are likely to reach a record of 6.1 million with expenditure, excluding air fares, of at least $5 billion. The corresponding figures for 1984 were 5.6 million visitors who spent some $4.5 billion. The main reasons for the increase continue to be the strength of the dollar and the pent-up demand for travel to Europe which was postponed in the United States over the period of the recession there. The European countries most visited continue to be the United Kingdom, France and Germany.

There was a strong turn-round in Canadian visitors to Europe in 1984. The Commission estimates that the final figure for the year will be close to the record of 1 068 000 set in 1977 representing an increase of some 40 per cent over a three-year period. The market is growing again as the Canadian dollar maintains its strength against European currencies and the Commission is forecasting an increase of 15 per cent in 1985.

Visitors from Japan also increased from 438 000 in 1983 to an estimted 480 000 in 1984. The Commission is undertaking a series of promotional campaigns aimed at achieving a total of over 500 000 Japanese visitors in 1985.

I

GOVERNMENT POLICY AND ACTION

Chapter I of this Report consists of two parts. A consolidated summary of the overall short- and long-term policy objectives and programmes of Member countries was presented in section A of the 1983 Report. This comprehensive section will be republished every third year with the intervening reports being restricted to changes in overall policies. However, the 1985 Report includes some elements of overall policies, giving information which was not available for the previous Reports. Section B takes up in detail the specific actions and

measures which the OECD governments took in 1984 in pursuit of the overall objectives, with particular reference to development of supply, marketing and international co-operation. In addition, three tables annexed to this chapter provide information on: 1) Travel documents required to visit Member countries; 2) Currency restrictions imposed on residents of Member countries when travelling abroad; and 3) Limitations imposed on foreign tourists concerning importation or exportation of the currency of the country visited.

A. POLICY OBJECTIVES AND PRIORITIES, PLANS AND PROGRAMMES, AND INSTITUTIONAL FRAMEWORK

Australia. The Australian Government has maintained its strong commitment to the development of the tourist industry during 1984 in line with the general tourism policy objectives adopted when it came to office in March 1983. The Government recognises the importance of tourism to the Australian economy and in particular its significance as an employment generator. The Government's overall tourism policy stems from the philosophy which recognises Australia's tourism industry to be a key economic accelerator as well as a key social and educational benefactor.

With its overall policy commitment to the development of Australia's tourism industry, the Government has continued to pursue the two major policy objectives of significantly increasing the number of overseas visitors to Australia, and of encouraging substantial increases in domestic tourism. In this respect increasing the number of visitors to Australia has been targetted to achieve a doubling of numbers by 1988, Australia's bicentenary year. To attain this objective as well as increasing the promotion of tourism domestically, there was an increase in the 1984/85 budget of the Australian Tourist Commission, the national tourism marketing

and promotional body, of 27 per cent to A$24.8 million. This represents an accumulated increase over the past two years of 148 per cent and has enabled the Commission to expand its overseas and domestic promotional activities substantially.

Other proposals and programmes formulated to achieve these objectives include:

- Continued development and upgrading of roads and highways servicing Australia's major tourist destinations;
- Creation of special employment opportunities in tourism projects under special employment generation schemes established by the Commonwealth Government;
- Commencement of the National (formerly Domestic) Tourism Campaign, designed to encourage Australians to see more of their own country and to enhance the awareness of the importance of tourism;
- Negotiations with the airlines for more innovative fares on both international and domestic airlines;
- Negotiations with the States and Territories on uniform licensing legislation for travel agents; and

– Approval for introduction of facilities for limited duty free shopping at Australia's international airports.

In December 1984 the Department of Sport, Recreation and Tourism was re-structured to facilitate the transfer of two offices from other Federal Government Departments. The incorporation of the Australian Information Service (AIS) within the Department creates potential for closer co-operation between the 24 AIS overseas offices and those of the Australian Tourist Commission. The primary role of the Service is to provide information, media material and public relations services to all Australian diplomatic posts. Similarly the Department's second new responsibility, that of the administration of Australia's participation in world expositions, should increase awareness of these events as further opportunities for the promotion of Australia's tourism product.

The functions of tourism policy formulation and tourism promotion remain separate, with the Department of Sport, Recreation and Tourism having responsibility for the former and the Australian Tourist Commission the latter. The Commonwealth Government maintains close links with the State/Territory Governments on tourism matters. A consultative group was established in July 1984 to explore the future of the conventions and meetings industry in Australia. The group, which is chaired by the Department of Sport, Recreation and Tourism, consists of representatives from the Australian Tourist Commission, State/Territory Tourism Authorities, industry organisations and the airlines. The group is supported by an industry/government working party which is expected to submit its draft report in early 1985.

Austria. The Austrian Conference on Tourism was held by the Federal Ministry of Trade and Industry in October 1984, the previous one having taken place in 1980. This Conference is the major meeting held in the Austrian tourism sector; it is a forum for discussion of all essential issues and proposal of policy measures, in the form of resolutions. This particular Conference was, in fact, a centenary event, for it was in 1884 that the first of its kind was held in Graz. This time the Conference set out to define the principles and guidelines of Austrian tourism policy not simply for the four years ahead but, more broadly, up to the end of the century.

One particular question examined at the Conference was the over-use of the natural environment and its relationship to tourism. The discussions resulted in a series of resolutions aimed at improving the situation.

In order to strengthen the position of Austrian tourism on the foreign market even more, a new, supplementary type of incentive was introduced on 1st July 1984. The aim is to encourage the production of leaflets and brochures in foreign languages, as well as promotion tours taking in fairs, exhibitions and other events related to tourism. Funds allocated in the context of aid to agriculture can be used only to modernise holiday flats.

In the framework of the Federal Government's regional policy, special arrangements for promoting tourism in problem regions have been worked out with the Federal *Länder* of Burgenland, Upper Austria, Salzburg and the Tyrol. These special promotion efforts provide for additional aid to be given to regions in difficulty, on the basis of existing schemes for promoting tourism.

The activities related to tourism undertaken by the Ministry of Trade in 1984 were mainly based on the Government Declaration of 31st May 1983, the Ministry's current programme for promoting tourism, covering the period 1980-1989, and the resolutions passed at the 1980 Austrian Conference on Tourism.

Canada. The Progressive Conservative Party was elected to power in Canada in September 1984. This signalled a new era for tourism with the appointment of a Minister of State solely responsible for Tourism.

The major thrust of the new Government will be to encourage co-operation with and within the industry in order to accomplish more, given the limited financial resources available. A document outlining facts and ideas to stimulate discussions was released early in 1985. This is being followed by a series of consultations and seminars across Canada with representatives of all levels of government and the private sector. It is expected that a comprehensive tourism strategy will be developed as a result of these discussions.

The major new directions will be established in more co-operative relations with provincial governments and the private sector. Recent changes in policy already signal a positive thrust in federal/provincial relations. In federal marketing programmes as well, the recent thrust has been to greater co-operation and co-ordination with provincial marketing programmes as well as the private sector. The result has been a shift away from the domestic market for the federal government to avoid duplication of effort with provincial governments, with greater emphasis on the United States and overseas markets.

Denmark. On several occasions, the Danish Tourist Board's target has been discussed, and a political decision has been taken to the effect that the Danish Tourist Board shall direct its efforts to increasing the foreign currency income but not to encourage the Danish domestic market in an attempt to limit foreign currency expenditure. On the basis of this political decision, the Danish Tourist Board started a strategic planning project in the autumn of 1984 with the purpose of defining its role within the Danish tourist trade up to 1990. The project is intended to be finished during autumn 1985.

The national Nordic tourist organisations have come to an Agreement on Co-operation with regard to marketing in the United States. The starting point will be promotion of the Nordic countries as a whole in the United States instead of promoting each country individually. As a result of this co-operation during 1984, the former Swedish office in Chicago is now run as a joint Swedish-Danish tourist office and in Los Angeles the former Danish office is now run as a joint Danish-Swedish office. In Japan, similar co-operation has transformed the former Danish tourist office into a joint Danish-Swedish-Norwegian tourist office.

Finland. As hotel capacity is sufficient in relation to growth in demand and since there has been a tendency to overinvest in certain regions of the country, a bigger part of Government investment subsidies is directed to developing activities and attractions. Government support is also given to the planning of a nationwide reservation and information system based on electronic data processing.

In the marketing field more emphasis is put on opening up new markets, especially outside Europe.

Scandinavian co-operation through the Nordic Tourist Board, for the years 1983-86, was headed by the Finnish Tourist Board.

France. Progress towards the general objectives of France's tourism policy, as outlined in the 1984 issue, is summarised below:

– Continuing priority has been given to enhancing France's tourism products. A further drive has been made to develop a range of products (winter sports, cultural tourism, thalassotherapy, etc.) suited to foreign markets. Facilities for promotion abroad were stepped up in 1984, including a new "business tourism" office in Chicago. The *"Bienvenue France"* (Welcome to France) agency has been reorganised and enlarged to facilitate promotion campaigns in foreign countries;

– Within France itself, the aim has been to improve the way tourism is organised at regional and local level. A policy designed to promote tourist information, local activities and the quality of accommodation and facilities has been implemented at all levels at central government instigation;

– Agreements have been concluded with most agencies, commercial and social, in the tourism sector, to guarantee a continuing high standard of services, improve marketing, and further develop training for staff now dealing with increasing numbers of foreign tourists;

– Lastly, policy on paid holidays and measures to enhance utilisation of leisure time have increased domestic tourism and led to more splitting of holidays, to the benefit particularly of the winter period.

Germany. The Federal Government sets the framework conditions for economic development in all sectors, including tourism, by adopting appropriate principles and measures of economic policy. The Federal Republic's leading position in international tourism is based primarily on a successful policy guided by market economy principles. A major element of this policy is the guaranteed freedom of choice for the consumer and, thus, the unrestricted choice of destinations by tourists. For this reason, the Federal Government's prime tourism-policy objective is to ensure the maintenance and improvement of the conditions necessary to preserve this freedom.

Greece. The 1983-87 programme of economic and social development of the country contains the following objectives for the tourism policy:

– To increase the international competitiveness of the sector through the improvement of the quality of the services offered; increased productivity; the re-organisation of bodies responsible for tourism in order to limit the activities of intermediaries and the underground economy in general; a better determination of the price/quality ratio, taking into account the prospects of development of demand; the blunting and staggering of seasonality with new forms of tourism (spas, winter sports, congresses, social, rural tourism etc.); and revalorisation of demand on a regional basis;

– To make the best use possible of idle or under-utilised capacity with: the creation of the necessary infrastructure; the granting of incentives and the proper organisation and promotion of individual units; and the necessary measures to create employment opportunities, training and education; and

– To implement the proper supply policy aiming at: harmonious relations between areas, accommodation and services; valorisation of traditional settlements; widening of the distribution and promotion of investments with priority given to underdeveloped areas which do not have alternative possibilities; careful development of supply in areas where tourism is competitive with other branches of the economy; and the creation of infrastructure and installations for various types of tourism such as marine and winter tourism, spas, etc.

In order to attain those objectives, measures are being taken and enforced and special programmes will shortly be put into effect to modify the institutional framework and improve programmes of technical education.

More specifically, this re-organisation of responsibilities among the bodies responsible for tourism policy will contain the following elements:

– The regional decentralisation of the services offered by the National Tourist Office of Greece (NTOG);

– The organisation of all tourist agents in each region on a "co-operative basis" with the implementation of the programmes aimed at solving particular prob-

lems in those areas where the tourist enterprises are facing serious survival problems; and
- The promotion of locally administered bodies so that they may participate actively in determining the means to be implemented, indicate the type of tourist development they wish for the regions under their jurisdiction and undertake important activities in co-operation with other bodies, in the protection of the environment, cultural manifestations, the promotion of free access to camping, etc.

Within these frameworks, 1983 and 1984 saw the implementation of the first stages of the transmission of responsibilities for NTOG property to the locally administered bodies.

Ireland. A revised tourism policy objective was adopted in 1984. Its purpose was to optimise the economic and social benefits to Ireland gained by the promotion and development of tourism both to and within the country consistent with ensuring an acceptable economic rate of return on the resources employed and taking account of:
- The quality of life and development of the community;
- The enhancement and preservation of the nation's cultural heritage;
- The conservation of the physical resources of the country; and
- Tourism's contribution to the programme of regional development.

The implications of this change in policy is that greater emphasis in the short to medium term will be placed on economic factors. In pursuance of this policy, primacy will be given to promotions and projects which are aimed at encouraging export tourism.

The responsible body for tourism is *Bord Failte* (the Irish Tourist Board). This is a quasi-independent state agency which reports to and is funded by the Minister for Industry, Commerce, Trade and Tourism. Servicing local tourism development and promotion are the responsibilities of eight (reduced to seven in the course of the year) regional tourist companies. These are independent organisations but rely for most of their funding on the national tourist board.

Italy. The institutional framework of tourism constitutes a complex whole based on relations between the State, as central authority (with policy and co-ordination functions), local authorities responsible for planning and promoting service provision, public bodies engaged in promoting and supporting social, cultural, sport and youth-oriented tourism, and lastly private firms which operate tourist facilities.

In 1984 the structure of tourism in Italy developed in accordance with the policy and objectives set out in the general Act on Tourism of 17th May 1983. Against this background the Ministry of Tourism started talks with the Regions on matters transferred to them at local level.

A recovery in supply was noted as regards diversification and quality of services, thanks to the distribution of available funds (L 300 billion in the three-year period 1983-85) and the adoption of the new classification of hotel and other accommodation (star system) together with a negotiated policy to promote tourism at home and abroad.

In this respect, it should be understood that the attempt to bring Italian tourism within the framework of a single Act can be explained firstly on legal grounds: the "policymaking and co-ordination" functions that central government exercises vis-à-vis the regions had to be made a reality, and an attempt made to reconcile differing local needs and realities while moving towards a common goal. Another problem concerns co-ordination of finance from different sources and to different recipients, i.e. the State, the regions, public bodies, tourist information bureaux, tour operators.

Japan. In accordance with the Japanese Tourism Basic Law which sets out the national tourism policy, the general tourism policy objectives are as follows:
- To stimulate the inflow of foreign tourists and improve reception services for them;
- To establish tourist resorts and routes for foreigners on a comprehensive and integrated basis;
- To ensure the safety of tourists while travelling and make it more convenient for them;
- To facilitate family travel and other travel by the general public;
- To relieve excessive concentration of tourists in specific tourist resorts;
- To develop tourism in under-developed regions;
- To protect, cultivate and develop tourist resources; and
- To maintain the beauty of tourist resorts.

The following objectives were continuously pursued in 1984:
- The development and promotion of international tourism, by encouraging travel to Japan from all over the world by improving the reception services for foreign visitors, by facilitating the smooth travel of Japanese tourists abroad, and by promoting international co-operation in tourism, including technical and financial assistance;
- The protection of tourist resources, by safeguarding the natural and cultural heritage and by maintaining the green areas within cities;
- The improvement of public areas and facilities for tourism and recreation, particularly large-scale recreation areas for appreciating natural resources and the provision of facilities for working people and the younger age groups;
- The improvement of public tourist facilities, notably by developing Youth Hostels, People's Lodges,

National Vacation Villages, and Youth Travel Villages; and

- The protection of the tourist as a consumer and the improvement of facilities for the tourist.

To cope with the changes over recent years in the situation at home and abroad concerning international tourism, the Tourism Policy Council, which was established under the provisions of the Tourism Basic Law, submitted to the Prime Minister in March 1984, the following proposals concerning possible measures and the means to enforce these measures by the Central Government, local governments and tourism-related private organisations working in close co-operation with one another:

- Measures should be taken to equip roads, means of transport and tourism-related facilities with directional signs or explanations written in foreign languages. Furthermore, to assist the safety of foreign visitors, lists of hospitals for foreigners' use, information pamphlets on disaster prevention and information on emergency escape measures in accommodation facilities should be made available. To eliminate many of the inconveniences encountered by foreign visitors because of the language barrier and to respond more adequately to their various needs, the information function of the tourist information centres operated by the JNTO (Japan National Tourist Organisation) and by local governments should be strengthened.
- The information service on inexpensive hotels/ryokan (Japanese-style hotels) suitable for foreign visitors' use should be expanded and the number of those hotels/ryokan should be increased. Minshuku (the Japanese equivalent of a guest-house-type lodging), which more and more foreign visitors have wished to utilise in recent years, provide them not only with inexpensive accommodation but also with an opportunity to experience the Japanese lifestyle. However, minshuku which can be used by foreign visitors are still insufficient in number and geographically limited. In order to increase the number of such minshuku, a grading system should be considered which might enable those well-equipped with the facilities peculiar to minshuku but satisfying approved standards to be registered as "International Tourist Minshuku".
- More Asian languages should be covered by the guide-interpreter system and travel literature in more Asian languages should be produced.
- The following measures should be taken in certain sectors where an increasing interest has been shown by foreign visitors in recent years:
    - i) to meet the demand of foreign visitors for person-to-person contacts with Japanese people and their life, the Home-Visit-System should be made more nationwide and the number of host families should be increased;

    - ii) to meet the demand of foreign visitors for seeing high technology developments in Japan, travel agents should be further encouraged to organise industrial tour routes, visiting plants with modern production equipment and efforts should be made to create an environment that may encourage more plants to accept foreign visitors.

- Eating out constitutes an important part of pleasure travel. The International Tourist Restaurants, registered with the Ministry of Transport, should be increased. At present their number is limited and they are concentrated in large city areas.
- For further promotion of foreign tourist traffic to Japan, a framework of overseas publicity activities, using each overseas office of JNTO as the centre, should be consolidated, particularly in Asia. In conducting tourist publicity activities abroad, efforts should be made to project the total image of Japan's society, economy and culture. Tourist publicity activities abroad should be generally strengthened and made efficient through developing joint projects with host governments in public relations work, travel seminars designed for the overseas travel trade and media assistance programmes for foreign journalists. Joint undertakings with neighbouring Asian countries in the European and American markets should also be strengthened.
- With the rising status of Japan in the world, the number of international conventions or exhibitions held in Japan is increasing. Since these international gatherings are also of importance to the promotion of international tourism, the following measures should be taken to attract more international gatherings to Japan:
    - i) Overseas publicity activities and domestic consultancy services for the planning and operation of international gatherings, which are now undertaken by the Convention Bureau, JNTO, should be improved;
    - ii) It is thought that international gatherings to be held in Japan will be further diversified and major gatherings will increase in number in the future. However, Japan is short of large-scale international convention halls at present, and this constitutes a serious obstacle to attracting international gatherings to Japan. It is satisfactory that interest in the construction of international convention halls is growing in some cities, including the Metropolitan district. Particularly, in the latter where there is a relatively large demand for international meetings, there is an urgent need for the construction of a large-scale international convention hall capable of accommodating major international gatherings. The various problems relating to its construction should be investigated without delay by the Central Govern-

ment, local governments and individuals with appropriate experience.

In the field of international tourism in Japan, the Ministry of Transport functions as the central administrative agency, representing the nation in international organisations and at international gatherings relating to tourism. As far as domestic tourism is concerned, other governmental agencies are also concerned with tourism within their respective scopes of activities, including the Environment Agency, the Ministry of Health and Welfare, the Ministry of Education, the Ministry of Construction and the National Land Agency.

With the reorganisation of the Ministry of Transport which was completed in July 1984, the Department of Tourism forms part of the Bureau of International Transport and Tourism, in the Ministry of Transport.

The Department of Tourism is in charge of administrative functions relating to the development, improvement and co-ordination of the tourist industry. It has three divisions: Planning Division, Travel Agency Division and Development Division, which are responsible for the following matters:

- Planning Division: overall co-ordination and planning of tourism administration; the supervision of the Japan National Tourist Organisation; the improvement of reception services for foreign visitors; research and study on tourism; subsidies to the tourist industry; matters relating to the acquisition of stocks by foreign investors in the tourism sector; collection and compilation of tourism-related documents; and the handling of general affairs for the Tourism Policy Council. In order to improve international relations in the field of tourism, the International Affairs Office was established in 1978, and is now within the Planning Division, with the responsibility for: liaison, co-operation and exchange of information with tourism administration authorities in foreign countries and international tourism organisations; research and study on tourism policies and situations in foreign countries; planning and guidance concerning international tourism publicity; and collection and compilation of international tourism documents.
- Travel Agency Division: supervision of the travel agency business; supervision of travel agents' associations; and supervision of the guide-interpreter system.
- Development Division: financial affairs and taxation relating to the tourist industry; the registration of hotels and ryokan which satisfy certain conditions and standards, and supervision of registered hotels and ryokan; the improvement of the quality of tourist souvenirs; planning and guidance concerning tourism publicity; planning the development of tourist facilities; and giving guidance for the improvement of tourist facilities including the Youth Hostel Centre.

The Tourism and Recreation Planning Office, which is a part of the Development Division, is responsible for: investigating and improving tourist resorts and resources; matters relating to tourism promotion in the comprehensive national land development plans; planning, co-ordination and financial aid for the improvement and development of the Tourism and Recreational Areas and the Youth Travel Villages, etc.; and developing systems for their consolidation; and investigation and research on tourism and recreational activities.

The Youth Hostel Centre, which was established in Otsu City in 1961, is under the control of the Development Division. The Centre gives guidance to the operation of youth hostels in Japan in addition to research and study. It also manages affairs pertaining to the operation of accommodation facilties mainly designed for youth.

The position of Senior Planning Officer for Tourist Industry was established within the Development Division in 1984 with the purpose of investigating and planning the development of the tourist industry.

In accordance with the provisions of the Tourism Basic Law, the Tourism Policy Council was set up in 1963 so that the views and opinions of private and academic circles might be reflected in the tourism administration. The Council is made up of 30 private individuals with learning and experience in the sector, and it investigates and deliberates on important matters relating to tourism. It also responds to inquiries made by the Government and offers opinions to the Government when deemed necessary. In March 1982, the Council submitted to the Prime Minister recommendations concerning "The Theory and Method of Forming Desirable Domestic Tourism", and in March 1984, it submitted recommendations "For the Future Development of International Tourism in Japan".

Luxembourg. The Ministry of Tourism, as in the past, continues to upgrade tourism infrastructures. The 3rd five-year tourism infrastructure investment plan (1983-1987) includes the following objectives:

- Improvement of tourism infrastructures (subsidies to *communes*);
- Upgrading hotels (modernisation, extension, rationalisation);
- Turning cultural assets to advantage;
- Promotion of rural tourism (farm holidays, e.g. lodging at farmhouses).

New Zealand. To assist in achieving the overall policy objective of maximising the economic returns from tourism while at the same time preserving New Zealand's unique lifestyle and environment, the following programmes were undertaken:

- A joint publication, by the Tourism Council and Tourist and Publicity Department, of a report setting goals and strategies for tourism's further development and recommending the policies needed to achieve them;

- The Government has launched initiatives to assist the establishment and further development of regional tourism. It sees particular value in regions preparing their own Regional Marketing Plans (RMP's) and has extended funding to assist with grants for initial RMP's and subsidies for an annual review, regional research and ongoing consultation leading to a partnership between government and regional tourism interests;
- The Tourist Industry Federation has also placed importance on regional involvement. It has three levels of membership, one of these being regional. It encourages representative groups of all tourism's interests to become involved as members;
- The Tourist and Publicity Department has been actively involved in the Te Maori exhibition (an exhibition of Maori Art) in New York and St. Louis, and to date has spent NZ$195 000 from the Department's vote. At both openings, the Department sponsored a ten person Maori cultural group.

Norway. The tourist trade is now becoming increasingly accepted as an export trade, and has been given the opportunity to participate actively in "1985, the Year of Export".

The volume of public loans and support for a further increase in hotel capacity has been somewhat hampered by the tendency to a reduced use of the capacity of existing enterprises. More emphasis has been put on activity measures and on marketing.

The Association of Norwegian Travel Organisations decided on a reorganisation of its general assembly on 4th April 1984. On 1st July 1984, the Norwegian Travel Council was established as a private tourist organisation for the tourist trade. From 1st January 1985, its business activities have been transferred to an independent body. The marketing services are administered by the new commercial enterprise, called NOR-TRAVEL, organised as a foundation. Its capital has been raised jointly by the trade and the government. Governmental marketing support to the tourist industry will be channelled through this foundation and may not exceed 50 per cent of its total income.

Portugal. As part of two moves to build up a regional tourism structure, the region "Verde Minho" has been created. It covers nine municipalities. With this new region there are now thirteen tourism regions in all. They cover 146 municipalities, i.e. over half the *communes* in continental Portugal (excluding Madeira and the Azores). The Government intends to give these regions greater power with regard to the planning and promotion of tourism.

The General Directorate for Tourism has responsibility at national level.

Sweden. The government policy in the tourism and recreation field was presented in the spring of 1984 and was confirmed by Parliament in May 1984. The political guidelines are a further development of the policy laid down in 1976. The objectives of this tourism and recreation policy are:

- To achieve improvement in the Swedish balance of payments and to reach positive effects for regional development and employment by increased development and marketing efforts in tourism;
- To improve the possibilities for all residents to engage in tourism and recreation.

The Government has emphasized the need of investing more resources in European markets, particularly in nearby continental countries. The action programme of the Government to support the development of tourism and recreation includes a wide range of subjects. These activities to which priority should be given include:

- The improvement of the facilities for marketing within the tourism sector;
- The protection of basic resources for tourism and recreation by reserving land in particularly valuable areas and by nature and environment preservation measures;
- The encouragement to construction and enlargement of tourist accommodation establishments and infrastructure in development areas and in regions with underemployment, through loans and subsidies within the framework of the labour market and regional development policy;
- The mandate to be given to the Swedish Tourist Board to develop a structural plan for tourism and recreation with the objective of arriving at a closer co-ordination of measures taken by Government agencies and by local and regional authorities within the framework of tourism and recreation policy;
- The development of tourism facilities for all social groups, particularly for those who at present do not avail themselves of the facilities and arrangements offered in the tourism and recreation field. Action will be initiated through the Swedish Tourist Board to make the necessary adjustments of the products offered, improve information, facilitate booking procedures, etc; and
- The enhancement of research and vocational training in the tourism sector.

The Government's guidelines state clearly that public measures must primarily be directed towards supporting initiatives taken by individual companies and by the tourist industry. The capacity of the enterprises for renewing and developing their establishments will provide the basis for the ability to compete within the tourism sector.

The Government decision on tourism and recreation policy has also brought about some administrative changes. The Swedish Tourist Board has thus from 1st July 1984 been entrusted with a general responsibility for tourism and recreation questions. This implies that certain matters, which were earlier dealt with by the Co-ordinating Committee for Tourism and Recreation and the National Environmental Protection Board have been transferred to the Swedish Tourist Board. The Board has consequently been given statutory power in defined fields of activity.

The organisational structure of the Swedish Tourist Board has been adapted to these additional tasks. The board of directors has a new constitution. A delegation for planning and development questions, with representatives of authorities, has been attached to the board of directors. Representatives of the tourist industry have been appointed delegates to a consultative reference group of the board of directors. The internal organisation has also been adjusted and a new planning department has been established. Marketing will, however, remain the primary task of the Swedish Tourist Board.

Switzerland. The Federal Administration is bound by the tourism policy objectives set out in the "Swiss tourism strategy" *(Conception suisse du tourisme)* and is required to direct its resources accordingly. The main effort is devoted to improving the quality, comfort and utilisation of existing facilities, while preserving the quality of the social and ecological environment.

Over the period 1985-87 the two traditional instruments of tourism policy in the Confederation – i.e. tourism promotion and hotel loans – will be reviewed. Preliminary work has already started. In 1984 the development fund for infrastructures in mountain areas was increased by SF 300 million. Various tourist projects will benefit from this fund. The introduction of a new tourism law in Switzerland is now being considered.

With the transfer of responsibility for tourism and the Tourism Service to the Federal Economic Department, the measures directly linked with tourism could be concentrated in a single office. The Tourism Service now comes under the *Office fédéral de l'Industrie, des Arts et Métiers et du Travail* (OFIAMT) (Federal Office for Industry, Arts and Crafts and Labour). The tasks of this new platform for tourism at federal administrative level are as follows:

- Tourism policy for the Confederation;
- Supervision and funding of tourism promotion (National Tourist Office);
- Supervision and funding of loans for hotels *(Société Suisse du Crédit hôtelier);*
- Financial aid for tourism infrastructure projects;
- Contribution to tourism planning;
- Funding of vocational training for the tourism industry;
- Action on the tourism labour market;
- Secretariat of the Advisory Commission on Tourism;
- Secretariat of the Group of Parliamentarians on Tourism;

- Co-operation with intergovernmental tourism organisations;
- Bilateral tourism agreements with other countries.

United Kingdom. The Government's overall objective is to encourage the development, growth and international competitiveness of the United Kingdom as a tourist destination. The Government aims to achieve this by creating a favourable economic climate for the industry's development and by the provision of financial support through the statutory tourist boards. However, the Government considers that the vast majority of tourism investment should be funded by the private sector.

The statutory tourist boards have drawn up their own objectives which will be reviewed annually in consultation with their sponsoring Departments. The British Tourist Authority (BTA) and the English Tourist Board (ETB) objectives include giving greater emphasis to the promotion of London, which is recognised as the United Kingdom's main tourist attraction.

The tourism review completed in 1983 found there was a need for closer co-ordination and better use of resources by the statutory tourist boards. As a result in 1984 the BTA and ETB moved to shared accommodation and began a rationalisation of many of their functions. Around 60 per cent of the Board's United Kingdom staff are now employed in common services divisions reporting to both Boards. On 1st November 1984 the Chairman of the BTA was also appointed as Chairman of the ETB. As Chairman of both Boards he will be examining the scope for further collaboration between the two Boards and in particular, whether a full merger of the two Boards would be desirable. The latter would require primary legislation.

The Tourism (Overseas Promotion) (Scotland) Act 1984 came into force on 13th May 1984. This Act enables the Scottish Tourist Board to carry out promotion of Scotland overseas. Previously only the BTA was empowered to carry out overseas promotion. The new powers supplement but do not replace the overseas promotion of Scotland by the BTA. Within the existing framework the BTA and the Wales Tourist Board (WTB) have developed closer links to improve the promotion of Wales abroad. The WTB has appointed an Overseas Marketing Director to give added impetus to the development of Wales as a tourist attraction for overseas visitors and the BTA has appointed a Liaison Executive to act as a focus within that organisation for promotional activity overseas on behalf of Wales.

Apart from the above changes the institutional framework of the four national tourist boards remains unaltered. Outside this framework, a number of other bodies also have some responsibility for tourism matters. In particular, the Development Commission (which is wholly financed by the Government) and its agency, the Council for Small Industries in Rural Areas (CoSIRA) are also engaged in developing tourism enterprises and tourism related projects as part of their role of developing the economy of the English Rural Development Areas designated by the Commission.

United States. The United States Travel and Tourism Administration (USTTA) was created by the National Tourism Policy Act of 1981. The Act redefined the national interest in tourism and designated USTTA as the nation's Government tourism office.

The National Tourism Policy Council, an interagency committee which co-ordinates policies and programmes of federal agencies having a significant effect on tourism, met four times during 1984. Meetings concentrated on visitor facilitation and travel-related research and economic development.

The United States Travel and Tourism Advisory Board, composed of public and private industry representatives to advise the Secretary, met twice. The Board reviewed USTTA's international marketing plan, the strategic planning system, accelerated entry procedures, personnel systems and the USTTA marketing concept and test programme.

To increase the effectiveness and productivity of its programmes, USTTA developed a strategic market planning system enabling it to set a series of measurable goals, strategies and programmes consistent with the legislative mandate of the agency and the goals of the Department. This system precipitated automation of many of USTTA's management, policy, marketing and research functions.

Yugoslavia. In pursuit of the basic objectives set in the Social Development Plan 1981-1985, general guidelines to complete the first stage of a long-term economic stabilization programme were determined. Work on the preparation of the new middle-term tourism development plan for the period of 1986-1990 was intensified in accordance with the Resolution on the preparation and implementation of the Social Development Plan for Yugoslavia from 1986-1990 adopted in November 1983 and its related documents.

B. ACTIONS AND MEASURES TAKEN IN 1984

a) Development of supply

Australia. In pursuit of the Government's overall tourism policy the measures taken during 1984 concern funded projects and schemes, conservation and management plans and infrastructural arrangements.

Government Funded Projects and Schemes: The Australian Government increased the depreciation allowance for non-residential income producing buildings and short-term traveller accommodation buildings from 2.5 per cent per annum to 4 per cent per annum. This allows capital costs to be written off over 25 years instead of 40. The Australian Government provided A$26 million for a replacement vessel for the Bass Strait passenger and vehicle ferry service and associated terminal works. The doubled carrying capacity of the proposed vessel is expected to have a significant effect on tourism to the island State of Tasmania. An allocation of A$2 million in 1984/85 was made to support the growth of tourism in the economically depressed Hunter and Illawarra steel regions of New South Wales. This is part of an on-going programme for federally funded infrastructure projects in the regions which will provide A$20 million to 1987/88 for tourism projects. The diesel fuel subsidy scheme provided A$500 000 in 1984/85 for grants to Queensland to assist with the electricity generating costs of Great Barrier Reef island tourist resorts, where reticulated power is unavailable. The Australian Government provides grants to the States and Northern Territory to construct and main-tain roads including roads servicing tourism destinations. In 1984/85, the Government allocated A$1 290 million for roadworks under various programmes.

Conservation and Management Plans: Zoning and management plans for the Great Barrier Reef are continuing to be developed by the Great Barrier Reef Marine Park Authority. The Government's objectives in this area are based on the belief that enjoyment and use of the Reef should be encouraged while at the same time ensuring that its unique natural qualities are preserved for future generations. Conservation and development of the Port Arthur region of Tasmania continued as part of Australia's ongoing programme to maintain the area as one of Australia's most important heritage sites and a focal point for tourism in the area. Funding for the Port Arthur Restoration project will amount to A$9.2 million over the seven years to 1985/86. The Federal and Tasmanian Governments have established joint management arrangements for the Western Tasmania Wilderness National Parks World Heritage area. This follows the Federal Government's decision to provide Tasmania with up to A$5 million over two years for the development of tourist facilities in the region consequent on cessation of work on the Gordon-below-Franklin Dam.

Negotiations with the Northern Territory Government and Aboriginal groups are being undertaken to develop a programme for the development of visitor facilities and park infrastructure in Kakadu National

Park. This programme will bring forward the development of recreation facilities providing for bush walking, nature observation and water based activities and provide visitors with better opportunities to enjoy the Park while not endangering its natural and cultural treasures.

New Infrastructure Arrangements: The Government approved, in principle, the introduction during 1984 of inwards duty-free shopping at Australian international airports. Sales of goods will be limited to the existing passenger concession entitlements for liquor, tobacco products and perfume. From 1st July 1984 new arrangements for awarding car rental concessions at Commonwealth airports have resulted in a greater number of car rental firms being given the right to operate at airport locations, with benefits to travellers. At the Government's urging, in February 1984 the two major domestic airlines introduced new touring fares for international visitors arriving in Australia on international promotional fares. A similar fare structure became available to Australian residents in April 1984. Cairns international airport commenced operations in March 1984. Coinciding with the opening, Qantas commenced a direct air service with the United States West Coast. Major upgrading works commenced or are continuing at Brisbane, Perth and Darwin international airports. Qantas, in conjunction with CAAC (China's national airline), offered special introductory holiday packages to China on commencement of direct air services between the two countries in September 1984. Qantas received the first of its Boeing 747 Extended Upper Deck aircraft in September 1984, as part of its major fleet modernisation programme.

In the tourism industry there has been a growing recognition by both the Government and the private sector that without co-operation between industry, educational institutions and Government, the reconciliation of both industry and tourist market needs will not be achieved. A Tourism Training Review Group has therefore been established with a broad cross-section of representation, to prepare a Report on the state of tourism training in Australia, aimed at ensuring that the future needs of industry are met. The Review Group is considering most aspects of tourism training – including the supply and demand to trained staff, on-the-job and extension training – and the training situation overseas. The Report of the Review Group was to be completed in the first half of 1985. The National Tourism Industry Training Committee is very involved in the Review Group and continues its work through State Industry Training Committees with Federal assistance of A$600 000 in 1984/85.

Austria. In addition to the continuing action which was mentioned in the last OECD report, a new promotion measure must be mentioned. This aims at strengthening the presence of Austrian tourism on foreign tourism markets (see Part A).

In order to ensure that hotels and restaurants can obtain the considerable labour force they require, the Labour Office is organising re-training courses which provide both theoretical knowledge and practical experience.

Canada. As the result of a very positive response and endorsement to the Financial Management Programme – "Tourism is Your Business" – introduced by Tourism Canada in October 1983, the development of a Marketing Management Programme in this series has recently been initiated and will include a similar print/video format. Its primary objective is to demonstrate how sound management practices can lead to improved business performance and increased industry productivity through well planned and executed marketing strategies and techniques.

Tourism Canada actively supported the Canadian Federation of *Chefs de Cuisine* (CFCC) in its participation at the World Culinary Olympics in Frankfurt, Germany, 12th-18th October 1984. The CFCC National Team entry was acclaimed the overall "best team" among 28 competing countries and honoured by the German Association of Chefs as follows: "In all the categories, in all the disciplines of the World Culinary Olympics, the CFCC National Team of Canada has earned the title of culinary world master". This international honour and recognition will make a significant contribution in the promotion of Canadian tourism and its cuisine and firmly establishes a strong awareness of the culinary professionalism by members in Canada's catering and foodservice industry.

A review of the foodservices and hospitality sector is being undertaken by the Canadian Tourism/Hospitality Advisory Council on Human Resources (which is sponsored by Tourism Canada) with a view of studying Canadian tourism/hospitality programmes as to their ability to meet Canada's employment needs for an expanding tourism industry. A study is also being undertaken by the Canadian Tourism/Hospitality Advisory Council on Human Resources on the need for a national certification programme that will include: standardization of courses and programmes, a certification of graduates and programmes and a national accreditation process.

Domestic Air Transportation: A new liberalised air policy was announced in May 1984. The initiatives taken represent the first comprehensive reform of Canadian air policy and include:

– The easing of price regulations;
– Removal of restrictions on competition among carriers;
– The development of community air service projects;
– Direction to the Standing Committee on Transport to determine how further liberalisation should occur;

- Direction to Air Canada to operate in a business-like manner with no unfair competitive practices;
- Equal access to airports for new and existing airlines; and
- Direction to the Canadian Transport Commission to speed up the regulatory process, to acknowledge the benefits of increased competition when examining licence applications and to hold hearings to review air services in the North.

The objectives of the policy are to grant Canadian consumers more attractive fares and services and revitalise the airline industry. In addition, improved service will not only stimulate domestic travel, but research has shown that a drop in air fares prompts an increase at least twice as large in pleasure travel.

Major reconstruction of Canadian airports, including the expansion of airport terminal buildings, was undertaken at Charlottetown, Saskatoon, Sault-Ste-Marie and Whitehorse.

Cultural Heritage Preservation: During 1984 the Government of Canada granted C$five million to the Heritage Canada Foundation, a non-government and non-profit association. The purpose of the grant is to fund the resources necessary to assist up to 70 communities across Canada to restore principal downtown streets, urban cores and street-scapes. This special programme is called Main Street Canada and is designed to preserve cultural heritage and to attract tourists to discover and experience the quality of small town life in Canada.

Important actions taken for National Parks were:
- One World Heritage Site was accepted; Rocky Mountains National Parks (Banff, Jasper, Kootenay, Yoho);
- Mingan Archipelago National Park Reserve was estalished;
- Northern Yukon National Park was established via the Committee for Original People's Entitlement (COPE) land claim settlement – COPE is an Inuit group from the Western Arctic;
- The final draft of the National Marine Park Policy was prepared following consultations with the public and various government departments;
- Studies are continuing for the establishment of a national park in the Bruce Peninsula of Ontario and a national marine park in the west isles of New Brunswick;
- A commitment to establish Pingo Canadian Landmark was set out in the COPE land claim settlement;
- The Canadian Heritage Rivers System was formally announced. Active participants include six provinces, two territories, Parks Canada and the Department of Indian and Northern Affairs. Eight rivers have been nominated to the system; and
- Management plans for Gros Morne and Wood Buffalo National Parks were approved by the Minister of Environment Canada after extensive public consultation.

Important actions taken for national historic parks and sites were:
- The restoration, interpretation and utilities/services development at the Halifax Citadel were significantly advanced;
- The construction of an interpretation centre was undertaken at Restigouche National Historic Site to house the remains of the vessel Machault;
- The fortifications of Quebec were substantially advanced through major restoration and stabilization work;
- The interpretation centre at *le Vieux Port de Québec* was completed;
- The major part of the restoration of St. Andrews Rectory was completed;
- The new visitor interpretation centre at Rogers Pass, Glacier National Park, was opened; and
- Twenty-six historic sites and monuments board plaques were erected.

Tourism Financial Aid Programmes: The Federal Business Development Bank made 499 loans to tourist enterprises, a 42 per cent decrease over the previous year, for a total of C$90.7 million, which accounted for 28 per cent of the Bank's aggregate lending during the year. The Small Business Loans Act authorised loan guarantees in the tourist industry. Under the series of Canada/Provincial Tourism Subsidiary Agreements, Economic and Regional Development Agreements, Department of Regional and Industrial Expansion (Tourism Canada) at the federal level, collaborated with the provincial tourism departments in planning tourism development strategies, special programme assistance for infrastructure, destination area development, industry organisation, manpower standards and various forms of financial incentives for private sector facilities improvement and expansion. These agreements ensure that tourism development is in line with regional as well as national priorities. All agreements are expected to be signed and in effect by mid-1985, with six already signed in 1984.

Under the national tourism incentive programme entitled "Industrial Regional Development Programme", Tourism Canada made direct federal assistance to the tourism industry throughout all of Canada. Financial assistance activity to the tourism industry during 1984 was C$29.5 million. This programme provided financial assistance to tourism businesses and tourism non-profit organisations through grants, contributions, repayable contributions, participation loans and loan guarantees.

Tourism Canada Initiatives: Tourism Canada continues to provide sectoral expertise and a planning framework focused on national and international tourism development concerns. To maximise the net economic benefits of tourism development, Tourism

Canada has designed a planning methodology entitled "Process For Identification, Analysis and Selection of Tourism Destination Areas in Canada" which permits consistent and more detailed tourism factor analysis on a regional basis. To assist this planning and to identify evolving opportunities, work continues on the development of a national computerised data base of resource, product and market data to be linked to an auto-cartographic system. This system will, through a series of internal map overlays, produce a final map displaying those locations in Canada (or in a part of Canada) most suited to a given set of market specifications. The system will also identify those supply factors which need to be influenced so as to increase tourist visitation. Demonstration of this system has been eagerly received in Nova Scotia, Manitoba and British Columbia. Future demonstrations of the system across Canada are being planned.

Denmark. Among its special nation-wide activities in 1984, the Danish Tourist Board:

- Harmonized terms for renting holiday cottages through co-operation with a number of appropriate agencies in order to determine consistent terms of reference with regard to seasons, off-season reductions, cancellation and renting conditions;
- Carried out and consolidated the three nation-wide hotel cheque systems existing in Denmark;
- Developed the national tourist menu system – Danmenu – with the participation of over 700 Danish restaurants;
- Produced, in co-operation with the conservation authorities and the outdoor life organisations, a report on establishing a Danish Ranger system;
- Began establishment of a national electronic data processing system for registration of information about Danish products for tourists, in co-operation with local Danish tourist organisations. This system, called Dandata, will be ready as an on-line information base during 1986;
- Drafted, together with the handicap organisations, special information material for handicapped tourists;
- Elaborated, in co-operation with customs authorities and retail shops in Denmark, more advantageous rules for tax-free tourist shopping.

Finland. Hotel capacity in Finland grew by 4 per cent. As during earlier years, most of the new capacity was added in southern Finland where the use of capacity is also the highest. Government investment support to hotel building in the developing ports of Finland was Mk 69 million.

The emphasis in the training provided by the Finnish Tourist Board was on the organisation of courses held in conjunction with other tourist sectors and on the production of teaching material for training and instructional purposes. The fifth national Symposium on Tourism held in May was the most important seminar on

tourism to have taken place in Finland in 1984. The symposium was attended by 300 delegates and initiated a medium-term plan for tourism marketing. A joint Nordic seminar for senior tourist officers was held in Lappeenranta in November. This third seminar was held on "Culture and Tourism". Other national training events included a national entrepreneur seminar for rural tourism, in-service training for guides, a training session for fishing guides, and a seminar on marketing for marketing and sales managers in the tourist trade. At regional level, a tourist marketing seminar gathered personnel from tourist undertakings and locally elected officials.

The hotel and catering trade employed about 59 000 persons in 1984 and the estimated rate of unemployment was 8 per cent.

The "Ruokasuomi/A la Finlandia" project begun in 1981, was continued both at home and abroad. This project, organised jointly by agricultural producers, the foodstuffs industry, catering services and the tourist and export trades, aims at making their products and services better known both in Finland and abroad. It also included a "Finland menu" campaign involving the largest hotel and restaurant chains in Finland and a number of individual establishments.

France. *Accommodation:* The main event in 1984 was the promulgation on 29th March 1984 of the decree concerning camping and caravan sites, with a new procedure for approval, now in the hands of mayors in *communes* with approved land-use plans. Further regulations are in preparation, pursuant to the decree, setting standards for the facilities at camping and caravan sites run on a strictly seasonal basis, and adjusting standards for existing sites of other types, to align facilities on present-day requirements.

Where hotels are concerned, a study was launched in 1984 on possible changes to the present standards for tourism-class hotels. The industry and a range of official bodies were associated with this work.

Lastly, it was decided that approval of holiday villages managed by non-profit making groups should be decentralised, and lie with the *préfet* in each *département*. The purpose is to safeguard the social and family character of services, and the fiscal and social welfare departments are involved as well as tourism. This move is still in preparation.

Employment and occupational training: Job vacancies in activities directly related to tourism increase at some 4 per cent per year. Only the retail trade (particularly supermarkets) is growing as fast. All other sectors are stationary. In 1984, this increase was slightly less than in previous years in the hotel, catering and collective accommodation sector. It ranged between 7 500 and 10 000 according to the quarter, compared with 12 000 to 15 000 in previous years (the number of jobs created, taking annual turnover into account, may be estimated at about 20-25 000). In the travel agency sector, the number of job vacancies appears to have slightly declined in 1984.

The number of people trained each year (initial and further training) continued to be higher than the number of paid jobs created, but it should be remembered that employment is also available abroad and outside the monitored field of tourism (transport, canteen managers, agri-food, etc.).

To assist manpower adjustments to trends in the tourism sector, the Ministry of Commerce, Crafts and Tourism has launched an in-depth study to determine profiles of the people enterprises will be needing around 1990. The main originality and merit of this study is that it is based on analysis of likely changes in products, marketing, technology and management.

Discussions are also being held concerning the introduction of employment exchanges in the tourism sector, in liaison with the National Employment Agency *(ANPE)*. The aims are threefold:

i) To improve the functioning of the labour market, particularly with regard to seasonal employment;
ii) To organise the training system to meet the requirements of the job market more adequately;
iii) To forecast the trend in job numbers, taking into account the introduction of new technologies, so as to adjust both recruitment patterns and further training for those already in jobs.

Aid and incentives for enterprises for construction, modernisation and investment in the social tourism sector: Following the decentralisation act and the re-allocation of responsibilities between central government and local communities, the range of funds available for financing accommodation and tourist facilities has increased considerably and there are now four main types:

i) Financial assistance granted by the central government and local communities for the associative tourism sector;
ii) Low-interest loans for the creation, extension and modernisation of tourist accommodation and related collective facilities;
iii) Aid granted by the central government and the regions under their "plan contracts"; and
iv) Apart from these contracts, regions and *départements* may make specific grants to further their own policies. A survey of these various types of additional aid is currently being made.

Greece. A study was undertaken to prepare a new institutional framework for the organisation and operation of accommodation establishments and entertainment centres and new specifications were drafted for all categories and types.

The list of available tourist accommodation was expanded by the inclusion of those establishments which had not been formally designated but which fulfilled the relevant specifications of the National Tourist Organisation of Greece (NTOG).

In the transport sector, old projects were completed and new ones started for the improvement of airports and better servicing of passengers. Within the context of implementation of the Governmental policy for decentralisation and regional development, four new airports were put into operation, in Skyros, Leros, Sitia and Araxos and three other airports are under construction on the islands of Kastellorizo, Astipalea and Alonissos. Various institutional measures were taken with regard to tourist coaches and the implementation of a system of technical control of all means of road transport was started.

In order to assist areas with under-developed tourist infrastructure, programmes of financial assistance were implemented to promote coastal communications and more specifically included:

– Subsidy of marginally economic shipping routes by the Ministry of Merchant Marine;
– Subsidy by NTOG with the distribution of free tickets for those shipping lines connecting certain small islands with larger ones.

The relevant NTOG services are making continuous efforts through the press media and the organisation of special seminars to keep the public well informed of the importance of environmental protection.

In the area of professional education and employment, a three-year course was introduced for tourist enterprises within the scope of operations of certain educational institutions in technology. Vocational training for professionals at the "School of Tourist Professions" has been intensified: in 1984, 60 branches in 23 towns received 1 400 persons, against only 9 branches in 4 towns and 150 participants in 1981. In order to fight seasonal unemployment, an experimental training programme is under way in Nauplion which has enrolled 149 employees of the Xenia Hotel of Akronauplia. Financial incentives were given to maintain the continuity of employment in the sector (e.g. by subsidy on salaries) and a law is being drafted which will contain measures safeguarding the employment of the graduates of the School of Tourist Professions.

For the tourist enterprises, the financial assistance and granting of loans by law was continued for the creation of new units in areas in need of assistance and included in the framework of regional development as well as for the conversion of traditional buildings into tourist accommodation establishments.

The development of new forms of tourism is well under way. The procedure for the approval of the operation of nudist centres was finalised and the first of those centres was opened during the summer of 1985.

An institutional framework for the development of rural tourism was established. The programme of social tourism for the domestic market was implemented with success with the participation of NTOG, the Under-Secretariat for Youth and Sports, the Social Insurance Services and the transport companies. Winter and marine subsidised programmes enabled 1 500 workers to take three-day cruises on the Aegean. Infrastructure work is also being carried out for the development of the convention market and an important congress centre was inaugurated in Athens with a capacity of 13 000.

In 1984, credits were mainly available for the construction of tourist infrastructure projects and more specifically for:
- The promotion of three main systems aiming at the development of new forms of tourism (spas, winter sport centres and marinas);
- The implementation of projects included in special programmes (traditional settlements, border stations, golf installations, etc.);
- The creation of supplementary means of accommodation (e.g. camping sites);
- Promotion, publicity and research;
- Promotion of Social Tourism Programmes on the domestic market; and
- Execution of special EEC programmes.

Ireland. A system of grant incentives to encourage the provision of tourist accommodation was continued. This was financed both from the Central Exchequer and the European Regional Development Fund (non quota section) as follows:
- Hotel bedroom improvements: Ir£373 600;
- New hotel rooms: Ir£2 500;
- Caravan and camp sites: Ir£346 500;
- Self catering: Ir£319 500; and
- Supplementary accommodation: Ir£330 100.

The tax on all air and sea tickets issued in the state increased to Ir£5 per ticket. VAT on a range of tourism services including car rental and cruiser hire was reduced from 23 per cent to 18 per cent. A tax-free personal export scheme similar to those in other EEC countries was introduced.

The Government financed the Council for Education, Recruitment and Training in the tourist industry. This body is directly and indirectly involved via the state educational system in the management and craft training of hotel, catering and trade personnel. The Council sets standards and determines curricula requirements for all aspects of tourist industry training provided through hotel and catering schools and other educational establishments.

A fund of Ir£1 003 million from the Central Exchequer plus Ir£0.64 million from the European Regional Development Fund (non-quota section) was made available to provide a range of tourist amenities other than accommodation. These included infrastructural investment projects, environmental protection and preservation of the cultural heritage.

Italy. In accordance with a directive of the Interministerial Committee on Prices, "administered" prices, which include the prices of regional and local transport and hotel and other accommodation, were not in 1984 to rise more than the target for average annual inflation which was fixed at 10 per cent as against 15 per cent for 1983. In addition, the obligation to provide a receipt for tax purposes was to protect customers against uncontrolled price increases.

This heading also covers regional financing of accommodation either from own funds or by additional appropriations from the Ministry of Tourism under the general Act and which amounted to L 125 billion in 1984.

Bank loans at reduced interest rates backed up by regional grants are available for the development and modernisation of hotel accommodation and also for other activities, mainly sporting and thermal facilities.

With regard to tourism supply, the professional qualifications of operators are of great importance. In 1983 hotels and other accommodation employed 720 000 persons against 710 000 in 1982 and accounted for 3.5 per cent of the total working population; labour market prospects are currently fairly good and there is no unemployment in this sector. The general Act on Tourism sets out the basic conditions required of tourist undertakings and travel agencies, and for the different jobs in the tourist trade, while a bill on the reform of higher secondary education emphasizes the importance of "tourism" education by putting it on the same footing as "classical" and "scientific" education.

Japan. In last year's Report, three types of projects to develop public recreation areas and facilities, which will be available at modest prices, were described:
- The Large-Scale Recreation Areas. In 1984, four areas designated as "Recreation Cities" were developed in city planning parks with other related facilities.
- The Recreation Areas for Nature. In 1984, three "Family Villages", the East Hakkoda Area in Aomori Prefecture, the Iizuna Area at the east foot of the mountain in Nagano Prefecture and the Kuma Heights Area in Ehime Prefecture, were newly opened to the public, thirteen "Family Villages" were under continuous development and detailed design surveys for three new "Family Villages" were completed.
- The Recreation Areas and Facilities for Working People and the younger age groups. In 1984, two "Youth Travel Villages" were under development by the Japan Tourism Development Foundation.

Under the International Tourist Restaurant System, introduced in 1981, 144 restaurants had been registered by 31st March 1985.

As an aid for the language problems of foreign visitors, a network of tourist information offices (called "I" system), where tourist information can be provided to foreign visitors in their own languages, was established in 1983 by the JNTO (Japan National Tourist Organisation) under the direction of the Ministry of Transport with the co-operation of local governments. In 1984, 5 information offices were under development, and special seminars were sponsored by JNTO for information officers at the tourist information offices in these 5 cities: Sendai, Kumamoto, Miyazaki, Nagoya and Nara. In total, 21 information offices in 15 cities had been opened by March 1985. In order to help foreign visitors who have problems on the streets or in other public facilities, the "Goodwill Guide" programme was launched in the Tokyo area by JNTO in 1979 using volunteers. By the end of 1984 this programme covered the Nagasaki Prefecture in addition to the areas in and around Tokyo, and Kinki, Chukyo, Sapporo, Miyagi, Ibaragi, Kanazawa, Hiroshima, Fukuoka, Beppu, Kumamoto and Kagoshima Areas, and the total number of volunteers had reached 16 515.

Japanese National Railways (JNR) has continued to upgrade its services by introducing new technologies, as exemplified by its super express service (Shinkansen). In addition to the Tokaido-Sanyo Shinkansen services between Tokyo and Hakata in Kyushu, JNR extended the Tohoku and Joetsu Shinkansen services (which started to operate in 1982) from Omiya to Ueno in Tokyo on 14th March, 1985. For railway travel-loving tourists from abroad, the Japan Rail Pass was introduced by the JNR in 1981. The Pass, which is exclusively available for foreign tourists, offers unlimited travel throughout the entire JNR rail, bus and ferry network at a specially reduced price. There are three types of passes: 7-day, 14-day and 21-day. Vouchers that travellers are required to exchange for the actual passes after arrival in Japan can be purchased at overseas Japan Air Lines ticket offices or authorized travel agencies. According to JNR, the number of passes purchased by foreign visitors totaled 51 150 in 1984, a 53.4 per cent increase over the previous year.

Information services, using the telephone, which were started by the Japan Tourist Association (JTA) in 1983 for sea bathing in summer and skiing in winter were extended in 1984 to cover sea bathing and climbing in summer and skiing and skating in winter. They include weather conditions and forecasts, sea, snow or ice conditions, availability of accommodation, road traffic, transport services and tourist attractions.

With the theme of "Dwelling and Surroundings – Science and Technology for Man at Home", the International Exposition, Tsukuba, Japan which is popularly called "TSUKUBA EXPO '85" was held in Tsukuba Science City, Japan, for six months from 17th March to 11th September 1985. Tsukuba Expo is showing how people can adapt the recent tremendous progress in the science and technology of information and communications to contemporary living.

Since the National Parks were established in 1957, their social surroundings have changed. To allow for this, the plans for five areas in four National Parks, such as Shiretoko National Park and Japan Alps National Park, etc., were reviewed in 1984 and the revised plan for Ise-Shima National Park includes an inspection every five years. Based on the general regulation "Outline for Motorcar Use in National Parks" established by the Environment Agency in 1974, vehicular traffic except buses and taxis was not permitted to enter the five controlled areas in the Japan Alps and Nikko National Parks during the busiest periods in summer and autumn which extended for 59 days in 1984.

In order to deepen the national understanding of the social, cultural, educational and political significance of tourism, as well as its economic importance, the Government of Japan has annually sponsored a "Tourism Week" with the co-operation of the Japanese National Railways, Prefectural governments and other tourism-related organisations during the first week of August ever since 1965. In 1984, this campaign was directed to the enhancement of the beauty of tourist resorts; and to ensuring tourists' safety. In commemoration of the 20th anniversary of "Tourism Week", a nationwide "Tourism Recreation Fair" was held in Shinjuku in Tokyo from 18th to 24th June 1984 under the auspices of the Japan Tourist Association and the Japan National Tourist Organisation in order to deepen the national understanding of the important role of tourism in national life.

In addition to "Tourism Week", the following national campaigns for the protection of natural and cultural resources take place every year:
– Nature Protection Month (21st July to 20th August)
– Municipal Tree-Planting Month (during October)
– Cultural Properties Protection Week (1st to 7th November)
– Fire Prevention Day for Cultural Properties (26th January)
– The "Green Day" in National Parks (the first Sunday of August).

Though all vocational training in the field of tourism is left to private enterprises, three national examinations are held annually. In the 1984 examinations, 218 qualified as Guide-Interpreters, 1 633 passed as Certified General Travel Service Supervisors and 1 339 passed as Certified Domestic Travel Service Supervisors.

Luxembourg. While the main objective of the 3rd five-year plan is still the modernisation of hotel bedrooms, the coverage of the capital grants awarded has been extended so that more emphasis is placed on reception facilities (foyer, lounge, dining room) and on the sports and recreational facilities which hotels and similar establishments are expected to provide for tourists.

Grants at the rate of 15 per cent of the total cost may be made for hotel investment not exceeding LF 25 million; this rate is reduced to 7.5 per cent for the LF 25-35 million bracket. In certain circumstances the ceiling may be raised from LF 25 to 35 million for the 15 per cent grant and from LF 35 to 60 million for the 7.5 per cent grant.

Conversion of holiday cottages and exploitation of cultural assets for tourism purposes are the chief innovations of the 3rd five-year plan.

The Ministry of Tourism may grant substantial aid to private individuals who convert farm buildings, whether still in use or abandoned, in order to provide tourist accommodation. This kind of economic changeover finds a new use for country dwellings and helps to maintain or even create jobs in areas which urgently need them.

The Ministry of Tourism attaches a great deal of importance to the preservation of cultural assets and their exploitation for tourism purposes. In association with the Ministry of Cultural Affairs and other authorities, it encourages and subsidises activities concerned with preserving typical village architecture and showing it to its best advantage.

The amount of the capital grant awarded to a private individual who converts holiday cottages or turns cultural assets to advantage cannot exceed 15 per cent ot the total cost of the investment.

When an investor in activities of the latter type is a *commune,* tourist office or other non-profit-making association, the amount of the grant cannot exceed 40 per cent of total investment costs.

The Ministry of Tourism encourages the upgrading of camp sites and especially the provision of extra facilities (reception areas, sports and play grounds, wooded areas, etc.).

Hitherto, only *communes* and tourist offices were eligible for grants for the opening or upgrading of camp sites; private individuals were not entitled to State aid. The Ministry of Tourism now wants to change this rule, and in 1985 aid will also be available to the owners of private camp sites. This should encourage owners to invest even more substantially to upgrade their property.

Netherlands. In December 1984 the Tourist Policy Memorandum for the period 1985-1990 was published. An important element of this memorandum is the new public infrastructure investment scheme. In all provinces, tourist development plans have been or are being worked out, with a view to improving the tourist infrastructure in regions or sub-regions of the provinces.

On the basis of these development plans, the provincial authorities will submit projects to the State-Secretary of Economic Affairs, responsible for tourism. The State-Secretary will select the most urgent projects which will be supported by financial contributions from the Ministry of Economic Affairs up to 75 per cent of the investment costs. An important criterion for judging the merits of the various projects will be the improvement of the accessibility of the tourist infrastructure in the regions concerned and the level of employment created and/or maintained.

New Zealand. A special first year depreciation allowance is available to encourage the development of modern tourist accommodation. In 1980, to alleviate a specific shortage in Auckland, a cash grant of 9.5 per cent in lieu of first year depreciation was introduced for international standard hotels. This scheme was extended to Wellington, Christchurch and Queenstown in 1984.

A new second-level carrier, Newmans Air, has commenced flying Dash 7 aircraft on the Auckland/Rotorua/Christchurch/Mt Cook/Queenstown route. Negotiations with Canada have resulted in a Direct Air Services Agreement. It will commence in September 1985 with two flights per week. Aerolineas Argentinas recommenced fortnightly flights. The first-level carrier, Air New Zealand, announced the purchase of 10 new aircraft. Deregulation of road transport has resulted in the expansion of some passenger services.

Two new Forest Parks, Whirinaki and Northland, have been created and the National Parks and Reserves Authority have recommended that Punakaiki be designated a National Park. The proposed Wanganui River National Park is currently under consideration. The creation of the new Ministry for the Environment is recognition of the importance placed on the environment and nature conservation. There is a greater awareness amongst Maori people of how tourism can work in a positive way for them. A closer liaison is developing between the Tourist and Publicity Department and interested Maori groups.

A Training Needs Analysis was commissioned by the Industry Training Boards and the Tourist and Publicity Department. It is to ascertain what training is required and by whom, and provide information to establish training priorities. It is funded on a 50/50 basis by the Government and the industry.

The 1984 Budget brought the phasing out of the Export Performance Incentive, and other export incentives are under review.

Norway. Tourism commitments of the Regional Development Fund made up 10 per cent of its total activities. In 1984 it gave NKr 65.2 million in loans and 35.2 million in investment support to the tourist industry.

The private sector shows an increasing interest in the expansion of hotel capacity in city areas. In 1984 construction activity regarding hotels and restaurants was higher than in 1983. Site completions increased by 4.1 per cent and the initiation of construction sites increased by 27.7 per cent.

Concerning ferries, the capacity has increased, expecially to Denmark. A new line to England is being planned. These initiatives were taken by the trade.

An investigation concerning fresh water supplies and drainage facilities for accommodation enterprises in mountains has been completed. Financial measures are under consideration. A comprehensive plan for construction work and preservation of the water system has been presented. Public means have been used to increase employment, including new jobs in the tourist industry. A new law concerning opening hours involved a liberalisation of the rules now in force.

Portugal. Existing tax incentives have been maintained. They aim at encouraging the modernisation of hotels and the installation of units whose characteristics and location make them of interest to tourism. Other tax incentives have been introduced with regard to camping facilities and accommodation (rural tourism and rooms in private homes).

The programme for building new State-run inns ("pousadas") has been stepped up and the running of those already open has been reviewed. The reorganisation of local activities and the provision of extra sports facilities has been encouraged. Support has also been given to the installation of equipment aimed at rationalising management, particularly in hotels. Additional support facilities and tax measures have been introduced with a view to improving the quality of the services provided in hotels and restaurants.

Decree-Law No. 49 399 of 24th November 1969 which regulates the tourist industry has been revised and will be published shortly. Decree-Law No. 251 was published on 25th July 1984. It regulates "tourism in private houses". This supplementary accommodation should provide some 1 450 extra beds.

An integrated plan for training in the tourism occupations aimed at improving external competitiveness and specifying criteria for access to these occupations or activities, has been developed. The existing education structure has been strengthened and a scheme has been introduced to encourage enterprises in the tourism sector to provide their staff with continuing training. International co-operation has been intensified, particularly with the new Portuguese-speaking countries and other countries in Africa.

Sweden. There has been an expansion in the hotel-building sector, particularly in the big city areas. In the Stockholm area the hotel capacity increased by 1 750 rooms, in the Gothenburg area by 1 450 rooms and in the Malmö area by 250 rooms. These new hotel investments have not come about by Government intervention or subsidies but strictly through market forces. The percentage of occupied rooms in these new constructions has been most satisfactory and the share of nights spent by foreign guests has been above the average in the new hotels.

Discussions are going on about the introduction of a holiday-cheque system, intended for residents in Sweden, along lines similar to those already practised in Switzerland.

Switzerland. *Trend in aid for tourism development:* Loans granted by the Confederation (mostly interest-free) under the Federal Act on aid to investment are designed to finance community facilities in mountain areas. Among the projects financially supported by the Confederation, many relate to infrastructure of a strictly tourist nature and therefore to the development of tourism supply. Between 1975 and 1984 the sums thus allocated amounted to SF 73.4 million (1983: SF 61.5 million), broken down as follows:

- Tourist transport: 18.3 million
- Sports facilities: 41.2 million
- Swimming pools: 7.5 million
- Museums: 5.5 million
- Conference centres: 0.9 million.

Under the Federal Act on aid to investment in mountain areas, the Confederation is in a position to support the activities of regional secretary/organisers. Up to the end of 1984, 40 of them had obtained federal financial assistance. It should be emphasised that in most mountain areas tourism is an important economic sector and that the activities of the secretary/organisers also focus on promoting the development of tourism.

Planning measures in mountain areas: Up to the end of 1984, the Federal Department for Public Economy had approved 51 regional development programmes, to the implementation of which the Confederation had contributed by allocating subsidies amounting to some 80 per cent of the total cost of the regional studies. The establishment of regional programmes is a prior condition for the granting of aid enabling community facilities or hotels in mountain areas to be financed on concessional terms. Given the importance of tourism for these regions, the development programmes always devote several chapters to tourism activities. The following items are given special attention: analysis of the current situation, development potential and outlook, identification of objectives and choice of development measures. These development programmes cover a period of between 10 and 15 years. They include a 4 or 5-year investment programme. By the end of 1984, twenty-seven of these programmes had been reviewed and approved.

Government aid in the form of loans and loan guarantees: In the context of the implementation of the Federal

Act on the promotion of credit for the hotel industry and holiday resorts, the aid granted by the *Société Suisse de Crédit Hôtelier (SCH)* is for the purpose of facilitating the construction and modernisation of hotels in mountain areas. In 1984, the SCH granted loans amounting to SF 11 million for the modernisation of hotels and holiday resorts, the construction of new hotels, and hotel purchase. The interest rate was 5.5 per cent per annum throughout the year.

For projects included in a programme of development under the Federal Act on aid to investment in mountain areas particularly worthy of support, the *Société* may for a period of not more than five years reduce the interest rates on the loans it grants. The rate was 3.5 per cent throughout 1984.

In 1984 the SCH provided guarantees for bank loans amounting to SF 14.4 million for the modernisation of hotels and holiday resorts, the construction of new hotels and the purchase of hotels, of which 75 per cent, i.e. SF 10.8 million, was guaranteed by the Confederation. The interest rate on these loans varied between 5.75 and 7 per cent in 1984. To the interest rate must be added a guarantee charge of ⅛ per cent per annum.

For projects included in the development programme under the Federal Act on investment in mountain areas particularly worthy of support, the SCH has in several cases taken under its aegis, initially for three years and up to a maximum of five years, the interest rates of 2 per cent per annum on the loans which it guarantees. Of the total guarantees and loans of SF 24 407 500, SF 12.1 million (47.6 per cent) are for the modernisation of hotels in tourist areas and mountain regions, 4 million for the replacement of hotels by new constructions (15.8 per cent), 1.4 million (5.5 per cent) for the construction of new hotels, 0.9 million (3.5 per cent) for the modernisation or creation of tourist facilities in holiday resorts and 7 million (27.6 per cent) to finance the purchase of hotels. With the assistance of guarantees and loans by the SCH in 1984, a total volume of investments of approximately SF 179 million was financed.

Government aid is confined to loans and guarantees for bank loans. There are no government subsidies or tax incentives.

Occupational training/employment: At 1st January 1984, the number of current contracts for the training of skilled workers was 8 546. The number of students at the hotel school of the *Société Suisse des hôteliers* at Chalet-à-Gobet training for medium and higher level executive posts was 490 at 30th September 1984. At 30th November 1984 there were 3 601 job seekers in the hotel and catering professions and 1 394 vacancies in this sector.

Environmental protection: As in previous years, expenditure on nature conservation and the cultural heritage increased by about 20 per cent and was estimated to represent some 1 per cent of total public expenditure. The number of areas placed under the full protection of the Confederation did not increase in 1984. In all, 13 per cent of the country is now under federal protection (in addition to conservation areas protected by the *cantons* and *communes*).

United Kingdom. The national tourist boards continued to provide assistance by way of grants under Section 4 of the Development of Tourism Act 1969. In 1983/84 the English Tourist Board (ETB) made a record number of grant offers to developers (503 totalling £12.3 million). This was the first year in which the Scheme was available throughout England. The anticipated investment to be generated through these projects amounts to a record £68 million and is expected to create some 1 600 jobs. During 1983/84 the Wales Tourist Board (WTB) approved 54 grants totalling £1.7 million and introduced the Resort Accommodation Incentive Scheme to assist small ventures whose capital costs do not exceed £5 000. In the same period the Scottish Tourist Board (STB) approved 250 grants totalling £5.5 million. In Scotland a moratorium on grants was imposed in September 1984 due to demand exceeding the funds available (£4.3 million).

For the Rural Development Areas (RDAs) in England, designated by the Development Commission in June 1984, local authorities and other agencies are drawing up Rural Development Programmes which will include many tourism-related projects calculated to benefit the rural economy. The Development Commission will consider contributing towards the cost of such projects in association with other agencies and authorities. Also for the RDAs, the Development Commission's agency, the Council for Small Industries in Rural Areas (CoSIRA), has a team of specialist tourism consultants and other expert advisers who provide advice to small tourism enterprises which benefit the rural economy. Assistance is also given in helping enterprises raise finance from the private sector including, where necessary, the provision of top-up loans for building and equipment at interest rates set by the Government.

During 1984, the grant scheme operated by the Department of Economic Development, aimed at encouraging the development of tourist accommodation in Northern Ireland, remained closed for the receipt of new applications. The Department's financial resources were fully committed as a result of selections for grant made when the scheme was last open in early 1983. During 1984, local authorities in Northern Ireland with grant assistance from the Department of Economic Development and the European Communities, invested £3 million (approximately) in tourist amenity infrastructure, ranging from picnic sites to major visitor centres in key tourist areas.

ETB has been engaged in identifying and encouraging the development of tourist potential in inner cities and areas of industrial, cultural and other heritage. In

Bristol it is collaborating with the City Council and the Bristol Marketing Board on an extensive range of tourism and marketing projects aimed at developing the attractions of the historic city. Co-operation has also resulted in the production of a "Tourism Development Action Plan" for the city which it is hoped will serve as a prototype for other cities in the future.

During 1984 an important tourist event which has also benefited inner city regeneration was the Liverpool International Garden Festival. This was financed by the Government through the Merseyside Development Corporation and was the first event of its kind in the United Kingdom, attracting some 3.3 million visitors between May and October. A National Garden Festival is to be held at Stoke-on-Trent in 1986 and following an announcement in November 1984 a further series of national festivals is to be staged: at Glasgow in 1988, at Gateshead in 1990 and in Wales in 1992. All these will be designed to regenerate derelict areas but will also represent significant promotional opportunities for tourism in their regions. As with the Liverpool Festival the tourist boards will be fully involved in advising and assisting the marketing effort.

The new equity capital company for tourism and leisure investment, which the ETB helped to establish, was launched as Leisure Development Ltd. in January 1984 with the backing of 5 financial institutions. This has made two investments to date and is looking actively for further opportunities, particularly in health-related tourism and in budget hotels, both of which are seen as important growth areas.

The National Heritage Act 1983 provided for the establishment of a new body with responsibilities for historic buildings and ancient monuments. Under this provision the Historic Buildings and Monuments Commission became operative on 1st April 1984.

In 1983 the Government introduced a major new scheme of vocational preparation for young people, the Youth Training Scheme. This offers a full year of planned work experience and off-the-job training. Most of the training places are with employers, and the tourism industry is providing a significant number of these places. For example, in the hotel and catering sectors, around 7 000 places were made available and around 5 200 were filled in the 1983/84 financial year. During the first 9 months of financial year 1984/85 around 6 500 places were made available and around 5 000 were filled.

Yugoslavia. During 1984, tourist supply was increased and improved by the opening of new facilities for tourists. Bed capacity in hotels was increased by 16 182 units in hotels and 23 551 in supplementary accommodation (an increase of 5.3 per cent and 2.6 per cent respectively over 1983). Some 5 000 new berths were added to marinas. The new capacity was most notable in Bosnia and Herzegovina, concentrating on

winter sports and holidays, in Croatia, directed to yacht tourism, and in Montenegro. A large part of the investment in tourism went towards modernisation and reconstruction of tourist establishments, and to the expansion and improvement of various other facilities.

Special attention was paid to improving the quality of services offered to tourists. Foreign tourist passage through the border crossings was improved and speeded up. Buses and goods vehicles were directed towards less crowded border crossings. Technical facilities at certain border crossings were improved, notably at Sentilj. The border crossing staff were given special training and a system of inspection controls was introduced in order to ensure the most efficient flow of international tourist traffic.

Petrol coupons which give foreign tourists a 10 per cent reduction on the retail price of petrol are now sold at a larger number of places both in Yugoslavia and abroad and unused coupons can now be refunded. In the course of the tourist season, special attention was paid to the regular supply of petrol to stations and to their opening hours, the control of traffic and the provision of assistance to motorists so as to meet the needs of foreign tourists in the best possible way. Railway services were also improved by offering better facilities for the transport of private cars to the more popular tourist resorts. Increased attention was paid to improving the overall conditions for foreign tourists including health protection, the general arrangement of tourist resorts and the overall quality of services provided including modification of working hours to meet the needs of tourists.

The use of Dinar cheques issued by the National Bank of Yugoslavia, introduced in 1983, was extended and their re-conversion was made easier. These give a discount of 19 per cent on all tourist services offered by participating tourist organisations and their associated labour unions.

By a decision on foreign exchange policy, $60 million were granted for the import of goods in order to increase foreign tourist consumption, of which $5 million were used for the import of foreign newspapers and magazines.

In 1984, tourist agencies and the catering industry employed 220 000 people (figure based upon average over the period from January to August), a 5 per cent increase compared with 1983.

b) **Marketing**

Australia. A major television and radio campaign on the West Coast of the United States was launched by the Australian Tourist Commission early in 1984. The campaign has since been extended to the East Coast. Response to the campaign was excellent and initial

30

indications are that it will achieve a significant increase in the number of United States citizens visiting Australia.

The Bureau of Industry Economics published in 1984 the results of a Survey of Expenditure on Domestic Travel. In addition the Domestic Tourism Monitor (DTM) and the International Visitors Survey (IVS) were conducted. The DTM is the main source of information on Australia's domestic travel behaviour while the IVS provides information on the characteristics and travel behaviour of overseas visitors to Australia.

Austria. The Ministry of Trade drew up and/or helped to finance the following studies:

- Forecasts for the summer of 1984 and the winter of 1984/85;
- A list of holidaymakers' requirements in Austria, indicating key areas in the relationships between tourists and their hosts and identifying the main things tourists expect to find;
- A study on youth tourism, updating a study on the same subject made in 1976;
- Participation in the "Survey of tourists in Austria". In the summer of 1984, the first survey of Austrian and foreign tourists in 160 tourist areas was made. A particularly important set of questions concerned the structure of expenditure, and whether tourists were pleased with what they had found on holiday;
- Participation in the analysis of holiday plans for 1985, undertaken by the Tourism Study Group in Germany; and
- Participation in an analysis of tourism, "Tour A 85", a survey concerning holiday travel by Austrians, undertaken by the Institute for Social and Market Analysis.

Canada. A task force on tourism statistics headed by the Chief Statistician of Canada has been established. The task force composed of representatives of the federal, provincial and territorial governments as well as of the private sector is charged with developing a comprehensive data base for Canadian tourism. In addition a complete review of the tourism research needs of the federal and provincial governments has been started. The task force report is expected in late 1985 while the research review should be completed by March 1985.

The Canadian Travel Survey was conducted in all four quarters of 1984, and analysis of the 1982 study was completed. A desk research report was prepared that brought together much of the existing material on the United Kingdom market. Initial analysis of the results of the Canadian Tourism Attitude and Motivation Study started. Studies on the evaluation of specific advertising campaigns were done in Canada, the United States, United Kingdom and the Federal Republic of Germany.

The tourism marketing priorities for 1984-85 were to compete more effectively in the North American automobile market with major television campaigns based on Canada's unique marketing opportunities and to develop new domestic and foreign markets with particular emphasis on special interest markets such as meetings and conventions and package tours.

Extensive television, radio and print advertising campaigns were carried out in both Canada and in the United States, supported by a special one year C$10 million award from the Policy Reserve. The number of visits by United States tourists spending one or more nights in Canada by all modes were up 4.1 per cent in 1984 over 1983. The balance of payments on the travel account remained at approximately the same level as 1983. Although no domestic travel data is available for 1983, corroborating travel indicators suggested an increase in Canadians travelling within Canada between 1983 and 1984. Travel by Canadians to the United States decreased. This was offset however by increased travel overseas. It has been estimated that Tourism Marketing advertising has had little effect on inter-provincial traffic, the targetted market segment, and as a result the federal tourism programme is withdrawing from active domestic marketing.

Several new overseas markets have received increased and profitable attention, including Hong Kong and the Pacific Rim, Italy, Sweden and Switzerland. The meetings and incentive travel market was given a new priority in 1984-85, and indications are that this will pay off in increased business to the convention centres across Canada.

Denmark. The Danish Tourist Board undertook the following important surveys in order to improve the knowledge of the present and potential international demand for Danish tourist products:

- A visitor survey on personal interviews with one thousand foreign tourists which analysed the tourists' expenses, attitude towards Danish tourist products, duration of stay, forms of accommodation used, reasons for spending holidays in Denmark, organisation of trips and mobility during holidays in Denmark;
- An analysis based on interviews with one thousand foreign yacht tourists. The analysis, like the previous survey, examined expenditures, travel patterns, duration of stay, holiday expectations and the attitude to the Danish products offered in yacht tourism;
- A nation-wide analysis on the renting of holiday cottages which – for Danish tourism – is the most important accommodation product. This was done in co-operation with the National Statistical Office;
- A working group was also set up with the Danish hotel organisation, with the purpose of planning a survey which will disclose the circumstances determining the tourists' choice of Danish hotels – especially outside the main tourist season.

In co-operation with the planning authorities, the Danish Tourist Board has also carried out a descriptive survey of western Jutland, which is one of the most popular tourist areas in Denmark. Apart from describing factors of interest for tourism, it considers the general planning, occupation, attitude to tourism, urbanisation and nature. Using a methodological framework designed by the Danish Tourist Board, a great number of local tourist organisations have finally analysed the economic importance of tourism for the various local areas.

The overall strategy which stresses the importance of marketing efforts in the neighbouring countries has been continued, although new market possibilities are currently being evaluated. During recent years, the "direct-mailing" approach has turned out to be very successful in neighbouring markets. Such activities will therefore be increased in the coming years.

Finland. There were about 40 development projects and investigations in progress during the year. The most important surveys completed were a study of the Finns' holiday habits, a study of municipal marketing of tourism, an investigation into the most attractive winter tourist resorts, and a classification criteria for cross-country skiing centres. One extensive new project embarked on was an investigation into the regional structure of tourism in Finland. As regards the development of services, work continued on the development of various attractions, services and activities suitable for marketing in collaboration with the tourism industry. The emphasis was on the development of winter activities (such as cross-country skiing) and activities involving water (such as fishing, canoe safaris and rowing packages)..

The main goal in foreign marketing was on increasing demand for the summer season. Marketing of winter holiday-making and facilities for cross-country skiiing continued in central Europe. The main target countries were again Sweden, Norway and Germany. Efforts were mainly concentrated at sales level (travel organisers and agencies), the media and consumers.

Sales and training events and study tours were arranged for travel agents and operators. The biggest events were Finland Purpuri Travel Market, held in Helsinki for overseas buyers (380 participants), and Finland Omnibus, held in Lappeenranta, for Scandinavian coach tour organisers (150 participants).

Efforts were made by advertising in newspapers, magazines and the trade press and by taking part in travel exhibitions to make Finland known as a high-quality, safe and varied tourist country. Briefing sessions were held for the press and training and study trips were arranged to Finland for about 700 travel agents and 300 representatives of the media. The Finnish Tourist Board again produced a large number of publications for foreign readers in 1984. A total of around two million copies were published by the Finnish Tourist Board in support of marketing abroad. On the domestic market, two general, large-circulation booklets called *Lomas-uomi* were produced, covering activities in summer and in winter.

Germany. The Federal and the *Länder* Governments commissioned a study of spending patterns in tourism. The main objective of this study is to ascertain the volume of spending and the importance of tourism to the economy as a whole and to obtain basic data on the supply of tourist services.

Greece. A research project in three phases was carried out at the main border crossings for the collection of data and information on the characteristics of foreign tourism. It concerned a sample which represented 5 per cent of the tourists more than 16 years of age leaving the country.

In order to determine the correct policy line to be followed, taking into account present and potential foreign tourist demand and forecasts for 1985, the 1983/84 data were analysed, questionnaires were completed by the NTOG services abroad and views were exchanged with private tourism bodies during two Conferences organised by the NTOG in Crete and Corfu.

Ireland. The annual "Home Holiday Survey" was again repeated towards the end of the year. This assesses the extent and nature of holidays taken by residents at home and abroad.

The present and potential international demand was assessed through the following:

- A sample of all departures to determine visitor numbers by country of residence. This brief survey was carried out throughout the year;
- A second and more detailed sample survey of all international travellers departing from all sea and air ports in the state throughout the year. Personal interviews were conducted with travellers to establish visitor and trip characteristics;
- Surveys in various markets to establish the potential target markets for Ireland and its image abroad; and
- A survey of coupon enquirers in the Benelux countries.

Other research with relevance both to the national and international markets included:

- An annual hotel survey. This records the demand for overnight accommodation, the relative utilisation of various categories of premises and the sources of business;
- An annual inter-hotel comparative profitability study;
- Research on various products to measure overall demand and its characteristics, e.g. inland water-ways cruising;
- Advertising tests in various markets; and

- An update of tourist attitudes to hotels and other serviced accommodation.

The marketing objectives are to maximise foreign revenue to stimulate domestic short holiday taking in paid accommodation and maintain the home market's share of long holiday revenue. The strategy has been the following:
- To project an image of Ireland as a different, desirable and unique holiday destination;
- To concentrate the bulk of resources on identified market areas and segments where the rate of return on the investment is maximised; and
- To devote the major part of resources to direct consumer marketing (advertising, publicity and promotion) with support services provided for the travel trade.

Italy. The State is involved in marketing via bodies with statutory promotion and advertising functions or which organise major tourist events.

In 1984, L 60 billion were invested in tourist promotion abroad.

Among the cultural events organised in 1984 were the 500th Anniversary of the birth of Raphael, the Two Worlds Festival in Spoleto, the Verona Opera Festival, the Carnivals in Venice and Viareggio, etc.

The importance of cultural motivations in tourist development and the ever-growing interest – especially to foreign tourists – in cultural centres such as Rome, Venice, Florence, Siena, etc., should be emphasized.

Concessions for foreign tourists should be mentioned (petrol vouchers, toll reductions on motorways and services offered by the Italian Automobile Club).

Tourism is well on the way to becoming a major factor in education – as well as a social and economic phenomenon – an understanding of which also requires considerable research and investigation. Italy wants to give a scientific basis to the study of tourism. In this respect an International Seminar was organised by the Italian National Association of Scientific Experts on Tourism (ANIEST) and the *Accademia Nazionale dei Lincei* in Rome in May 1984 on the application of the systems approach to tourism. The creation of a University of Tourism is also being studied.

However, the analysis of a phenomenon as complex as tourism presupposes increasingly detailed knowledge of its components and of the forces which affect supply and demand; the Ministry of Tourism is planning the creation of a computerised information system. This service, known as the "Observatory of the general state of tourism" will operate from 1985 and will provide consolidated data on general trends. For more detailed information, a first report on tourism in Italy has been prepared and gives a comprehensive description of the structure of tourism in Italy.

Japan. In 1984, the following surveys and study were made in the field of tourism:
- A survey and study on tourism and recreation for one-day trips;
- Surveys on the present state of the leisure-time-related industry and on the cost of leisure by the Ministry of International Trade and Industry;
- Surveys on overseas travel markets in Malaysia, Singapore and Thailand and on foreign tourists' routes in Japan by the National Tourist Office.

Luxembourg. The National Tourism Office (ONT) is responsible for promoting and advertising the country's tourist facilities, especially on the major overseas markets and in the medium and long term, its activities include keeping track of trends in demand; deciding what type of publicity is most suitable; obtaining the necessary resources; producing and distributing material; planning and carrying out advertising campaigns; issuing promotional literature; creating new products; and welcoming tourists.

In 1984, the ONT continued its action in all these fields but concentrated especially on three of its medium-term activities: the promotion of conferences and congresses, the German business travel market and the provision of information for visiting American ex-servicemen.

Netherlands. A survey of the structure of incoming tourism to the Netherlands was started.

Norway. Investigations into seasonal vacation habits were undertaken to explain the important changes now going on. Marketing analyses in Sweden, the United Kingdom, the Netherlands and Belgium were carried out by the Norwegian Travel Council in co-operation with the other Nordic countries. Marketing efforts in the United States were increased.

On 1st April 1984, Norway joined Sweden and Denmark in the operation of a joint tourist office in Tokyo. In 1985, Norway will establish its own tourist office in Finland.

Portugal. The survey of holidays taken by Portuguese and the frontier survey covering foreign tourists were carred out in 1984, as in previous years. Portuguese tourism offices abroad have also carried out market surveys and opinion polls.

Where promotion (commercial strategies and actions) is concerned, activities abroad have been intensified in order to maximise utilisation of tourism supply, by:
- Action aimed at staggering the main season and attracting sections of the market interested in off-season tourism;
- Orientation of high-season visitors to less-saturated destinations;
- Special campaigns focusing directly on the general

public (individual tourism), particularly socio-economic groups with greater purchasing power;
- Inauguration of new tourism programmes centered on specific requirements (spas and special climate stations, sport, culture, etc.);
- Co-ordination of the promotional activities of government departments and regional or local authorities with those of the various commercial agencies concerned (carriers, travel agents, hotels, etc.).

Sweden. On the domestic market a qualitative sample survey was conducted among Swedish tourists on camping holidays in Sweden. The aim of the survey was to find out what attitudes and motives made them choose camping for their holidays, what expections they have of camping holidays, etc. In the summer season a majority of European tourists to Sweden arrive by car. A comprehensive visitors' study was therefore made in the summer of 1984 among motorists from seven European countries, when leaving Sweden. This survey supplied valuable information on that market, such as forms of accommodation used, composition of the travel party, length of stay, expenditure, etc.

Marketing strategies and measures have also been increasingly directed towards specific target groups within defined segments of consumers and with priced products selected for each market. In 1984 more emphasis was put on Nordic countries and on off-season and weekend travel. Establishment in overseas markets has been given special priority. The markets of immediate interest are Japan and South America, completed with a larger engagement in the United States market. The domestic summer campaign "Sweden is fantastic" was carried out for the twelth year. A total of 2.5 million brochures distributed to all households in the more important population centres, and a nationwide advertising campaign were the main components of this promotion. For the second time, the Swedish Tourist Board launched a domestic campaign for the winter season: "Sweden is fantastic – also in wintertime". A brochure was produced in close co-operation with the trade and distributed in 1.2 million copies.

The production of a brochure specially intended for handicapped people has met with a positive response in and outside Sweden. In 1984 the brochure has been enlarged and co-operation on a Scandinavian basis has been initiated.

A marked increase has been registered in the number of visitors from the neighbouring Nordic countries, especially Norway. This may partly be explained by the fact that promotional efforts have been concentrated on marketing specific travel arrangements aimed at defined target groups, partly as a consequence of the devaluation of the Swedish krona in 1982. Tourism from neighbouring Nordic countries is predominantly short and medium distance travel. The larger influx of Nordic visitors has also had the effect that there has been an increased demand for holiday destinations in Sweden involving long-distance travel from their home town.

In the markets outside Scandinavia the same principle on marketing has been applied, concentrating on specific travel arrangements for defined target groups. In all markets the campaigns have been carried through in close co-operation with interested parties in the tourist industry and with their financial support.

Increased promotion of tax-free shopping for foreign visitors has been made in co-operation with the retail trade. Several campaigns on the tax-free project have been conducted in the Federal Republic of Germany and the United States. Between 1983 and 1984, tax-free purchases by tourists in Sweden increased from SKr 220 million to 300 million.

The Swedish Tourist Board took an active part in the launching of the first international travel fair in Sweden, "TUR 84" in Gothenburg. On this occasion the total Swedish supply of tourist products was presented to the trade as well as to consumers. The results were most encouraging and the experience will be renewed with "TUR 85", also in Gothenburg.

In the United States market, special efforts were made to attract more incentive travel to Sweden. An encouraging result of this promotion was that a leading American incentive travel operator nominated Sweden the best incentive travel destination of the year.

The Swedish Tourist Board and the Danish Tourist Board opened joint offices in Los Angeles and Chicago in co-operation with Scandinavian airlines. In Tokyo the Scandinavian Tourist Board, operated jointly by the Tourist Boards of Denmark and Sweden, was opened.

Switzerland. The TOMAS survey undertaken on behalf of the regional tourism directors, with the backing of the *Office National Suisse du Tourisme* (ONST) and other bodies, continued. Some 15 000 Swiss and foreign tourists staying in hotels and holiday flats in 125 resorts and towns were interviewed during the winter of 1983/84 and the summer of 1984. According to the findings, a good proportion of visitors confirmed the wide appeal of Switzerland and expressed satisfaction with their stay.

An analysis of the South-East Asian market, excluding Japan, was carried out jointly by the ONST and the German and Austrian tourist offices. For visitors from the Far East, the main attraction in Switzerland is the beauty of the landscape, and particularly the mountains.

Promotion strategy was backed by a special grant of SF 3.5 million made by the Federal authorities to ONST. The latter stepped up its publicity on the European and overseas markets. The number of journalists and travel agents invited for trips in Switzerland increased considerably, as did participation in trade fairs and general exhibitions. In Switzerland itself, the

ONST is the main organiser of a working party on "Tourism and the new media". It has also successfully launched an intensive campaign on "One hundred years of winter sports in Switzerland". Marketing, however, remains in the hands of the regional and local tourist offices and the private sector.

United Kingdom. The British Tourist Authority (BTA) and the English Tourist Board continued to carry out a wide variety of research projects. New reports on the Conference and Exhibition Market, English Churches and Visitors, and a Strategy for Growth for the period 1984-1988 were published in 1984.

In 1984, the Scottish Tourist Board (STB) initiated a new, continuous survey of tourism in Scotland by British residents – the National Survey of Tourism in Scotland. Each month, around 2 700 British residents are interviewed and asked for details of any tourist trips they may have taken in Scotland in the preceding 3 months. The results from this survey will provide the STB with accurate and up-to-date information on the very important British market. The various promotional campaigns undertaken by the STB are also the subject of extensive monitoring to gauge their efficiency.

In April 1984 the Wales Tourist Board set up new marketing planning procedures, supported by an extended marketing research programme. The first of a regular series of marketing plans is in preparation, which sets out policy objectives and outlines a variety of joint marketing initiatives available to local authorities and the trade.

During 1984, the Northern Ireland Tourist Board carried out extensive market research of a qualitative and quantitative nature in the Republic of Ireland. Market Research of a qualitative nature was also carried out in the United States.

On the domestic market, the National Boards have introduced a number of programmes which have a particularly strong bearing on spreading the season. Examples include the "Let's Go" autumn/winter/spring promotion, the Spring into Summer promotion, and the encouragement of the sale of new products through the retail travel trade. STB's main promotion was augmented by a major joint STB/Area Tourist Board advertising campaign, designed to link individual area advertisements under a Scottish identity and so achieve greater impact for the country as a whole.

On the international markets, in promoting incoming tourism, BTA aims to increase the overall level of travel throughout Britain with emphasis on London as Britain's principal tourist centre and international gateway and on the regions of England, Scotland and Wales. They also aim to improve traffic in off-peak periods which relieves congestion and improves profitability of tourism services.

Following the enactment of the Tourism (Overseas Promotion) (Scotland) Act, STB has initiated a programme of activities supplementing those of BTA. STB agreed to concentrate on proven areas such as America and Europe and create initiatives aimed at developing business potential through the travel trade. The general publicity material, print, generic advertising and joint scheme assistance remain the task of BTA who retain the role of principle promotional agency for Scotland overseas.

United States. The United States Travel and Tourism Administration (USTTA) promotes export earnings through trade in tourism. It does this through a comprehensive international marketing programme tailored to each key foreign market and based on marketing research. USTTA develops programmes with travel suppliers to promote and sell their products or services to the foreign travel buyer at the wholesale, retail and consumer levels.

The USTTA marketing plan has four principal objectives:

i) Trade Support
ii) Consumer Information
iii) Technical Assistance
iv) Media Services.

The various marketing activities performed by USTTA in 1984 include the following:

i) *Trade Support:* USTTA regional offices serviced 134 000 enquiries from the travel trade in their markets, and initiated 28 000 trade contacts to make recommendations on tour planning and construction. USTTA conducted or supported 106 training workshops and seminars, for more than 10 000 tourism industry staff members abroad. Included was special workshop training for travel trade personnel in Australia and New Zealand. More than 2 500 foreign travel agents and wholesalers inspected US travel facilities on trips conducted in co-operation with the airlines, State travel offices, city convention and visitors bureaux, and private sector travel companies and attractions. Nearly one million copies of brochures, booklets and maps were given to foreign travel sellers for distribution to prospective travellers. Each of USTTA's six regional offices sends monthly or bi-monthly information on the latest US tourism industry developments to approximately 5 000 travel firms in its market. Nearly 50 000 foreign travel trade representatives and 600 000 members of the foreign public were brought together with US travel sellers at 29 international travel shows.

ii) *Consumer Information:* The six USTTA regional offices serviced a total of 399 000 enquiries.

iii) *Technical Assistance:* To aid US tourism interests in marketing abroad, USTTA introduced a "Foreign Tour Operators Directory". Listed are more than 900 sellers of travel to the United States from 23 countries which are the source of 88 per cent of all foreign visitors. The booklet provides addresses as well as telephone and telex numbers. USTTA assisted 41 travel missions with more than 700 participants from the US private and public sectors, and made available "A Guide to Planning and Conducting a Successful Travel Mission Abroad". This booklet contains instructions to be followed from beginning to completion of a travel mission. Several USTTA offices provided other travel mission guides tailored specifically for their markets.

iv) *Media Services:* More than 1 000 foreign journalists came to the United States and gathered their own information on destinations, facilities, attractions, events and prices, and produced stories and TV programmes which would have cost USTTA $60 million if purchased as advertising. These efforts to place US tourism stories in print and broadcast media abroad resulted in international consumer media coverage equivalent to an estimated $44 million had it been paid advertising. Further, through the travel trade press and its own trade newsletters, USTTA informed travel agents and tour operators abroad about low-cost accommodation, air and surface transport, cruises, special interest tours, incentive travel, and US convention centres.

USTTA also expanded a new programme initiated in 1982 to gather comprehensive consumer marketing data, heretofore unavailable, on the volume and characteristics of travellers to and from the United States. An In-Flight Survey was designed for distribution aboard international flights from the United States to all regions of the world. More than 30 US and foreign air carriers co-operated in the distribution of questionnaires to passengers aboard selected sample flights. The In-Flight Survey is partially subsidised by the sponsorship of public and private tourism agencies and companies. In-Flight Survey data were made available in 1984, covering foreign visitors to the United States in the four quarters of 1983. Comparable reports analysing responses of Americans going abroad were also issued on a subscription basis.

Yugoslavia. During 1984, more money was spent on overall tourist promotion and information activities abroad (calculated on a basis of 1 per cent of the foreign currency receipts from tourism in 1983). The various marketing and promotional activities of Yugoslavian offices abroad led to more foreign tourists being attracted to visit Yugoslavia. The XIVth Winter Olympic Games in Sarajevo, and the various activities organised in connection with them made a considerable contribution to a favourable presentation of tourist possibilities in the country.

Research was conducted on the position of Yugoslavia in the following markets: Germany, Austria, Switzer-land, France, Great Britain, the Netherlands and Scandinavia. The main purpose of these studies was to adapt the supply to demand and to establish a common strategy in these markets, strategy aimed in particular on reinforcing the competitive position of Yugoslavia as a tourist destination for the forthcoming season.

The Nordic countries. Under the sponsorship of the Nordic Tourist Board and the Nordic Council of Ministers (from Denmark, Finland, Iceland, Norway and Sweden), a number of joint research projects have been conducted in recent years. In 1984 two comprehensive image studies have been made in the French and Belgian markets. The results were published in December 1984.

c) Protection of the tourist as a consumer

Australia. In September 1984 the Government approved the preparation of a model licensing Bill which could be adopted by the States and Territories in drafting their own travel agents licensing legislation. Approval was also given for the drafting of a Bill to establish a National Compensation Fund. The legislation would provide protection of, and where necessary compensation for, consumers and ensure that agents within the industry provide services of at least a minimum standard. Bills were drafted and circulated to the State Governments. In April 1985 the Federal Government decided not to proceed with the establishment of the National Compensation Fund leaving the remaining work on implementation of licensing to the States.

Canada. The ACTA (Alliance of Canadian Travel Association) Performance Plan is not yet a reality but it is far more than a "somewhat idealistic plan" as mentioned in last year's report. The principle upon which it is based is that the user would be required to make a small payment on each purchase of prepaid travel services. The accumulated monies would be used to buy an insurance policy, the proceeds of which would respond in the event of a financial default on the part of any of the suppliers involved. With the insurance money and the expertise of those in the travel industry, alternate arrangements would be provided to the traveller. A refund of money would be considered as a second alternative but the major attraction of the "Performance" is the aspect of actual performance.

In 1984, considerable time was spent in aligning support of Government, consumers, and the industry. The major focus of attention was on Government. Each of the ten provincial Ministries was visited on at least one occasion and an extensive brief was presented to the annual meeting of Consumer Ministers in the autumn.

In the most recent Throne Speech, the Government of British Columbia indicated an intention to return the administration of the Travel Industry Registration and Compensation Fund to the trade. The industry objected to this proposal, feeling that without the resources that are available to a Government, it would not be able to administer the existing regime adequately. In the autumn of 1984, the Government was convinced to maintain the existing system, and to try to streamline existing procedures within present parameters. The trade is convinced that this will better serve the interests of the consumer.

With the urging and co-operation of ACTA-Ontario, the Government of Ontario passed a series of Advertising Guidelines that are intended to reduce the prospect of consumer confusion. These guidelines have the power of law as they are official regulations passed pursuant to the Travel Industry Act.

Finland. Through legislation and the establishment of a guarantee fund, the requirements for tour operators have been strengthened in order to protect the consumers against bankruptcy, non-fulfilment of contract, etc. Tour operators are further obliged to inform the public of their membership in the fund.

Japan. In 1982, the Japanese Travel Agency Law was amended to ensure greater fairness in transactions between travel agents and tourists, safety in travel and benefits for tourists. The newly amended law entered into force on 1st April 1983. In order to attain its objectives, the Law established five systems: i) the registration system; ii) the business guarantee bond system; iii) the Certified Travel Service Supervisors system; iv) the regulations for fair transactions, and v) the travel agents association system. Those systems are as follows:

- The Registration System: According to the law, travel agents in Japan are classified into three groups: General Travel Agent, who may deal in both international and domestic travel agency business; Domestic Travel Agent, who may deal in only domestic travel agency business; and Travel Sub-Agent, who may deal in travel services on behalf of a travel agent as its representative. Only a person who is registered with the Government can conduct travel agency business. An applicant must meet several conditions for registration, which include his commercial probity, fairness of business, legal and financial abilities.
- Business Guarantee Bond System: A travel agent (except a travel sub-agent) is required to deposit a business guarantee bond before he starts his business for the protection of his clients. When a travel agent becomes insolvent, those who have made transactions with the agent for travel services are compensated for their loss, if any, by the guarantee bond deposited by the agent.
- Certified Travel Service Supervisor System: A travel agent must assign one or more Certified Travel Service Supervisors, who have passed the national examinations, to each of his offices.
- Regulations for Fair Transactions: The law makes several stipulations in order to protect travellers' interests. These are as follows:
    i) A travel agent must establish his handling fees for travel services and display the tariff prominently in his office;
    ii) A travel agent must have his general terms and conditions for travel contracts authorised by the Government. These must be set out in a place where travellers can easily read them or may have free access to them;
    iii) A travel agent, when entering into a contract with travellers, must explain to them the conditions of transactions and must deliver to them documents specifying the particulars of travel services to be rendered.
- Travel Agents Association: The Government may designate a group consisting of travel agents as a Travel Agents Association. There are two designated travel agents associations at present. They are the Japan Association of Travel Agents (JATA), whose members are General Travel Agents, and the Japan Association of Domestic Travel Agents. A travel agents association is required by the law to undertake the following activities: settlement of complaints from clients regarding travel arrangements made by any of the members; compensation business for those who dealt with their members; arrangements of educational programmes for members' employees; and guidance to members to ensure the sound and healthy development of the travel industry.

As a part of the travel trouble prevention campaign, the "Have a Nice Trip '85 Campaign" was conducted by the Ministry of Transport and local governments in co-operation with the National Police Agency, JATA and the Japan Association of Domestic Travel Agents from 9th to 15th March 1985. The outlines of this campaign were as follows:

- In accordance with the Travel Agency Law, the officials of the Ministry of Transport and of local governments entered the business offices of travel agents and inspected whether they had obeyed the Travel Agency Law;
- Facilities for reporting on unregistered travel agents were created in the Ministry of Transport and local governments and JATA, and the system of co-operation with the police was secured;
- Information media and advertising agents were required to practise self-regulation not to run advertisements for unregistered travel agents; and
- Tourists were encouraged to use registered travel agents.

Norway. Through legislation and the establishment of a guarantee fund, the requirements for tour operators have been strengthened in order to protect the consumers against bankruptcy, non-fulfilment of contract etc. Tour operators are further obliged to inform the public of their membership in the fund.

Portugal. Campaigns have been launched to alert the general public to the need to improve the welcome given to tourists and the services provided for them.

Switzerland. Legislation on tourism is being discussed that would considerably improve the situation of tourists. They would in particular, be protected against "intermediary clauses" and other unilateral provisions in travel contracts. It is important to lay down rules concerning the damages to be paid by an agent when his clients' holidays have been spoilt by his shortcomings or mistakes. The introduction of licences for travel agencies and clear conditions for agency operation (security, professional competence, etc.) are also being discussed. Bodies concerned are at present being consulted on reform of the law concerning travel agencies and contracts.

United Kingdom. The Government has announced proposals for legislation to prevent false and misleading price indications generally. These proposals extend to display of exchange rates and commission charges by bureaux de change operators which have been a source of complaints in recent years.

d) Staggering of holidays

Canada. The tourism marketing strategies do take into account the need to influence consumer demand and travel trade development in off seasons in order to assist Canada's tourism industry in maximising revenues and optimising operational efficiency.

Denmark. Legislators and labour market organisations have not come to any agreement with regard to possible staggering of holidays. However, since the seasonal problem is very important in Denmark, the Danish Tourist Board has started the following activities in order to make the most of off-season capacity:

- Information and brochure material for the German market has been developed to present Denmark as a holiday destination outside the tourist peak season;
- In its general production of brochures, the holiday possibilities of Denmark which are not exclusively related to the peak season have been stressed to a greater extent than previously;
- When supporting product development of private product suppliers, the Danish Tourist Board has particularly backed projects that can attract tourists outside the crest of the high season.

Finland. The *"Hiihdä Halvalla"* (Ski Cheap) campaign was continued. The goal of the campaign is to increase sales of tourist services outside the peak winter season by means of specially reduced rates. The campaign also includes extensive advertising and a brochure produced in collaboration with the trade.

France. In 1984, the Secretary of State for Tourism set up a scheme of awards, administered by a country-wide panel, for firms making noteworthy efforts to adjust working-time and holiday arrangements.

The economic aspect of staggered holidays: Specific action was taken with the *Préfets, Commissaires de la République,* in three employment areas (Blois, Troyes and Clermont Ferrand), in conjunction with employers, trade unions, associations, etc. Assessments and technical assistance were available for firms wishing to introduce new arrangements in order to stagger holidays. A brochure for managers *"Gérer l'entreprise, Gérer les vacances"* (Run the company, Run the holidays) was published by the *Documentation Française.* It is a practical guide to the organisation of production, and hence greater staggering of holidays. In November 1984, in conjunction with the *Direction de la Sécurité et de la Circulation Routières* in the Ministry of Transport, and the *Direction du Temps Libre et de l'Education Populaire* in the Ministry for Youth and Sport, an information file was sent to over 9 000 industrial firms. At the same time the Ministry of Transport surveyed firms about their holiday planning.

These efforts are bearing fruit and the results are encouraging. The proportion of enterprises closing down for holidays, 54 per cent in 1982, fell to 48 per cent in 1983 and to 45 per cent in 1984.

Staggering of school holidays: Since 1967, a number of experiments have been made to reconcile the needs of schoolchildren and the interests of the tourist industry. They have mainly focused on "zoning" policies. The solutions for the winter holidays have on the whole given satisfaction but opinion is more divided about the summer. The Ministry of Education is currently considering a change in school schedules, which would entail a further review of summer holidays.

Tourism reception services also have an essential role to play in promoting staggered holidays. Emphasis has for some time been placed on improving reception services in June and September. There was two-pronged action for the summer of 1984:

- Extensive information about the opening of resorts: Half a million maps were distributed showing France's "long-playing resorts", i.e. places open in June and September, with the facilities they offer. Now covering 670 resorts, the map offers tourists a much wider choice than in 1983, when only 80 resorts had undertaken to remain open from June to September. The incentive to stagger holidays was thus much greater.
- Encouragement to resorts to provide good quality facilities from June to September: the communes on the map were notified by the *Préfets, Commissaires de la République,* that special awards would be given to those providing noteworthy new activities in June

and September, judged on reports submitted to the *Mission de l'Aménagement du Temps*. The first awards for "long-playing resorts" were given by the Minister of Commerce, Crafts and Tourism, to 25 winners (one *département* and 24 tourist resorts) at a ceremony on 15th January 1985. The prize-winners were from everywhere in France, ranging from a commune with 31 inhabitants (Méjannes Le Clap, in the Gard) to a whole *département* (Gironde) and included both well-known tourist resorts, Cap d'Agde (Hérault) and rural communes, Vimoutiers (Orne).

All these studies and activities show that the staggering of holidays is closely related to the extent of tourism products, from luxury hotels to camping sites on farms, from culture to sport, and from discovery to relaxation. Each product caters for a specific clientele and a particular place and time, so it is only by diversifying products very widely that the tourist industry can secure a steady throughput.

Greece. The extension of the tourist season was assisted by incentives provided to hotels in accordance with a law which encourages their opening in winter. Hoteliers therefore receive allowances which are equivalent to what the employees would receive as unemployed persons, if the hotels had been closed. Programmes have been drawn up for the development of winter tourism from abroad. Important foreign travel agencies initiated air-charter holidays during the winter season to Athens, Delphi and Parnassos. Cruises were organised up to 15th December 1984 and started again from 15th March 1985.

Ireland. No staggering of holidays takes place. All action to minimise the problems of the peak are taken by the Tourist Board and commercial bodies in the tourist sector through off season promotion and differential pricing.

New Zealand. The possibility of introducing staggered holidays in New Zealand has been studied several times in the past, particularly when seasonal fluctuations in visitor numbers and occupancy rates have been extreme. However, from the point of view of tourism there is little to be gained from staggered holidays. Concerted marketing efforts overseas have helped to overcome the problems of seasonality. The Trans-Tasman promotional airfares have proved very effective in inducing people to travel during off-peak months.

The Education Department's view on staggered holidays is that people generally want to integrate holidays on a family basis, so school holidays should be co-ordinated nationally. As with staggered holidays, the four-term school year concept has limited appeal to the tourism industry because of the changes in visitor patterns over recent years.

Portugal. The General Directorate for Tourism has carried out its usual annual campaign to encourage the Portuguese to take their holidays in their own country,

and more particularly to do so during off-season periods and in all regions.

Switzerland. Swiss tourism benefits from the staggering of school and business holidays as a result of the federal struture of the country. Experience shows that a satisfactory staggering of holidays has been achieved.

The problem of traffic jams on motorways at the weekends is above all the result of Switzerland's position in the centre of Europe, since there are a great many foreigners in transit. So the question of staggering has to be solved at the European level. One proposal is that holidays should start and end in mid-week.

Yugoslavia. The tourist and catering organisations are seeking to encourage off-season holiday tourism by offering substantial reductions in tourist service prices during these periods. Dependent on the category of tourist accommodation and level of occupancy, off-peak prices are 10 to 40 per cent lower than during the peak period.

To stagger the tourist season, a number of other actions have been undertaken including: lengthening the period of time within which enterprises close down for their annual paid holidays, changing the dates of school holidays to make full use of existing tourist capacities, and organising seminars, conferences, sports competitions, cultural and entertainment events, carnivals and traditional events.

e)   International co-operation

Australia. In the context of Australia's aid programme a tourism training seminar was planned for South Pacific countries. This involved a series of technical visits designed to share Australia's tourism industry development experience and parallel this experience with similar problems encountered in the South Pacific. The programme includes a conference to examine tourism in the context of national development objectives.

Canada. Canada is engaged in an airport construction programme for Trinidad and Tobago, Antigua and St. Kitts under a technical assistance programme.

International co-operation projects involved in the area of tourism and their respective objectives are as follows:

–   English Harbour Development in Antigua, (Leeward and Windward Islands) (C$3.1 million): To assist the Government of Antigua in the development of English Harbour as a national park for tourists. Specifically the Canadian Industrial Development Agency is to assist in the drafting of legislation establishing national parks, development of a plan for the new English Harbour Park and the conception of relevant infrastructure projects.
–   Tourism Sector Study in Leeward and Windward Islands (C$450 000): To determine the impact of

previous tourism related projects in the Region, to assess the role of tourism in the future economic growth of the Region, and to identify suitable interventions in providing the greatest net benefit to the recipient countries.

- Frigate Bay Sewage Plant, St. Kitts, (Leeward and Windward Islands) (C$10 million): To provide a sewage plant at the Frigate Bay, area which has been targeted by the Government of St. Kitts for major tourism development. In addition to provide technical assistance in sewage treatment and in tourism development.

Bilateral air agreements were signed with the following countries:

- *St. Lucia:* An agreement reached with St. Lucia in September 1983 was signed in January 1984. BWIA, the designated carrier for St. Lucia, has since inaugurated a service to Toronto.
- *Singapore:* A new agreement on air transport was signed in July 1984. Air Canada started a service in January 1985 from Toronto to Singapore via London and Bombay. Singapore obtained traffic rights to Montreal and Toronto across the Altantic as well as to Vancouver across the Pacific. Neither Singapore International Airlines, nor CP Air (which is authorised to serve Singapore across the Pacific) has announced any service plans.
- *Greece:* A new bilateral Air Transport Agreement was signed in August 1984. Olympic Airways is currently operating to Toronto and Montreal from Athens and Salonica.
- *Yugoslavia:* A new bilateral Air Transport Agreement was signed in November 1984. Yugoslav Airways is currently operating to Montreal and Toronto from Belgrade and Zagreb.
- *India:* Agreement was reached ad referendum in September 1984 on the terms of a revised bilateral Air Transport Agreement. Under the terms of this agreement, Air India has extended its existing Montreal service to Toronto. Air Canada began service to Bombay and beyond to Singapore in January 1985.
- *New Zealand:* Agreement was reached ad referendum in November 1984 on the terms of a new bilateral Air Transport Agreement. CP Air and Air New Zealand anticipate operating scheduled service as of November 1985.
- *United States of America:* Agreement was reached with the United States for a new route between Toronto/Montreal, and San Juan (Puerto Rico), for Western Airlines to stop at Salt Lake City on the Los Angeles – Calgary/Edmonton route, and for Empire Airlines to serve Syracuse – Ottawa/Montreal; for automatic approval for the operation of new transborder regional, local and commuter air services under agreed criteria; for unrestricted access to Mirabel with virtually unrestricted pricing flexibility, from any airport in the United States with few exceptions for a trial period, and for charter affiliates of Canadian air carriers to serve United States sunspot markets for at least a year.

Germany. A total of DM 5.94 million for technical co-operation was used for different projects which concerned: the provision of experts to catering schools; the building and extension of catering schools, including a training centre for teachers; and the assistance of an advisor to a tourist organisation. Subsidies totalling DM 254 000 were used to facilitate the participation of countries in the *Internationale Tourismusbörse* in Berlin in March.

The funds allocated to the training of specialised and managerial staff totalled about DM 0.6 million; they were used to provide 77 scholarships of an average of 3.1 months each.

On 13th July 1984, the Federal Government and the French Government reached an agreement on the step-by-step reduction of customs formalities at the Franco-German frontier. Similar arrangements were made with the Austrian Government. To inform the travellers of these new facilities, the Federal Government published plaquettes with instructions for customs formality facilitation at the Franco-German and the German-Austrian borders. Negotiations are currently being held with Belgium, Luxembourg and the Netherlands for similar arrangements.

Ireland. Close co-operation particularly in the research area was maintained with the British Tourist Authority and the Northern Ireland Tourist Board.

Japan. As a part of inter-regional co-operation, the Government of Japan assisted the ASEAN Promotion Centre on Trade, Investment and Tourism established in Tokyo in accordance with the Agreement which entered into force on 25th May 1981 between Japan and ASEAN countries for the purpose of promoting exports from ASEAN countries to Japan, accelerating the flow of investment from Japan to ASEAN countries and vitalising tourist traffic from Japan to ASEAN countries, through closer co-operation. ASEAN Centre's annual budget in 1984 was Y 602 million, of which Y 547 million was contributed by the Government of Japan. The main activities conducted by the ASEAN Centre during 1984 in the field of tourism were as follows:

- Five seminars on Japanese Tourism in Singapore, Kuala Lumpur, Manila, Bangkok and Semarang;
- The ASEAN Photos and Children's Drawing Contest in Tokyo;
- The ASEAN Handicraft Presentation (Konnichiwa ASEAN Fair) in Tokyo;
- The ASEAN Tourism Festival, Yokohama and Nagoya;
- A Travel Presentation for the Consumer Sector in Fukuoka; and
- A Travel Trade Seminar, Tokyo.

As a part of the Japanese Technical Co-operation Programme, Japan conducted a group training course called the "Tourism Promotion Seminar" sponsored by the Japan International Co-operation Agency. The Promotion Seminar, in which 20 persons from 20 developing countries participated, was held from 4th October to 5th December 1984 with the collaboration of the Ministry of Transport and the Japan National Tourist Organisation.

On the recommendation of the Ministry of Transport, the Japan International Co-operation Agency attached an expert in the field of hotel and catering services to the Government of Fiji as a part of the Japanese Technical Co-operation Programme.

Netherlands. In 1984 the second of a series of three multi-media campaigns subsidised by the Ministry of Economic Affairs, was launched by the Netherlands *Bureau voor Toerisme,* in co-operation with other tourist organisations.

Portugal. Co-operation with the new Portuguese-speaking countries has continued, particularly with Guinea, Cape Verde, Angola and Mozambique. Technical missions have visited these countries and their nationals have taken training courses in Portuguese hotel schools.

Switzerland. In the context of its technical co-operation programme in the tourism sector, Switzerland's commitments and disbursements in 1984 amounted to SF 4 845 000 and SF 2 345 121 respectively. They concerned four projects: technical co-operation with the hotel schools in Nairobi (Kenya) and Bandung (Indonesia), the training of mountain guides in Peru and scholarships to enable students from developing countries to train at the hotel school in Glion (Switzerland).

In addition, financial support was provided to a working party engaged in research on the impact of tourism in developing countries. Since 1981, Switzerland has provided annual credits amounting to some SF 15 000 to support information programmes and analyse the social and cultural problems to which the development of tourism may give rise in certain third world countries. These contributions are mainly intended to cover the cost of training guides employed by travel agencies specialising in third world travel and publishing information material (brochures, prospectuses, etc.) for tourists travelling to the developing countries.

United Kingdom. A grant totalling £75 100 was made by the Overseas Development Administration for the acquisition and tourism infrastructure of Little Bay Estate in Montserrat.

The United Kingdom signed annual Plans of Co-operation with three countries – all of which arose from individual Health Co-operation Agreements signed several years ago:

– Plan of Co-operation 1984/85, signed on 10th February 1984 with the German Democratic Republic (Agreement of 14th April 1977);
– Plan of Co-operation 1985/86, signed on 15th November 1984 with Hungary (Agreement of 1st November 1978);
– Plan of Co-operation 1985/86, signed on 13th December with Czechoslovakia (Agreement of 23rd April 1976).

Yugoslavia. An Agreement was signed between the Socialist Federal Republic of Yugoslavia and the United States of America on co-operation in the field of tourism.

f) Frontier formalities and currency restrictions for Member countries' residents

To gain an overall view of the present situation concerning frontier formalities world-wide, including the OECD area, the reader is invited to consult the annual study of the World Tourism Organisation entitled "Travel Abroad – Frontier Formalities".

With reference to the particular situations of OECD Member countries, the tables annexed to this Chapter set out the position as at 1st January 1985 as follows:

Table I.1. Documents required for visiting Member countries (for nationals coming from other Member countries);
Table I.2. Currency restrictions imposed on residents of Member countries travelling abroad;
Table I.3. Limits imposed on foreign tourists concerning the importation or exportation of the currency of the country visited.

In June 1984, the Member countries of the European Communities adopted a resolution mainly destined to cut down on waiting time and make checks quicker (Resolution 85/C159/01).

Other arrangements, which only apply to the citizens of Member countries crossing a frontier within the Community, are as follows:

– It is no longer necessary to present a national passport. A national identity card will be sufficient (except, temporarily, Greek nationals);
– In accordance with the Resolution of 23rd June 1981, a uniform European passport will be issued from 1st January 1985;
– Frontier checks on the international insurance certificate (green card) have been abolished for private cars but the driver must be in possession of a third party risk certificate (green card) to comply with Community legislation;
– A driving licence issued by one Member country is already recognised by every other Member country. A uniform multilingual community driving license is to be progressively introduced before 1st January 1986.

41

Table I.1. Travel documents required to visit Member countries
Position at 1st January 1985

Tourists from \ Country visited	Australia	Austria	Belgium	Canada	Denmark	Finland	France	Germany	Greece	Iceland	Ireland	Italy	Japan	Luxembourg	Netherlands	New Zealand	Norway	Portugal	Spain	Sweden	Switzerland	Turkey	United Kingdom[2]	United States	Yugoslavia
Australia[1]		–	–	–	–	–	–	–	–	–	–	–	V	–	–	O	–	–	V	–	–	–	–	V	V
Austria	V		IP	–	I	I	IP	IP	IP	I	–	IP	–	IP	IP	V	I	IP	IP	I	IP	IP	I	V	IP
Belgium	V	IP		–	I	I	IP	IP	IP	I	I	IP	–	O	IP	–	I	I	I	I	IP	IP	I	V	I
Canada[1]	V	–	–		–	–	–	–	–	–	–	–	–	–	–	V	–	–	–	–	–	–	–	O	V
Denmark[1]	V	–	I	–		O	–	I	–	O	I	I	–	I	I	–	O	–	–	O	–	–	I	V	–
Finland[3]	V	–	IP	–	O		–	–	–	O	–	–	–	–	–	–	O	–	–	O	–	–	–	V	I
France	V	IP	IP	–	I	I		IP	IP	I	I	IP	–	IP	IP	–	I	IP	IP	I	IP	–	I	V	I
Germany	V	I	I	–	I	I	IP		I	I	I	I	I	–	I	I	–	I	I	I	I	I	I	V	I
Greece	V	I	I	–	–	–	IP	I		–	I	I	–	I	I	I	–	I	–	I	–	I	–	V	V
Iceland	V	–	V	–	O	O	–	–	–		–	–	–	–	–	–	O	–	–	O	–	–	–	V	I
Ireland[1]	V	–	–	–	–	–	–	–	–	–		–	–	–	–	–	–	–	–	–	–	–	O	V	–
Italy	V	I	I	–	I	–	IP	I	I	I	I		–	I	I	V	I	–	I	–	I	I	I	V	I
Japan[1]	V	–	–	–	–	–	–	–	–	–	–	–		–	–	–	–	–	–	–	–	–	–	V	–
Luxembourg	V	IP	IP	–	I	–	IP	IP	IP	I	I	I	–		IP	–	I	IP	IP	I	IP	IP	I	V	I
Netherlands[1]	V	IP	IP	–	I	–	IP	IP	IP	I	I	IP	–	I		–	I	–	IP	I	IP	I	I	V	I
New Zealand[1]	–	–	–	–	–	–	–	–	–	–	–	–	–	–	–		V	V	–	–	–	–	–	V	V
Norway[1]	V	–	–	O	O	–	–	–	O	–	–	–	–	–	–	–		–	–	O	–	–	–	V	–
Portugal	V	IP	IP	–	–	–	IP	IP	IP	–	–	IP	–	IP	IP	V	–		I	–	IP	–	–	V	I
Spain	V	IP	IP	–	–	–	IP	I	I	–	–	I	–	IP	IP	V	–	I		–	IP	–	–	V	I
Sweden[1]	V	–	–	–	O	O	–	–	–	O	–	–	–	–	–	–	O	–	–		V	–	–	V	–
Switzerland	V	IP	IP	–	I	I	IP	IP	IP	I	I	IP	–	IP	IP	–	I	I	IP	I		IP	I	V	–
Turkey	V	–	V	–	V	V	V	V	V	V	–	–	–	V	V	V	V	–	–	V	V		–	V	I
United Kingdom[1]	V	I	–	I	–	–	–	I	I	–	O	I	–	–	I	I	–	I	I	I	–	I		V	–
United States[1]	V	–	–	O	–	–	–	–	–	–	–	–	V	–	–	–	–	–	–	–	–	–	–		V
Yugoslavia	V	–	–	V	–	–	–	–	V	–	–	–	–	–	V	–	–	–	–	–	–	–	–	V	

I Agreements under which identity cards (national cards or special tourist cards) are accepted.
IP Agreements under which passports having expired for less than five years or identity cards are accepted.
O Agreements under which control of identity documents is abolished.
– Valid passport is required.
V Visa and valid passport required for visits of any length.
1. Countries where no identity cards exist.
2. Nationals from Austria and Switzerland are required to produce a visitors' card in addition to their identity card.
3. Finnish nationals travelling outside the Nordic countries must be in possession of a valid passport.

Table I.2. **Currency restrictions imposed on residents of Member countries when travelling abroad**

Position at 1st January 1985

Country	Credit cards	Allowances in foreign currency or travellers' cheques[1]	Additional allowance *per journey* in domestic currency
Australia	UL	Unlimited. Amounts in excess of A$ 50 000 per person *per journey* require the completion of a declaration form for taxation screening purposes.	$A 5 000 in notes or coins.
Austria		The equivalent of Sch 26 000 *per journey* is granted automatically[2].	Sch 15 000.
Belgium	UL	Unlimited.	Unlimited.
Canada	UL	Unlimited.	Unlimited.
Denmark	UL	Unlimited.	DKr 25 000.
Finland	UL	The equivalent of Fmk 10 000 *per journey* in foreign and/or national currency[3].	
France	UL	The equivalent of FF 5 000 per person and *per journey*. For business purposes, a supplementary allowance of the equivalent of FF 1 000 per person and per day is granted automatically[2].	
Germany	UL	Unlimited.	Unlimited.
Greece		The equivalent of $250 per trip. For business educational or other purposes, higher allowances are granted upon request. For hospitalisation, unlimited amounts are granted. Use of credit cards by Greek nationals limited to the equivalent of $300 per year[4].	Dr 3 000.
Iceland		The equivalent of $1 350 per person and *per journey*. Amount reduced if the person is taking part in an organised tour or has paid for accommodation and other expenses through a travel agency in Iceland. The allowance for children is half the authorised amounts. Credit cards use limited to $1 350.	IKr 2 100 in notes of IKr 100.
Ireland	UL	The equivalent of Ir£500 *per journey* is granted automatically[2].	Ir£ 100.
Italy	UL	The equivalent of L 1 600 000 *per person*[5, 10].	L 400 000.
Japan	UL	Unlimited.	Y 5 000 000.
Luxembourg	UL	Unlimited.	Unlimited.
Netherlands	UL	Unlimited.	Unlimited.
New Zealand	UL	Unlimited.	Unlimited.
Norway		The equivalent of NKr 10 000 *per journey*[2].	NKr 2 000.
Portugal		Per person and *per journey* : Esc 70 000 for persons over 18 years: Esc 50 000 for persons from 12 to 18 years or independent; Esc. 30 000 for persons under 12 years. Authorisation required for all amounts exceeding the above limits for travel undertaken for educational, family, business or health reasons.	Esc 5 000[6].
Spain	UL	The equivalent per person *per journey* of Ptas 80 000 for private travel and the equivalent of Ptas 200 000 for business travel. Travel allowances for education or health are freely granted within the limits of expenses incurred[7].	Ptas 20 000.
Sweden	UL	Unlimited. Amounts in excess of the equivalent of SKr 6 000 *per journey* require justification of use.	SKr 6 000.
Switzerland	UL	Unlimited.	Unlimited.
Turkey		The equivalent of $1 000 per person and *per journey* for travellers over 18 years, and of $500 for travellers under 18 years. Business travellers may take up to the equivalent of $2 000 per trip, subject to bank approval.	LT 450 000 ($ 1 000).
United Kingdom	UL	Unlimited.	Unlimited.
United States	UL	Unlimited[8].	Unlimited.
Yugoslavia		Unlimited provided the currency has been derived from a foreign currency bank account.	Din 2 500[9].

UL : No limits on the use of credit cards for the payment of tourism services.

1. When the allowance is limited, travel tickets (return and circular) can generally be paid for in national currency without reducing the travel allowance.
2. Additional amounts are granted on request, subject to verification of the bona fide of the transaction.
3. Additional amounts are granted for business travel on special request.
4. For travel to EEC countries, up to the equivalent of 720 European units of account.
5. This allowance may be used within the following framework:
   a) foreign banknotes up to a total countervalue of L 1 000 000.
   b) travellers cheques and various other means of payment up to the remaining balance of the allowance.
   No limits are placed on business, health or study journeys.
6. For nationals over 18 years old and bearers of a passport.
7. Additional amounts are granted up to Ptas 320 000 for four private journeys or more per year and up to Ptas 1 400 000 for seven business journey or more per year.
8. Amounts in excess of $5 000 must be reported to United States customs.
9. On first exit and Din 500 for subsequent occasions in the same year.
10. Justifications for use of over L 5 000 000 per year may be requested up to five years after the year in question.

Table I.3. **Limitations imposed on foreign tourists concerning importation and exportation of the currency of the country visited**

Position at 1st January 1985

Country visited	Authorised importation	Authorised exportation
Australia	Unlimited	A$ 5 000
Austria	Unlimited	Sch 15 000
Belgium	Unlimited	Unlimited
Canada	Unlimited	Unlimited
Denmark	Unlimited	DKr 50 000[3]
Finland	Unlimited	Fmk 10 000[3]
France	Unlimited	F 5 000
Germany	Unlimited	Unlimited
Greece	Dr 3 000	Dr 3 000
Iceland	IKr 2 100[1]	IKr 2 100[1]
Ireland	Unlimited	Ir£ 100
Italy	L 400 000	L 400 000
Japan	Unlimited	Y 5 000 000
Luxembourg	Unlimited	Unlimited
Netherlands	Unlimited	Unlimited
New Zealand	Unlimited	Unlimited
Norway	Unlimited	NKr 2 000
Portugal	Esc 5 000	Esc 20 000[3]
Spain	Ptas 200 000	Ptas 20 000
Sweden	Unlimited	Unlimited[4]
Switzerland	Unlimited	Unlimited
Turkey	Unlimited	LT 450 000[5]
United Kingdom	Unlimited	Unlimited
United States	Unlimited	Unlimited
Yugoslavia	Din 2 500[2]	Din 2 500[2]

1. Restricted to denomination of IKr 100.
2. Restricted to denominations of Din 100 or less. Maximum of Din 2 500 on first visit and of Din 500 on subsequent visits in the same year.
3. A higher amount if traveller can prove that the amount does not exceed the sum imported in national or foreign currency.
4. Amounts in excess of the equivalent of SKr 6 000 require justification of their purchase abroad.
5. LT to the equivalent of $ 1 000.

II

INTERNATIONAL TOURIST FLOWS IN MEMBER COUNTRIES IN 1984

This chapter brings together, in the form of summarised tables, all available data concerning international tourist flows to OECD Member countries, broken down into the main regions, and to Yugoslavia, for the period from 1981 to 1984. Monthly data concerning the main generating countries together with annual information on the country of origin of tourists or visitors from abroad are set out in the Series II tables in the Statistical Annex.

Section A gives the available information on *arrivals at frontiers,* either of *tourists* (i.e. persons spending more

than twenty-four hours in the country), or, when this is not available, of *visitors* (which include excursionists).

Section B provides data on development in the *number of nights spent* by foreign tourists *in hotels and similar establishments* (generally speaking, hotels, motels, inns and boarding houses) and *in all means of accommodation* (without distinction of type of accommodation).

Finally, Section C assesses the international tourist flows coming from the four main generating countries, France, Germany, the United Kingdom and the United States.

A.   ARRIVALS AT FRONTIERS

In the fourteen Member countries which assembled data or made estimates concerning international tourist flows at frontiers over the last three years, there was, overall, an increase of 3 per cent in 1984, against zero growth in the previous year (Table II.1).

Apart from the United States, where there was a fall of 4 per cent, and Austria where the level has been constant since 1981, all the countries providing data recorded an improvement in the number of tourists or visitors over the previous years. In Australia and in three important Mediterranean countries, this was a reversal of a decline which took place in 1983; in Australia, there was a rise of 8 per cent (against – 1 per cent), in Greece 16 per cent (– 5 per cent), in Italy 6 per cent (– 4 per cent) and in Spain 4 per cent (– 2 per cent). The most marked expansion took place in Turkey (+ 30 per cent), New Zealand (+ 13 per cent), Portugal (+ 11 per cent), the United Kingdom and Iceland (both + 10 per cent).

An analysis of the figures in the tables by receiving country (Series II.1 in the Annex) which give the number of foreign visitors or tourists by country of origin makes it possible to show the more substantial impact that tourists or visitors from certain countries have on total tourist movements.

a)   Tourist movements recorded at the frontiers of European Member countries

Among the 19 European Member countries, only twelve compile data or make estimates on the movements of foreign visitors or tourists at frontiers. The 1984 data is not available for either France or Germany and Norway has discontinued gathering the information from 1st January 1984. It may be that this tendency will become more general in the future as a result of the attempts of Member countries to improve the unrestricted movement of their residents within the OECD

	T/V	% 82/81	% 83/82	% 84/83	1984 Millions of arrivals
Austria	V	−0.2	0.4	0.1	129.3
Belgium					
Denmark					
Finland					
France	T	9.8	1.6		
Germany	V	−0.3	−1.8		
Greece	T	−9.8	−5.1	15.6	5.5
Iceland	T	1.0	6.9	9.9	0.1
Ireland	V	0.8	0.1	1.0	9.9
Italy	V	11.0	−3.6	5.5	49.2
Luxembourg					
Netherlands					
Norway[2]	V	−0.6	1.4		
Portugal	T	4.7	17.4	10.9	4.1
Spain	V	4.7	−1.8	4.0	42.9
Sweden					
Switzerland	T	2.2	0.0	3.0	11.9
Turkey	V	−1.0	16.8	30.3	2.1
United Kingdom	V	1.6	7.4	9.7	13.7
Canada	T	−4.9	2.5	7.4	13.4
United States[3]	T			−4.0	20.8
Australia[4]	V	1.9	−1.1	7.6	1.0
New Zealand	T	1.3	7.2	12.7	0.4
Japan	V	13.3	9.8	7.2	2.1
OECD[1]		2.3	0.0	3.2	
Yugoslavia	V	−12.7	4.6	5.3	19.7

Table II.1 **Change in growth rate of number of arrivals of foreign tourists at frontiers**[1]

V   Visitors.
T   Tourists.
1. Overall trend for all countries with data available from 1981 to 1984.
2. End of series in 1983.
3. New series in 1983.
4. Data for 1984 are estimated.

area, particularly if they are travelling for tourism purposes. On the other hand, of these twelve countries, only Iceland does not have data on the number of nights spent by foreign tourists in various means of accommodation.

Greece.   After two years of decline, foreign tourists arriving at the frontiers of Greece rose by 16 per cent, bringing the level back to that of 1982. In comparing these two years, the following trends may be noted in the main markets. The share of the most important single contributor, the United Kingdom, remained relatively constant at about 19 per cent (the number of arrivals rose in 1984 by 17 per cent). The part played by German and United States tourists rose to 16 per cent and 9 per cent respectively and their numbers had risen steadily over the previous two years. France regained its 7 per cent share, since a rise of 36 per cent in the number of arrivals more than compensated for the 11 per cent fall in 1983. As far as the Yugoslav market was concerned it contributed 5 per cent of the total, as a result of a fourfold increase in the number of arrivals, from a 1983 level only one-tenth that of 1982.

Iceland.   After a deceleration of arrivals in 1982 (+ 1 per cent) the rising tendency has speeded up with a growth of 7 per cent in 1983 and 10 per cent in 1984. The expansion in 1984 was particularly due to an increase in visitors from the other Nordic countries, although the three main markets, which made up 55 per cent of the 1984 total, made their contribution with rises of 10 per cent from the United States and Germany and 6 per cent from the United Kingdom.

Ireland.   The number of foreign visitor arrivals has remained almost stationary since the beginning of the decade. A slight rise of 1 per cent in 1984 brought the total to 9.9 million. This sluggishness reflects the poor performance of the United Kingdom market which has an overwhelming impact since it contributes 93 per cent of the total. Among the other main markets there were changes in direction in both France (+ 1 per cent after − 14 per cent in 1983) and Germany (− 2 per cent against + 14 per cent).

Italy.   A 6 per cent rise in 1984 reversed the previous trend and more than counterbalanced the 4 per cent reduction in the previous year. The visitors from countries which contributed most to the total were all more plentiful in 1984, with the Germans, who make up 22 per cent of the total, rising by 4 per cent, the Swiss (22 per cent of the total) by 7 per cent, the French (17 per cent of the total) by 7 per cent and the Austrians (10 per cent of the total) by 8 per cent. Of four other countries, who each made up 4 per cent of the total, Yugoslavian visitors increased by 59 per cent, Americans and Dutch by 3 per cent, whereas there was a 5 per cent fall in the number of British visitors.

Portugal.   In 1984, both visitors and tourists grew at a similar rate of about 11 per cent. As a result the share of excursionists remained constant at 58 per cent of the total number of visitors, and amounted to 5.7 million. As far as tourist arrivals were concerned, Spain, whose tourists have not unnaturally made the largest single contribution (47 per cent of the total, 5 points more than in 1982), added 16 per cent which, together with a 15 per cent increase in British tourists (who made up 16 per cent of the total) ensured that there would be a substantial rise in spite of the decline in French and German arrivals, by 1 per cent and 6 per cent respectively.

Spain.   After a 2 per cent fall in the previous year, the number of visitors arriving at the frontier of Spain rose again, by 4 per cent, to reach a total of 42.9 million. Among OECD Member countries, who provide 91 per cent of Spain's visitors, the arrivals from four important categories declined. This was true for the two most important markets, France (− 3 per cent; 23 per cent of the total) and Portugal (− 1 per cent; 20 per cent of the total) and for one secondary market, Belgium (− 2 per cent; 2 per cent of the total) as well as for Spaniards resident abroad whose numbers have fallen slightly over the last two years, by 1 per cent in 1983 and 2 per cent in 1984. However, there were substantial increases in visitors coming from the countries which hold the third and fourth positions, the United Kingdom (+ 16 per cent; 14 per cent of the total) and Germany (+ 6 per cent; 12 per cent).

Turkey. The number of travellers to Turkey continued to rise spectacularly with a 30 per cent increase, following 17 per cent in the previous year. Four Member countries made particular contributions to the increase of 1983 and 1984, providing between them 36 per cent of the 1983 total. These were the United States (80 per cent and 13 per cent), Germany (3 per cent and 38 per cent), Greece (3 per cent and 29 per cent) and the United Kingdom (42 per cent and 6 per cent). In addition France reversed its trend and added 17 per cent in 1984 after an 11 per cent fall in the previous year.

United Kingdom. The growth rate of arrivals at frontiers has accelerated since 1982. In that year they increased by 1 per cent and then rose by 7 per cent and 10 per cent in the two following years. In 1984 the four main generating countries all increased their number of arrivals, the United States by 19 per cent, France by 8 per cent and Ireland by 4 per cent, with visitors from Germany rising by 8 per cent against – 5 per cent in the previous year. There was also a very marked rise in the numbers from the three Pacific Members of the OECD, which together come in fifth place as generators of tourists, whose 30 per cent increase in 1984 was primarily the result of the 38 per cent rise in Australian visitors.

b) Tourist movements at the frontiers of North American Member countries

The number of tourists arriving at the frontiers of the two North American Member countries in 1984 was the same as in the previous year, some 34.2 million. The effect of the 4 per cent fall for the United States whose arrivals made up 61 per cent of the total, was almost exactly balanced by the 7 per cent rise reported by Canada.

Canada. In 1984 the volume of tourists arriving at the frontiers of Canada grew more rapidly than that of visitors (by 7 per cent against 2 per cent), which implies a fall in the number of excursionists. This category (which made up 64 per cent of all visitors in 1983) went down from 21.7 to 21.4 million in 1984. Changes in tourist flows from the United States (which provides 95 per cent of visitors and 87 per cent of tourists to Canada) accounted for the greater part of this. Tourists arriving from other countries which are important markets for Canada increased by 19 per cent and 10 per cent respectively from Japan and from non-Member countries of Asia and Oceania, by 7 per cent from France (after an 11 per cent fall in 1983), whereas

tourists from the United Kingdom fell for the third consecutive year, by 2 per cent (against – 15 per cent and – 12 per cent in 1982 and 1983).

United States. The new statistical series which was started in 1983 (see Chapter II of the 1984 Report) does not permit comparisons with earlier years. In 1984 the volume of tourist arrivals fell by 4 per cent. The only increases recorded were for tourists from Latin America, including Mexico (+ 21 per cent), from Japan (+ 10 per cent) and from France (+ 8 per cent), which did not by any means balance out the 8 per cent reduction in those coming from Canada, which is by far the most important market, contributing 53 per cent of the total in 1984.

c) Tourist movements at the frontiers of Member countries in the Pacific Basin

The total number of arrivals at the frontiers of the three Pacific Member countries of the OECD continued to increase and reached 3.7 million in 1984, an 8 per cent rise on the previous year. New Zealand was the country where the increase was most pronounced with 11 per cent more visitors and 13 per cent more tourists. Japan passed the 2 million mark and provisional estimates suggest an 8 per cent growth in Australia, making more than a million arrivals in 1984.

New Zealand. The number of tourists arriving in New Zealand has accelerated over the last three years with a 1 per cent growth in 1982 and + 7 per cent and + 13 per cent in the successive years. This has essentially resulted from the increasing amount of tourists from Asia and Oceania (which together constituted 61 per cent of the 1984 total), with 12 per cent more from Australia (+ 3 per cent in 1983), from Japan (+ 29 per cent against + 19 per cent) and from the non-Member countries in the zone (+ 15 per cent against + 9 per cent).

Japan. In 1984 visitors to Japan exceeded 2 million for the first time. Although the growth rate has slackened over the last three years from + 13 per cent in 1982 to + 10 per cent in 1983 and + 7 per cent in 1984, these levels have been substantially higher than the general trends for Member countries as a whole. The most significant increases because of the importance of their markets, were recorded for the United States (+ 11 per cent; 24 per cent of the total) and for the non-Member countries of Asia and Oceania (+ 7 per cent; 50 per cent). Among non-Member countries, Taiwan and South Korea were most prominent although visitors from China increased by 92 per cent over 1983 to reach a total of 51 010, reflecting the rapprochement between the two countries.

B. NIGHTS SPENT IN THE VARIOUS MEANS OF ACCOMMODATION

Eleven European countries have comparable data on the nights spent by foreign tourists *in hotels and similar establishments* for the period 1981-84. In 1984 these rose overall by 5 per cent (compared to + 1 per cent in 1983). All these countries recorded an increase in 1984 except for Italy which declined for the second consecutive year, by 1 per cent compared to – 2 per cent in 1983. Seven countries maintained a positive direction for at least the second consecutive year: Portugal (+ 12 per cent), Spain (+ 12 per cent), Sweden (+ 8 per cent), France (Ile de France only, + 8 per cent), Norway (+ 7 per cent), Finland (+ 3 per cent) and Denmark (+ 2 per cent). In several other countries there was renewed growth notably in Yugoslavia (+ 17 per cent against – 1 per cent in 1983), Switzerland (+ 2 per cent against – 1 per cent), Luxembourg (+ 2 per cent against – 2 per cent) and Austria (+ 1 per cent against – 2 per cent). (Table II.2).

For the ten countries which provide information covering *all means of accommodation* from 1981 to 1984, there was a 4 per cent rise in 1984 (against + 1 per cent in 1983). Six countries continued to increase in 1984, specifically Spain (+ 11 per cent), Luxembourg (+ 10 per cent), the United Kingdom (+ 7 per cent), Portugal (+ 5 per cent), Sweden (+ 4 per cent) and Ireland (+ 3 per cent). In Yugoslavia and Greece, there was a substantial positive switch respectively of + 20 per cent (compared to – 1 per cent) and + 17 per cent (against – 8 per cent), Switzerland (– 3 per cent), Italy (– 2 per cent) and Austria (– 1 per cent) continued to decline and were joined by Denmark with a 4 per cent fall (after + 3 per cent in the previous year). (Table II.3).

An analysis of the data on nights spent by foreign tourists in the various means of accommodation, for those countries for which a breakdown by tourists' country of origin is available (see Tables in Series II.1 in the Annex), shows the impact that the residents or nationals of certain tourist generating countries had on the 1984 trends.

Table II.2 **Change in growth rate of nights spent by foreign tourists in hotels and similar establishments[1]**

	% 82/81	% 83/82	% 84/83	1984 Millions of bed-nights
Austria	–1.6	–1.7	1.0	55.5
Belgium	8.3	4.2		
Denmark	–0.7	1.2	2.4	4.6
Finland	–1.4	1.8	2.5	2.1
France[2]	–3.7	4.2	7.8	17.9
Germany	–2.6	1.1		
Greece	–2.5			
Iceland				
Ireland				
Italy	9.6	–1.9	–0.6	63.0
Luxembourg		–1.8	2.4	0.9
Netherlands	4.5	–5.0		
Norway	–7.9	2.2	7.3	2.5
Portugal	2.1	3.5	11.5	11.0
Spain	8.3	4.0	11.7	89.1
Sweden	0.4	10.2	8.3	3.3
Switzerland	–5.7	–0.7	1.7	20.2
Turkey		45.3		
United Kingdom				
Canada				
United States				
Australia				
New Zealand				
Japan[3]	11.4			
OECD[1]	3.6	0.8	5.0	
Yugoslavia	–5.9	–0.5	17.0	23.9

1. Overall trend for all countries with data available from 1981 to 1984.
2. Concerns Ile-de-France region only.
3. End of series in 1982.

Table II.3 **Change in growth rate of nights spent by foreign tourists in all means of accommodation[1]**

	% 82/81	% 83/82	% 84/83	1984 Millions of bed-nights
Austria	–2.8	–2.8	–0.8	86.7
Belgium	18.7	4.5		
Denmark	3.4	3.3	–4.4	9.1
Finland				
France		3.0		
Germany[2]			9.9	26.2
Greece	–2.2	–7.6	17.2	32.4
Iceland				
Ireland	–0.5	8.6	2.9	19.3
Italy	9.1	–3.5	–2.1	95.2
Luxembourg		9.5	10.0	2.5
Netherlands	8.8	–2.7		
Norway	–18.3			
Portugal	0.7	0.6	5.0	12.5
Spain	8.5	3.7	10.9	92.9
Sweden	1.5	18.3	3.9	7.5
Switzerland	–6.3	–2.1	–2.8	35.0
Turkey	19.7	50.2		
United Kingdom	1.0	6.3	6.8	155.3
Canada	–5.5	–4.1		
United States				
Australia				
New Zealand				
Japan				
OECD[1]	2.1	1.1	4.0	
Yugoslavia	–10.4	–0.6	19.6	42.3

1. Overall trend for all countries with data available from 1981 to 1984.
2. New series from 1983.

Trends in the nights spent by tourists in individual countries

Austria. For the third year running, the number of nights spent in all means of accommodation fell, bringing the 1984 total to 86.7 million, 6 per cent lower than in 1981. During the last year this decline can essentially be attributed to a reduction in the use of supplementary means of accommodation since in hotels and similar establishments the number of nights went up by 1 per cent over 1983, a figure which would have been higher had it not been for the 4 per cent contraction in the German market which, with 61 per cent of the total, is by far the most important. The other most significant markets all recorded gains with + 29 per cent for France, + 28 per cent for the United States, + 8 per cent for the United Kingdom and + 3 per cent for the Netherlands.

Denmark. 1984 saw a substantial regression of supplementary means of accommodation in relation to the hotel sector in contrast to the previous year. This is shown by the following figures; nights spent in hotels and similar establishments rose by 1 per cent in 1983 and 2 per cent in 1984 whereas nights spent in other means of accommodation increased by 5 per cent in 1983 and fell by 10 per cent in the following year. As a result foreign tourists to Denmark in 1984 spent more nights in hotels than in supplementary accommodation. The decline in the use of other means of accommodation was particularly notable for German tourists who spent 12 per cent less nights than in 1983 as well as for the other Nordic countries, who with Germany, made up 68 per cent of the market in 1984. The only exception appeared to be France, whose use of the supplementary sector fell by 35 per cent in 1983 but then rose again by 65 per cent in 1984 after the removal of the French currency restrictions.

Finland. The nights spent in hotels has continued to rise slowly, by 3 per cent in 1984 after 2 per cent in the previous year. This rise was due mainly to the contribution of tourists from Germany (+ 9 per cent; 13 per cent of the total) and the United States (+ 5 per cent; 8 per cent). On the other hand tourists from its two Nordic neighbours went on dropping from Norway by 2 per cent (− 3 per cent in 1983) and from Sweden by 4 per cent (against − 10 per cent) and their combined share fell to 26 per cent in 1984. Russian tourists remained at the level of the previous years after a rise of 8 per cent in 1983.

France. After a 4 per cent drop in 1982 the record of nights spent in hotels in the Ile de France region has progressively increased, by 4 per cent in 1983 and 8 per cent in 1984. This was due to the continued growth in tourists from three of the four most important generating countries, the United States (+ 31 per cent compared to + 25 per cent in 1983), the United Kingdom (+ 8 per cent against + 3 per cent) and Italy (+ 6 per cent against + 3 per cent). On the other hand there was

a downturn in the markets in Germany (− 7 per cent against + 7 per cent) and Japan (− 6 per cent against + 2 per cent).

Italy. The declining attraction of supplementary means of accommodation continued in 1984. There was a 5 per cent decline in the nights spent by foreign tourists in such establishments after a 6 per cent reduction in the previous year. In hotels on the other hand the decline was much less pronounced with less than 1 per cent reduction compared to 2 per cent in 1983.

Norway. Foreign tourists again spent more nights in Norwegian hotels, with a 7 per cent increase in 1984 against + 2 per cent in the previous years. Among the main markets there were increases in tourists from the United States (+ 11 per cent; 20 per cent of the total), from Germany (+ 8 per cent; 15 per cent), from the United Kingdom (+ 4 per cent; 12 per cent) and from Denmark (+ 17 per cent; 12 per cent). On the other hand the Dutch, Swedes and Finns spent fewer nights in Norway, a continuing trend, with respectively − 22 per cent (− 7 per cent in 1983), − 2 per cent (− 9 per cent) and − 1 per cent (− 3 per cent).

Portugal. Over the last two years the total nights spent in hotels and similar establishments has grown more rapidly than in all means of accommodation (by + 10 per cent and + 4 per cent, against + 5 per cent and + 1 per cent). In Portugal too, this is due to a decline in the supplementary sector which fell from 2.2 million nights in 1982 to 1.5 in 1984. This took place for all of the six most important markets for Portugal, which together make up three quarters of the total. In the hotel sector, the growth in nights spent by tourists resident in these generating countries, by decreasing order of importance, was as follows: United Kingdom, + 9 per cent; Germany, + 8 per cent; Spain, + 13 per cent; Netherlands, + 13 per cent; United States, + 19 per cent; France, + 19 per cent.

Spain. The number of nights spent by foreign tourists in *"estrellas de oro"* and *"estrellas de plata"* hotels (gold and silver star category) continued to rise to a total of nearly 9 million, 12 per cent up on the previous year. Tourists from individual Member countries all increased their nights except for Portugal (− 7 per cent). The most vigorous increases were by those from Italy (+ 51 per cent), North America (+ 18 per cent), the United Kingdom (+ 17 per cent) and Belgium (+ 11 per cent).

Sweden. Here also the number of nights spent in hotels and similar establishments went up rapidly, by 8 per cent, whereas those in supplementary accommodation stagnated. The only country whose tourists recorded a decline in both cases was the Netherlands by respectively 30 per cent and 24 per cent. On the other hand the nights spent in all means of accommodation rose for the other Nordic countries, Norway (+ 8 per cent), Finland (+ 7 per cent) and Denmark (+ 7 per

49

cent) and for the United States (+ 6 per cent) which together made up 53 per cent of the total in 1984.

Switzerland. The number of nights spent in all means of accommodation fell for the third successive year, by – 3 per cent compared to – 2 per cent and – 6 per cent in the previous years. In 1984 this decline only affected supplementary accommodation in which a 9 per cent drop (– 1.4 million nights) was recorded, while the nights in hotels increased by 2 per cent. The fall in nights spent by tourists from Europe as a whole and the rise in those from outside Europe which has occurred since the record year of 1981, continued in 1984, with a 6 per cent decline for Europeans and a 13 per cent increase for non-Europeans. Among individual countries German tourists were reduced by 9 per cent whereas those from the United States went up by 27 per cent. These two groups constitute 51 per cent of the total. Among other important generating countries there were increases for France (+ 2 per cent), Japan (+ 3 per cent) and Italy (+ 6 per cent) and decreases for the United Kingdom (– 3 per cent), Austria (– 5 per cent) and Belgium (– 8 per cent).

United Kingdom. Nights spent by foreign tourists have been on a rising curve since 1982 with annual growth rates of 1 per cent, 6 per cent and 7 per cent. In 1984 the only important markets which recorded falls were Italy (– 3 per cent; 4 per cent of the total) and Africa as a whole (– 6 per cent; 7 per cent). However, increases (by order of market importance) were recorded by the United States (+ 15 per cent), non-Member countries of Asia and Oceania (+ 10 per cent), Germany (+ 1 per cent), France (+ 14 per cent), Australia (+ 16 per cent), Canada (+ 5 per cent) and Ireland (+ 5 per cent).

Yugoslavia. After two years of decline the number of nights recorded in all means of accommodation rose by 20 per cent, more than recuperating the losses of 10 per cent and 1 per cent in 1982 and 1983. This rise was caused by visitors from both halves of Europe which made up 96 per cent of the 1984 total. The revivals of two very important markets should be noted; Germany added 9 per cent (– 2 per cent in 1983) and Austria gained 13 per cent (– 2 per cent). There was also continued advances by tourists from Eastern Europe (+ 31 per cent following + 5 per cent), from the United Kingdom (+ 30 per cent after + 3 per cent) and Italy (+ 29 per cent after + 8 per cent).

C. MAIN GENERATING COUNTRIES

a) Arrivals at frontiers

For the thirteen countries which have information for 1984 on the arrivals of visitors or tourists at frontiers broken down by country of origin, the overall flow of tourists increased by 5 per cent over the previous year. Each of the main generating countries also recorded rises in 1984. For the French market, this was a reversal of the 1983 trend with a 2 per cent rise following a drop of 5 per cent in the previous year. The other main markets were characterised by strengthened expansion, for the United States by 10 per cent (after 8 per cent in 1983), for Germany by 6 per cent (after 2 per cent) and for the United Kingdom by 5 per cent (after 2 per cent). (Table II.4).

The tourist flows from France increased in all reporting countries except Portugal (– 1 per cent) and Spain (– 3 per cent) where in 1984 they constituted 8 per cent and 23 per cent respectively of total arrivals. The most notable recoveries took place in Greece (+ 36 per cent after – 11 per cent in 1983), in Canada (+ 23 per cent after – 23 per cent), in Iceland (+ 24 per cent after – 11 per cent) and in Turkey (+ 17 per cent after – 11 per cent).

All reporting countries recorded an increase in the number of arrivals of tourists/visitors from the United States. These were most important in those countries where this market made up a substantial part of the total, such as Canada (+ 7 per cent; 87 per cent of the total), Iceland (+ 10 per cent; 32 per cent), Japan (+ 11 per cent; 24 per cent) and the United Kingdom (+ 19 per cent; 20 per cent).

As far as the German market was concerned, only four countries reported declines, two European countries, Portugal (– 6 per cent) and Ireland (– 2 per cent) and two Pacific countries, Australia (– 9 per cent) and New Zealand (– 1 per cent). On the other hand, in a number of countries in which German tourists play a major role, there were increases significantly higher than the average growth rate. This occurred in Turkey where they constituted 11 per cent of the total and increased by 38 per cent (compared to an overall growth of 30 per cent), in Greece (16 per cent of the total with an increase of + 19 per cent against an average of + 16 per cent) and in Spain (12 per cent of the total; + 6 per cent compared to + 4 per cent).

Tourists arriving from the United Kingdom increased, particularly in Greece (+ 17 per cent; 19 per

Table II.4 **Tourist flows from the four main generating countries**

Number of arrivals at frontiers

	T/V	Total Variation % 84/83	From France		From Germany		From United Kingdom		From United States	
			Relative share % 84	Variation % 84/83	Relative share % 84	Variation % 84/83	Relative share % 84	Variation % 84/83	Relative share % 84	Variation % 84/83
Austria (R)										
Belgium (R)										
Denmark (N)										
Finland (R)										
France (R)										
Germany (R)										
Greece (N)	T	15.6	7.3	35.5	15.6	18.6	18.9	17.4	8.6	16.7
Iceland (N)	T	9.9	5.7	23.6	11.3	9.7	11.0	6.0	32.0	9.5
Ireland (N)	V	1.0	0.8	1.2	0.9	-2.2	93.1	0.6	3.1	13.1
Italy (N)	V	5.5	17.2	7.2	22.0	4.3	3.6	-5.4	3.6	3.3
Luxembourg (R)										
Netherlands (R)										
Norway (N)										
Portugal (N)	T	10.9	7.6	-0.9	7.2	-5.6	15.5	15.4	4.0	43.9
Spain (N)	V	4.0	23.3	-3.4	12.2	5.6	14.0	16.2	2.2	15.3
Sweden (N)										
Switzerland (R)										
Turkey (N)	V	30.3	4.9	17.2	11.4	38.2	4.2	6.2	10.1	12.9
United Kingdom (R)	V	9.7	11.9	7.6	10.8	8.0			20.2	19.3
EUROPE		6.0		2.2		5.7		5.8		13.8
Canada (R)	T	7.4	0.8	22.5	1.3	6.7	2.6	-2.2	87.3	7.3
United-States (R)	T	-4.0	1.6	8.1	2.6	-4.1	4.4	-9.0		
NORTH AMERICA		0.2		11.4		-1.7		-7.2		7.3
Australia (R)[1]	V	7.6	1.1	11.3	3.1	-8.8	14.3	-1.7	15.9	15.1
New Zealand (R)	T	12.7	0.3	14.1	1.7	-1.0	7.2	2.7	17.9	19.8
Japan (N)	V	7.2	1.6	18.4	2.3	12.8	7.9	-4.3	24.2	10.8
AUSTRALASIA-JAPAN		8.0		16.5		2.8		-2.6		12.6
OECD		4.8		2.4		5.4		4.8		9.7
Yugoslavia (N)										

V Visitors.
T Tourists.
(R) Tourist count by country of residence.
(N) Tourist count by country of nationality.
1. Data for 1984 are estimated.

cent of the total), Portugal (+ 16 per cent; 16 per cent) and Spain (+ 16 per cent; 14 per cent). However there were moderate reductions in Italy (– 5 per cent), Japan (– 4 per cent), Canada and Australia (both – 2 per cent).

b) **Nights spent in the various means of accommodation**

For the twelve countries of Europe which provide data on nights spent by foreign tourists broken down by country of origin, the overall trend was a growth of 5 per cent. In these countries, tourists from three of the four main generating countries of the OECD increased the number of nights they spent, with those from the United States, adding 16 per cent, from the United Kingdom, 12 per cent and from France, 10 per cent. However, there was a decline of 3 per cent for those from Germany (Table II.5).

Tourists from the United States spent more nights in 1984 than in the previous year in all these countries, except Ireland where a 6 per cent fall was reported. Taking into account the importance of this market, the most significant increases took place in the Ile-de-France (+ 31 per cent, where they constituted 19 per cent of the total), Norway (+ 11 per cent, 20 per cent), the United Kingdom (+ 15 per cent, 17 per cent) and Switzerland (+ 27 per cent, 10 per cent).

Only three countries saw a decline in the nights spent by British tourists in 1984: Denmark (– 11 per cent), Switzerland (– 3 per cent) and Sweden (– 1 per cent). In none of these, does the British market exceed 8 per cent of the total. On the other hand, the most vigorous expansion took place in Yugoslavia (+ 30 per cent), Spain (+ 17 per cent), Luxembourg (+ 9 per cent) and in the Ile-de-France, Portugal and Ireland (all + 8 per cent).

51

Table II.5 **Tourist flows from the four main generating countries**

Number of nights spent in the various means of accommodation

	H/A	Total Variation % 84/83	From France		From Germany		From the United Kingdom		From the United-States	
			Relative share % 84	Variation % 84/83	Relative share % 84	Variation % 84/83	Relative share % 84	Variation % 84/83	Relative share % 84	Variation % 84/83
Austria (R)	A	−0.8	2.7	28.7	66.2	−5.1	5.0	6.9	2.5	26.6
Belgium (R)										
Denmark (N)	A	−4.4	1.6	31.2	40.4	−10.7	4.2	−11.4	6.1	5.5
Finland (R)	H	2.5	2.8	26.6	13.2	8.9	5.1	3.8	7.5	5.0
France[1] (R)	H	7.8			10.9	−6.8	11.7	8.2	18.9	31.2
Germany (R)										
Greece (N)										
Iceland (N)										
Ireland (N)	A	2.9	4.5	−19.5	6.4	−7.2	56.3	7.8	17.4	−6.1
Italy (N)										
Luxembourg (R)	A	10.0	3.4	23.1	6.7	27.4	2.9	9.0	3.8	29.0
Netherlands (R)										
Norway (N)	H	7.3	3.2	10.6	15.1	7.8	12.4	4.0	19.8	10.7
Portugal (N)	A	5.0	7.6	1.2	12.8	−3.2	32.2	8.3	5.8	17.3
Spain (H)	H	11.7	7.1	5.7	26.0	3.4	39.5	17.2	3.2	18.3
Sweden (N)	A	3.9	2.0	26.8	19.2	−0.5	4.7	−0.5	5.7	5.8
Switzerland (R)	A	−2.8	7.1	2.4	41.2	−8.4	7.8	−2.6	9.5	26.9
Turkey (N)										
United Kingdom (R)	A	6.8	8.4	13.7	9.2	1.4			17.2	15.3
EUROPE		4.8		9.9		−3.3		12.2		15.6
Canada (R)										
United States (R)										
NORTH AMERICA										
Australia (R)										
New Zealand (R)										
Japan (N)										
AUSTRALASIA-JAPAN										
OECD		4.8		9.9		−3.3		12.2		15.6
Yugoslavia (N)	A	19.6	3.5	43.2	37.9	8.9	8.4	29.6	1.4	35.3

H   Hotels and similar establishments.
A   All means of accommodation.
(R)   Tourist count by country of residence.
(N)   Tourist count by country of nationality.
1.   Concerns Ile-de-France region only.

Compared to the previous year, in which the great majority of countries had recorded a substantial retreat in tourists from France, there was a strong revival in 1984. The only exception to this was Ireland, which dropped by 20 per cent (compared to − 3 per cent in the previous year). The resurgence was most prominent in Yugoslavia (+ 43 per cent), Denmark (+ 31 per cent), Austria (+ 29 per cent), Finland and Sweden (both 27 per cent).

The impact of the falling-off in the nights spent by German tourists was most significant in three countries where Germany is by far the most important customer. These were Austria (− 5 per cent and 66 per cent of the total), Denmark (− 11 per cent, 40 per cent) and Switzerland (− 8 per cent, 41 per cent).

III

THE ECONOMIC IMPORTANCE OF INTERNATIONAL TOURISM IN MEMBER COUNTRIES IN 1984

This chapter brings together the most recent data which is available concerning receipts and expenditure related to international tourism in the 24 Member countries in the OECD Area and its constituent regions, together with Yugoslavia. As far as possible, this data excludes material related to international fare payments unless otherwise indicated (see Statistical Annex, Series III).

Part A of the chapter considers receipts *a)* first in terms of national currency and U.S. dollars (both in current terms) and then in real terms, excluding the effects both of inflation and of exchange rate movements against the dollar. It then takes up expenditure *b)* in national currency and current dollars. Finally the "tourism balance" is struck in dollar terms *c)*.

Part B enables the foregoing data on receipts and expenditure to be related to other macro-economic indicators such as gross domestic product, private final consumption, and imports and exports of goods and

services, up to 1983, the most recent year for which the data is available for all OECD Member countries.

Part C (which appears for the first time) contains a certain amount of information about the importance of tourism as an economic activity in a number of OECD Member countries. The data was provided in response to an annual questionnaire circulated by the Tourism Committee.

The problem of international comparability of receipts and expenditure related to international tourism has been recognised by the Tourism Committee as one of the top priorities for the work of its Statistical Working Party. This body has completed a study on the matter, along similar lines to those of the work on "international comparability of arrivals and nights" which was derestricted in January 1983 and is available on request to the OECD Secretariat. Suggestions for improving the situation are also expected to be put forward within the near future.

A. INTERNATIONAL TOURIST RECEIPTS AND EXPENDITURE

a) International tourist receipts

International tourist receipts expressed *in national currencies at current prices* increased in 1984 as compared with the previous year in all Member countries except for the United States where a zero growth was reported. Reversals of a previously unfavourable trend in 1983 were recorded by Austria, (with a 7 per cent rise compared to a 3 per cent fall in 1983), by Finland (+ 6 per cent against – 1 per cent) and by the Nether-

lands (+ 17 per cent against – 2 per cent). (Table III.1).

When these figures are converted into *U.S. dollars at current prices,* the common unit of account used in the "Travel" account of the balance of payments, international tourist receipts rose in 1984 in about half the Member countries (Table III.2). The most striking increases took place in Turkey (+ 36 per cent), New Zealand (+ 31 per cent), Iceland (+ 25 per cent) and Japan (+ 18 per cent). On the other hand there was a

Per cent change over previous year

	Receipts	Expenditure
Austria	6.6	0.2
Belgium-Luxembourg	10.6	5.3
Denmark	12.0	14.7
Finland	6.2	18.2
France	20.6	15.6
Germany	11.9	2.4
Greece	42.2	20.2
Iceland	59.4	77.8
Ireland	13.3	4.4
Italy	10.0	33.2
Netherlands	16.7	2.8
Norway	7.9	3.8
Portugal	50.9	29.4
Spain	26.0	5.0
Sweden	8.9	9.8
Switzerland	12.5	11.3
Turkey	120.2	251.1
United Kingdom	14.2	14.1
Canada	15.1	4.2
United States	0.2	13.1
Australia	18.0	18.8
New Zealand	54.4	24.4
Japan	17.9	4.7
Yugoslavia	123.3	

downturn in Italy (– 5 per cent compared to + 8 per cent in 1983) and in Belgium/Luxembourg (– 2 per cent against + 9 per cent).

In the OECD area as a whole, receipts in current dollars rose by 2 per cent to reach a total of $70 billion in 1984. This positive development can be attributed to an increase of the same magnitude which took place in Europe (which contributed 76 per cent of the OECD total in the previous year). In the other parts of the OECD, the Pacific region recorded a vigorous growth of 18 per cent in 1984 after near stability in the previous year. In North America, after two successive years of decline (– 12 per cent in 1982 and – 4 per cent in 1983), 1984 was marked by a growth of 2 per cent.

In real terms i.e. after excluding the effects of both inflation and variations in exchange rates against the dollar, international tourist receipts rose in the OECD as a whole at an increasing rate over the last two years, growing by 7 per cent in 1984 after a 2 per cent growth in the previous year. (Table III.3). This was entirely due to the continued improvement in the receipts recorded by the European Member countries (+ 8 per cent compared to + 6 per cent). The European share in the OECD area total reached 79 per cent. Although its impact on the overall OECD results was less since its

Table III.2 **International tourists receipts and expenditure in dollars at current rates**

Rounded figures in million dollars

	Receipts			Expenditure		
	1983	1984	%	1983	1984	%
Austria	5 253.0	5 028.6	–4.3	2 897.1	2 607.1	–10.0
Belgium-Luxembourg	1 711.5	1 675.8	–2.1	2 096.0	1 954.6	–6.7
Denmark	1 306.5	1 292.0	–1.1	1 205.0	1 220.1	1.3
Finland	497.4	489.7	–1.5	622.3	682.0	9.6
France	7 226.5	7 597.9	5.1	4 281.6	4 316.8	0.8
Germany	5 457.2	5 478.9	0.4	15 141.5	13 910.3	–8.1
Greece	1 179.9	1 309.4	11.0	322.8	302.7	–6.2
Iceland	27.4	34.3	24.9	49.0	68.3	39.3
Ireland	484.7	479.0	–1.2	451.1	410.7	–9.0
Italy	9 033.2	8 594.9	–4.9	1 821.7	2 098.2	15.2
Netherlands	1 476.0	1 532.1	3.8	3 297.8	3 016.1	–8.5
Norway	673.0	649.4	–3.5	1 588.0	1 474.1	–7.2
Portugal	840.2	959.4	14.2	228.8	224.1	–2.0
Spain	6 898.0	7 759.9	12.5	896.0	839.7	–6.3
Sweden	1 063.0	1 072.6	0.9	1 624.9	1 653.3	1.8
Switzerland	3 153.3	3 170.7	0.5	2 300.7	2 287.6	–0.6
Turkey	414.5	561.8	35.5	128.0	276.6	116.1
United Kingdom	5 533.9	5 545.9	0.2	6 134.1	6 143.4	0.2
EUROPE	52 229.3	53 232.3	1.9	45 086.4	43 485.6	–3.6
Canada	2 582.0	2 828.6	9.5	3 915.2	3 883.4	–0.8
United States	11 408.0	11 426.0	0.2	13 977.0	15 805.0	13.1
NORTH AMERICA	13 990.0	14 254.6	1.9	17 892.2	19 688.4	10.0
Australia	1 070.3	1 228.3	14.8	1 706.0	1 969.9	15.5
New Zealand	236.1	308.7	30.7	452.8	476.9	5.3
Japan	825.3	972.9	17.9	4 431.2	4 639.2	4.7
AUSTRALASIA-JAPAN	2 131.7	2 509.9	17.7	6 590.0	7 086.1	7.5
OECD	68 351.0	69 996.8	2.4	69 568.6	70 260.0	1.0
Yugoslavia	928.9	1 053.7	13.4			

Table III.3 Trends in international tourist receipts in real prices [1]

	Per cent changes from previous year					Relative share in percentage of total	
	80/79	81/80	82/81	83/82	84/83	1983	1984
Austria	4.5	1.7	−1.8	−3.7	0.9	7.6	7.2
Belgium-Luxembourg	6.6	3.7	12.3	13.5	3.7	2.5	2.5
Denmark	−2.3	6.1	9.6	2.4	5.4	1.9	1.9
Finland	5.7	5.4	−14.8	−9.0	−0.8	0.7	0.7
France	−9.0	−3.0	26.3	9.2	12.4	10.8	11.4
Germany	6.4	4.7	−5.8	3.4	9.1	7.9	8.1
Greece	−0.1	14.1	−19.3	−14.1	20.9	1.9	2.1
Iceland	−7.7	−7.6	29.0	19.7	23.5	0.0	0.1
Ireland	−6.2	−28.8	27.5	0.2	4.4	0.7	0.7
Italy	−14.2	2.4	11.9	5.8	−0.8	12.5	11.7
Netherlands	13.6	17.3	−4.8	−1.1	13.5	2.2	2.3
Norway	−1.1	3.2	−7.5	−1.2	−0.5	1.0	1.0
Portugal	4.2	−8.4	−10.7	6.3	16.7	1.3	1.5
Spain	−0.3	9.1	9.7	11.9	13.2	11.4	12.1
Sweden	−4.5	7.2	18.9	15.9	0.8	1.7	1.6
Switzerland	17.3	6.0	−2.5	4.8	9.3	4.5	4.6
Turkey	0.8	15.9	12.3	17.0	46.5	0.6	0.9
United Kingdom	−9.1	−10.8	−0.8	9.4	8.6	8.6	8.7
EUROPE	−2.4	1.8	4.7	5.5	7.9	77.9	78.9
Canada	2.5	1.8	−10.9	0.3	10.7	3.5	3.6
United States	13.8	12.2	−9.4	−11.2	−2.9	15.6	14.2
NORTH AMERICA	11.6	10.3	−9.6	−9.3	−0.5	19.1	17.8
Australia	22.9	1.3	2.2	−0.3	10.6	1.6	1.6
New Zealand	7.0	16.6	−7.4	8.5	45.2	0.3	0.5
Japan	10.9	7.5	12.7	2.0	15.5	1.1	1.2
AUSTRALASIA-JAPAN	16.8	5.0	4.6	1.5	16.4	3.0	3.3
OECD	1.0	3.9	1.2	2.2	6.5	100.0	100.0
Yugoslavia	47.7	−14.1	−27.6	18.9	45.7		

1. After correcting for the effects of inflation in each country. For the regional and OECD totals, the receipts of the individual countries are weighted in proportion to their share in the total expressed in dollars.

volume is only 3 per cent of the total, the Pacific region has grown continuously since 1979 with a most notable rise of 17 per cent in 1984, compared to only 2 per cent in the previous year. In North America, Canada's 1984 increase of 11 per cent led to a slowing down in the decline of this region to 1 per cent after − 9 per cent and − 10 per cent in the two previous years.

Individually, only four Member countries recorded falls in the volume of receipts *in real terms* for 1984, the United States (− 3 per cent), Finland, Norway and Italy (all − 1 per cent). The most satisfactory increases took place in Turkey (+ 47 per cent), New Zealand (+ 45 per cent), Iceland (+ 24 per cent) and Greece (+ 20 per cent).

b) International tourist expenditure

The level of international tourist expenditure in 1984 in *national currency at current prices* increased in all of the OECD Member countries, except for Austria where they remained stable. As far as the four main tourist generating countries were concerned, the negative tendency of the previous year was reversed with a rise in expenditure by French tourists of 16 per cent (compared with a 4 per cent fall in 1983) and by German tourists of 2 per cent (against − 2 per cent). For visitors from the United Kingdom and the United States, their expenditure continued to increase, by 14 per cent for the former (against + 11 per cent) and 13 per cent for the latter, the same as in the previous year.

In *current dollars,* on the other hand, expenditure went up for only half of the Member countries of the OECD during 1984. Among these the most pronounced increase took place for Turkey (+ 116 per cent), Iceland (+ 39 per cent), Australia (+ 16 per cent), Italy (+ 15 per cent) and the United States (+ 13 per cent).

After three consecutive years in which the total OECD expenditure in current dollar terms has fallen, there was a slight improvement in 1984 with a rise of 1 per cent. This was the result of increases of 10 per cent in North America and 8 per cent in the Pacific region which counterbalanced the 4 per cent decline which took

Diagram III.1. Trend of international tourist receipts for European Member countries as a whole
1978 = 100

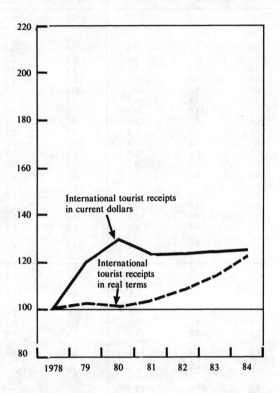

Diagram III.2. Trend of international tourist receipts for Canada and the United States
1978 = 100

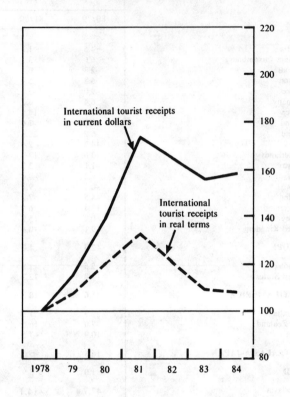

Diagram III.3. Trend of international tourist receipts for Australia, New Zealand and Japan
1978 = 100

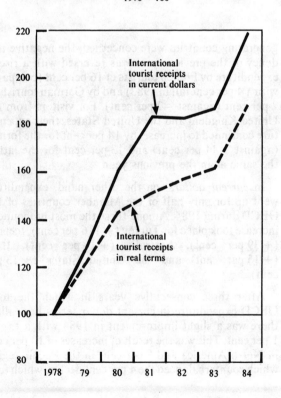

Diagram III.4. Trend of international tourist receipts for OECD Member countries as a whole
1978 = 100

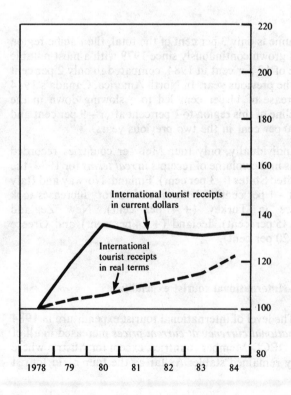

56

place in Europe. The European share in the total of OECD tourist expenditure has gone from 73 per cent in 1980 to only 62 per cent in 1984.

c) The tourism balance sheet

In the OECD area as a whole, the "tourism balance" expressed in current dollars has been virtually in equilibrium since 1982 which was preceeded by a deficit in 1981 of $2.2 billion. In 1984 both receipts and expenditure amounted to $70 billion (Table III.4). Between 1982 and 1984 this balance resulted from the steady rise in the outgoings from North America and the Pacific which grew from $22.1 to $26.8 billion, which was virtually balanced by the reduction in expenditure by the European OECD Member countries from $47.7 to $43.5 billion.

Table III.4 **Tourism balance sheet**
In billions of current dollars

	1982	1983	1984
EUROPE			
Receipts	52.1	52.2	53.2
Expenditure	47.7	45.1	43.5
Balance[1]	4.4	7.1	9.7
NORTH AMERICA			
Receipts	14.8	14.0	14.3
Expenditure	15.6	17.9	19.7
Balance[1]	–0.8	–3.9	–5.4
AUSTRALASIA-JAPAN			
Receipts	2.1	2.1	2.5
Expenditure	6.5	6.6	7.1
Balance[1]	–4.4	–4.5	–4.6
OECD			
Receipts	69.0	68.4	70.0
Expenditure	69.7	69.6	70.3
Balance[1]	–0.7	–1.2	–0.3

1. Minus signs indicate deficits.

B. THE ECONOMIC IMPORTANCE OF THE "TRAVEL" ACCOUNT IN THE BALANCE OF PAYMENTS

a) Ratio of receipts in the "Travel" account to gross domestic product

After rising to 1.0 in 1980, the ratio of "travel" account receipts to gross domestic product for the OECD area as a whole fell back for the most recent years for which data is available to 0.9, the level it had attained in 1979 (Table III.5). Between 1981 and 1983, the most marked increases took place in Spain (3.6 to 4.3) and Italy (2.1 to 2.6) whereas the greatest declines were recorded for Greece (5.1 to 3.4) and Austria (8.6 to 7.8).

b) Ratio of expenditure in the "Travel" account to private final consumption

Between 1981 and 1983 the ratio of expenditure in the "travel" account to private final consumption fell from 1.5 to 1.4 (Table III.6). For the two most recent years for which comparable data can be provided, three countries recorded a substantial increase; Austria (from 7.1 to 7.5), Iceland (4.4 to 4.7) and Canada (2.4 to 2.7). The only significant decline took place in Denmark (4.3 to 3.9).

c) Share of "Travel" account receipts and expenditure in international payments

It was in 1981 that the shares of "travel" account receipts and expenditure in the international payment of Member countries reached their nadir of 4.2. In 1982 and 1983 the shares rose again and reached 4.3 and 4.4 respectively (Tables III.7 and III.8).

Between 1981 and 1983, three major tourist receiving countries saw the share of travel receipts fall significantly. In Greece it fell from 20.5 to 16.4, in Portugal 16.3 to 13.3 and in Austria from 18.7 to 16.9. During the same period two other "tourist" countries increased their contribution, Italy rising from 7.7 to 9.4 and Spain from 19.7 to 20.9.

When travel expenditure is compared to total imports of goods and services there were falls between 1981 and 1983 in two main generating countries; France (from 3.4 to 2.9) and Germany (8.1 to 7.8). However it rose in the United States from 3.2 to 3.8 and remained virtually constant in the United Kingdom (from 4.7 to 4.6). Among other Member countries the most significant rises took place among the Nordic countries, in Norway from 6.2 to 7.1 and in Iceland from 5.1 to 5.8.

Table III.5 Ratio of the "Travel" account receipts to the gross domestic product (%)	1981	1982	1983
Austria	8.6	8.4	7.8
Belgium-Luxembourg	1.7	1.9	2.1
Denmark	2.2	2.3	2.3
Finland	1.4	1.1	1.0
France	1.3	1.3	1.4
Germany	0.9	0.8	0.8
Greece	5.1	4.0	3.4
Iceland	0.7	1.0	1.2
Ireland	0.3	0.3	
Italy	2.1	2.4	2.6
Netherlands	0.5	0.5	0.4
Norway	1.4	1.3	1.2
Portugal	4.3	3.8	4.1
Spain	3.6	3.9	4.3
Sweden	0.8	1.0	1.2
Switzerland	4.2	4.1	4.2
Turkey	0.7	0.7	0.8
United-Kingdom	1.2	1.1	1.2
EUROPE	1.7	1.7	1.8
Canada	1.1	1.0	1.0
United-States	0.4	0.4	0.3
NORTH AMERICA	0.5	0.5	0.4
Australia	0.7	0.7	0.7
New-Zealand	1.0	0.9	1.0
Japan	0.1	0.1	0.1
AUSTRALASIA-JAPAN	0.2	0.2	0.2
OECD	0.9	0.9	0.9
Yugoslavia			

Source: OECD, Balance of Payments Division and *National Accounts of OECD Member Countries.*

Table III.6 Ratio of the "Travel" account expenditure to the private final consumption (%)	1981	1982	1983
Autria	7.5	7.1	7.5
Belgium-Luxembourg	4.6	4.0	4.0
Denmark	4.0	4.3	3.9
Finland	2.2	2.3	2.3
France	1.6	1.5	1.3
Germany	4.4	4.3	4.1
Greece	1.5	1.5	1.6
Iceland	3.8	4.4	4.7
Ireland	0.5	0.5	
Italy	0.8	0.8	0.8
Netherlands	1.8	1.7	1.6
Norway	6.0	6.5	6.4
Portugal	1.5	1.6	1.6
Spain	0.8	0.8	0.8
Sweden	3.7	3.5	3.4
Switzerland	4.5	4.6	4.6
Turkey	0.2	0.4	0.3
United-Kingdom	2.2	2.2	2.2
EUROPE	2.6	2.5	2.5
Canada	2.5	2.4	2.7
United-States	0.6	0.6	0.6
NORTH AMERICA	0.8	0.8	0.8
Australia	1.9	1.9	1.8
New-Zealand	3.6	3.4	3.2
Japan	0.7	0.7	0.6
AUSTRALASIA-JAPAN	0.9	0.9	0.8
OECD	1.5	1.5	1.4
Yugoslavia			

Source: OECD, Balance of Payments Division and *National Accounts of OECD Member Countries*

Table III.7 Share of "Travel" account receipts in exports of goods and services	1981	1982	1983
Austria	18.7	18.3	16.9
Belgium-Luxembourg	1.8	1.9	2.2
Denmark	5.4	5.9	5.8
Finland	4.0	3.5	3.2
France	4.3	4.6	5.0
Germany	2.7	2.5	2.6
Greece	20.5	19.4	16.4
Iceland	1.8	2.4	2.4
Ireland	5.1	5.1	
Italy	7.7	8.6	9.4
Netherlands	1.8	1.8	1.8
Norway	2.7	2.7	2.5
Portugal	16.3	14.8	13.3
Spain	19.7	20.5	20.9
Sweden	2.6	2.9	3.0
Switzerland	9.4	8.6	9.1
Turkey	5.9	4.8	5.3
United-Kingdom	3.8	3.8	4.0
EUROPE	5.2	5.3	5.5
Canada	3.7	3.7	3.6
United-States	3.4	3.5	3.4
NORTH AMERICA	3.5	3.6	3.5
Australia	4.3	4.3	4.4
New-Zealand	3.6	3.3	3.4
Japan	0.4	0.4	0.5
AUSTRALASIA-JAPAN	0.9	1.0	1.0
OECD	4.2	4.3	4.4
Yugoslavia			

Source: OECD, Balance of Payments Division.

Table III.8 Share of "Travel" account expenditure in imports of goods and services	1981	1982	1983
Austria	8.8	9.0	9.4
Belgium-Luxembourg	3.1	2.5	2.7
Denmark	5.2	5.5	5.2
Finland	3.3	3.7	3.8
France	3.4	3.2	2.9
Germany	8.1	8.0	7.8
Greece	2.8	3.3	3.4
Iceland	5.1	5.6	5.8
Ireland	3.9	3.9	
Italy	1.5	1.7	1.9
Netherlands	4.2	4.1	4.2
Norway	6.2	6.8	7.1
Portugal	2.1	2.1	2.3
Spain	2.5	2.5	2.4
Sweden	5.6	5.0	4.6
Switzerland	6.9	6.8	7.0
Turkey	0.9	1.4	1.1
United-Kingdom	4.7	4.7	4.6
EUROPE	4.8	4.7	4.7
Canada	4.5	5.0	5.7
United-States	3.2	3.5	3.8
NORTH AMERICA	3.4	3.8	4.2
Australia	5.5	5.6	5.7
New-Zealand	6.4	5.6	5.3
Japan	2.5	2.4	2.8
AUSTRALASIA-JAPAN	3.1	3.0	3.3
OECD	4.2	4.3	4.4
Yugoslavia			

Source: OECD, Balance of Payments Division.

C. THE ECONOMIC IMPORTANCE OF TOURISM IN CERTAIN MEMBER COUNTRIES

Australia. In the 12 months to September 1982, Australians undertook an estimated 52.3 million trips of one night or more away from home in Australia, spending on average A$156 per person on each trip. A further 89 million day trips were taken with an average expenditure per trip of around A$20. During the same period, the Australian Tourist Commission estimated that 936 700 foreign visitors arrived in Australia and spent on average A$1 121 per trip.

During the survey period it was estimated that domestic tourists spent A$8.2 billion on overnight trips and A$1.8 billion on day trips, and foreign travellers spent A$1.033 billion, in Australia. A further A$1.1 billion was spent by domestic travellers on travel related equipment, holiday homes and a pro rata component of overall motoring costs.

After deducting transfers, imports and indirect taxes, tourist expenditure amounted to A$7 billion in 1981/82. This represented 4.8 per cent of GDP at factor cost. The Bureau of Industry Economics also estimated that tourist expenditure generated directly or indirectly, employment for 338 000 people or 5.2 per cent of the workforce. By way of comparison, the amount of income and the number of jobs attributable to tourism in 1981/82 was equivalent to the combined contribution of the textile, footwear, clothing and motor vehicle industries.

On average, it seems that A$1 million of tourist expenditure generates around 26 jobs. However foreign and domestic tourist expenditure naturally have a differential impact on employment generation. Only 26 overseas visitors undertaking a trip of average duration each year are required to create a job, whereas the corresponding number of domestic tourists is 247. This contrast primarily reflects the much larger average duration of trip associated with international visitors (31 days) compared with domestic tourists (4 days).

A separate Departmental study has revealed that, in the post-war period, the international tourism share of total overseas transactions increased significantly from 0.38 per cent in 1945 to 5.04 per cent in 1982/83. The travel credits share of total "invisible" credits increased from 0.17 per cent to 4.25 per cent while the share of travel debts to total "invisible" debits rose from 0.63 per cent to 5.68 per cent. The credit item represents expenditure by foreign visitors in Australia, while the debit item refers to expenditure overseas by Australian tourists.

France. There was an estimated expenditure on domestic tourism in 1983 of FF 314 billion. As a result, tourism represented 12.3 per cent of household consumption and between 8 and 9 per cent of GDP.

The tourist industry supported 637 000 persons directly employed (according to the 1982 Census of Population), equivalent to 3 per cent of the active population.

Furthermore an unofficial but authoritative estimate suggests that the total amount of employment associated with tourism, including direct, seasonal and indirect employment, is as high as 1.7 million people. Indirect employment covers those positions created by tourism in the non-tourism sectors such as commerce and the post and telegraphs etc.

Greece. The tourist industry in 1984 was an important source of foreign exchange since, according to provisional data of the Bank of Greece, its share in the total receipts from current transactions in the balance of payments represented 13.6 per cent, against 12.2 per cent in 1983. The share of foreign exchange earned by international tourism in total invisible transactions was 25 per cent as against 21.3 per cent in 1983.

Domestic and foreign tourism constitute an important source of income and contribute to the creation of employment opportunities in many areas of the country and thus substantially assisted regional development.

Ireland. A major study was undertaken during the year to determine the economic value of both export and domestic tourism.

The study assessed the appropriateness of input-output analysis in estimating the economic contribution made by tourism. Variations in the treatment of taxation were examined as a means of differentiating between short run effects and the economic contribution of the industry. It is argued that such Government receipts should be taken into account in examining the full economic effects of export tourism. An attempt was made to reconcile these for tourism derived by input-output methods and econometric models. When the direct import content and the indirect tax content are taken into account, both methods produce very similar results. A further check on results was made using input-output estimates for 1982. This confirmed that tourism's impact on the economy remained broadly unchanged between 1975 and 1982. The impact of supply constraints in a small open economy was also examined.

In the short run the multiplier for export tourism for Ireland lies in the region of unity. It is argued however that over the medium term any assessment of an industry's contribution should include some quantification of the impact of the tax revenue it generates. Proper management of the economy requires that Government expenditure should be closely related to revenues. This

medium term effect of an industry is not a "multiplier" in the strict sense of the word. Perhaps it should be termed a "GDP coefficient". Again a comparison of results suggests that they are independent of the method adopted. The GDP coefficient for expenditure by out-of-state visitors lies in the region of two, suggesting that two pounds of national income are generated for every pound spent by visitors to Ireland.

This approach sees exports and investment as the sectors which drive the economy and attempts to calculate the income arising from such sources. Similar coefficients were estimated for the other main sectors of the Irish economy. The coefficients for the main categories of agricultural exports were broadly similar but their manufacturing counterparts tended to have a much lower effect on national income. Some coefficients for sectors are presented below:

- Out-of-State visitor expenditure: 1.92
- Meat and meat processing: 1.88
- Dairy products: 1.86
- Chemicals: 1.05
- Office machines: 1.08
- Electrical goods: 1.11
- Beverages: 1.66
- Textiles: 1.23

Using a broadly similar approach the contribution of domestic tourism was estimated. In this case the key factor in determining its value is its lower import content compared to other forms of consumer spending. The net multiplier or coefficient on domestic holiday spending was estimated to be 0.63.

Thus while tourism (both domestic and foreign) accounts for some 5.5 per cent of GDP, the direct, indirect and induced effects of such activity create incomes totalling some 7.8 per cent of GDP.

Netherlands. The newly published Tourist Policy Memorandum, dated December 1984, pays some attention to the impact of tourism on economy activity employment in the tourist sector, compared with that of other sectors. Total employment in the tourist sector, i.e. direct and indirect employment, amounts to some 230 000 full time jobs (more precisely: 230 000 man-years of employment).

The contribution of domestic tourism to this amount is some 86 per cent while international tourism contributes the remaining 14 per cent. Direct employment makes up 175 000 man-years, some three-quarters of the total employment. Comparison with other sectors of the economy shows that direct employment in the electrical and electronic industry contributes 104 000, while it is 71 000 in the transport industries and 175 000 in the banking and insurance sector.

New Zealand. Foreign Tourism is New Zealand's fifth largest earner of foreign exchange. For the year ending December 1984, foreign exchange earnings from the main export industries expressed in millions of New Zealand dollars were as follows:

- Meat: 2 151.7
- Manufacturing: 1 769.3
- Dairy Products: 1 574.2
- Wool: 1 220.5
- Tourism and Travel: 1 035.0
- Other Primary Products: 797.1
- Forest Products: 751.1
- Other Animal Products: 543.5

The contribution of tourism to New Zealand's total foreign exchange measured by the ratio of travel receipts (excluding airfare receipts and domestic tourism) to all receipts from the export of goods and services, was 4.7 per cent for the year ending December 1984.

The best estimates of the combined value of domestic travel (NZ$600 million) and international arrivals (NZ$791 million) at NZ$1 391 million for 1983/84 show tourism providing 4 per cent of GDP.

Norway. The effects of tourism on the economy, employment and the environment has been studied in one of the Norwegian municipalities where tourism is most important. In economic importance, the tourist trade came second in this municipality. In 1983, the tourist trade had a turnover of NKr 133 million and, by application of the multiplier effect, NKr 251 million, or about 89 per cent more than the trade's direct turnover.

The effect of tourism varies according to the type of tourism. The multiplier effect of camping tourists is estimated to be 2.4. The responding effect of hotel guests however is only 1.5 but the total effect is much more important because of the higher initial volume/turnover.

Portugal. The tourism sector is increasingly important within the national economy as a whole.

According to recent studies, tourism has represented between 5.5 per cent and 7.0 per cent of GDP in recent years. Comparison with other sectors of activity shows it to be close to agriculture and fisheries and equivalent to construction and civil engineering and the banking sector.

Switzerland. Tourism comes third in the ranking of export sectors in Switzerland, after mechanical engineering and chemicals. It provided 10 per cent of export earnings.

Tourism is still an important source of foreign currency, since the tourism balance was estimated at SF 2.075 billion in 1984.

IV

TRANSPORT

Since the second oil shock, the main companies involved in international passenger transport have endured all kinds of difficulties arising from a situation of cost increases over which they had little or no control. During the same period, the expansion of international tourism demand slowed and then came to a halt at the beginning of the eighties. The most significant results of this were extensive losses in a number of sectors and the vanishing of a large number of companies who were ill-prepared to engage in competition which grew more and more bitter as the economic recession spread. It should be remembered that the basic characteristics of the tourist industries make them particularly vulnerable to macro-economic influence on the level of international trade in goods and services and to changes in the size and direction of international tourist flows.

From the second half of 1983, the economic recovery, which started in several OECD Member countries, was reflected in a revival, albeit modest, in the activities of certain parts of the international transport of passengers. In the international air transport sector, most notably, the provisional IATA statistics have shown for 1984 the first positive operating results since 1979.

Under the impact of all these relatively recent developments in the international transport, the political approach to the problems involved has also undergone changes. This was most notable in the aviation sector which involved many travellers whose movement would not have been possible without the air transport network (intercontinental travel, business trips, medium or long-range visits). From 1978, the laws which deregulated air transport in the United States foreshadowed the introduction of different concepts and practices in the future. In spite of the extensive controversies over the targets

towards which this approach was directed, the policy of deregulation had the advantage of helping other countries by providing them with background information for their various approaches.

In 1982, the first multilateral agreement between the United States and some of its European partners on the North Atlantic routes came into force, and was followed by several other similar agreements. Within the European Communities, ten years of work and debate directed towards the introduction of a common air transport policy has finally resulted in the establishment of a number of general guidelines and their practical implementation is expected in the near future. In all these negotiations the industry, the carriers and the international organisations involved have been able, in spite of positions which were at times divergent, to help the debate progress.

1984 may have been the pivot year in which the foundations for the future were laid down, but everything may go back into the melting pot if the various parties in the negotiations are unable to find common grounds for an understanding in a field which is vital to the development of international tourism. It is in this direction that both governmental and non-governmental bodies are working, as can be seen from the contents of this chapter, wherein the reader will find the main lines of the changes which took place during 1984 in the international passenger transport sector. Although the main emphasis has been on international air transport, there have nevertheless been considerable efforts made in the road and rail transport spheres. However, in these, the main problems which have been under study have concerned particularly goods transport where the political pressure has been more pronounced.

A. AIR TRANSPORT

a) World air traffic

According to provisional world data, the airlines of the 152 States belonging to the International Civil Aviation Organisation (ICAO) carried 832 million passengers in 1984, or 4.5 per cent more than in the previous year (the revised data for 1983 are 795 million, up 4.4 per cent from 1982). Expressed in passenger-km, the volume of world traffic on domestic and international flights rose by 6 per cent to 1 256 billion. As capacity expressed in available seat-km (+ 5 per cent) increased less than demand, the load factor came to 65 per cent, the best figure since the start of the decade.

The improvement in the economic situation since the second half of 1983 resulted in successive increases in the scheduled passenger traffic of the 134 members of the International Air Transport Association (IATA), which account for a high proportion of the world's scheduled air traffic. In terms of passenger-km, this traffic was up 3 per cent in 1983 and 6 per cent in 1984.

It seems that this situation enabled IATA airlines in 1984 to obtain the first positive operating result since 1979; the reference is to the result after interest. According to provisional data, the result was thus $1.2 billion in 1984, against respective deficits of $300 million in 1983 and $1.8 billion in the previous year. In an international economic context that is generally more favourable in the medium term, with prospects for yields keeping pace with cost rises, and at a time when capacity is being adapted more closely to demand, the positive trend could be maintained into 1985 and 1986 with respective profits of $1.5 billion and $1.7 billion.

Despite this rather optimistic outlook, the situation is affected by economic and policy factors. According to IATA, the financial balance is still precarious and sensitive to the slightest changes in trends. Future capital needs for replacement of the aircraft fleet and other equipment are heavy since it has been forecast that between $150 billion and $200 billion would have to be spent on them in the next ten years. Among the other financial problems confronting the industry, the Association also refers to blocked currencies, escalating insurance rates and a backlog in the development of EDP techniques, which is put at 9 000 man-years.

IATA is concerned at some of the moves being made in aviation policy. According to the Association, regional solutions to the industry's problems or the establishment of unilateral regulatory régimes may endanger the cohesion and progress of the multilateral system which is the very basis of aviation operation in the world today.

IATA took various kinds of action in the facilitation field in 1984. Continuing its efforts under Annex 9 of the ICAO Convention on Civil Aviation, IATA, for example, co-operated with the United States Department of the Treasury to set up a computer-based customs clearance system. The Association is also working with the Customs Co-operation Council with regard to certain provisions in the Kyoto Convention which concern the application of the dual channel (red/green) system of customs clearance to a larger number of countries.

IATA also expressed its views on many subjects concerning the future of international air transport, particularly in the following studies:

i) "US domestic deregulation concepts and their potential application to international aviation."
ii) "International air fares in Europe."
iii) "IATA comments on EEC Civil Aviation Memorandum No. 2."

The main events marking the international aviation policy trend in 1984 included certain action by the United States Civil Aeronautics Board (CAB), its sunset on 31st December and the transfer of its responsibilities to the Department of Transportation (DOT).

One of the main reasons for the interest shown in air transport developments in the United States is the importance of a network that connects almost every other country with this buoyant international market and the possible repercussions of a policy that may affect the bilateral or multilateral agreements between the United States and its partners worldwide.

The activities which attracted attention in 1984 were the deregulation of agencies and sales intermediaries and improved access to computerised reservation systems.

According to the schedule set by the United States Deregulation Act of 1978, the CAB sunset was ratified by a new Act signed by the President in October 1984, the *Civil Aeronautics Board Sunset Act of 1984*. The main tasks now assigned to DOT are as follows:

i) Protecting the public interest by ensuring observance of anti-trust law legislation at international level (unlimited authority) and at national level (authority limited to four years);
ii) Protecting the user, particularly by eliminating unfair or fraudulent practices; and
iii) Ensuring that the airlines are economically and technically fit for operation.

b) North Atlantic air traffic

Over 22 million passengers were carried by IATA and non-IATA airlines on North Atlantic routes in 1984, or 13 per cent more than in 1983 (Table IV.1). As capacity rose less than traffic performed, load factors were up by one point to 71 per cent on scheduled flights and to 88 per cent on non-scheduled flights.

Table IV.1. **Trend of North Atlantic air traffic**

IATA and non-IATA

Number of passengers carried in both directions
in 1984: 22 142 000

	81/80 %	82/81 %	83/82 %	84/83 %
Scheduled	3.7	−5.2	6.4	12.5
Non-scheduled	−6.9	23.3	5.7	13.6
Total	2.6	−2.5	6.3	12.6

Source: International Air Travel Association (IATA), Geneva.

Scheduled traffic rose by 13 per cent compared with a 14 per cent increase in non-scheduled activity. However, these overall data conceal network differences, as shown by the information broken down by group of routes in Table IV.2, for the only increase in traffic on non-scheduled flights in 1984 was on routes to and from the United States on which passengers numbered 1.8 million, or 25 per cent more than in the previous year. Since 1981 the share of charter activity in total North Atlantic traffic has risen from 5 to 8 per cent as a result of the constantly increasing demand for this type of flight. The possible reasons for this trend include the substantial increase in traffic from the United States to European destinations, particularly since 1982, the type of agreements concluded during this period between the United States and European countries on a wide range of promotional fares, and the advent on the market of a larger number of carriers operating charter flights at competitive prices.

Table IV.3 gives the monthly breakdown of passenger traffic in 1984 by type of flight and the percentage changes from the same months of the previous year. The breakdown remained much the same from one year to another with, in 1984, 74 per cent of traffic on non-scheduled flights being recorded between June and September, as against 47 per cent on scheduled flights.

c) Air traffic between the United States and European countries

Air passenger traffic in 1984 between the United States and the 19 European Member countries plus Yugoslavia was up for the second year running – by 14 per cent in 1984 against 3 per cent in the previous year (Table IV.4). As shown by the 1984 data provided by the US Department of Transportation, over 17.6 million passengers were carried on these routes, of which

Table IV.2. **North Atlantic air traffic in both directions**

IATA and non-IATA

	1982 Relative share %	1982/81 Variation %	1983 Relative share %	1983/82 Variation %	1984 Relative share %	1984/83 Variation %
North Atlantic						
Scheduled	88.2	−5.2	88.3	6.4	87.9	12.5
Non-scheduled	11.8	23.3	11.7	5.7	12.1	13.6
Total	100.0	−2.5	100.0	6.3	100.0	12.6
of which:						
United States						
Scheduled	75.6	−5.0	76.0	6.8	75.5	12.1
Non-scheduled	7.0	29.4	7.0	5.5	8.2	25.2
Total	82.6	−2.8	83.0	6.7	83.7	13.3
Canada						
Scheduled	11.1	−5.9	10.9	3.7	11.0	14.0
Non-scheduled	4.9	15.7	4.7	6.0	3.9	−5.4
Total	16.0	−0.2	15.5	4.4	14.9	8.3
Beyond						
Scheduled	1.4	−11.1	1.4	3.5	1.4	20.0
Non-scheduled	0.0	−69.4	0.0	−100.0	0.0	0.0
Total	1.4	−11.4	1.4	3.3	1.4	20.0
Number of passengers carried	18 538 000		19 688 000		22 142 000	

Source: International Air Transport Association (IATA), Geneva.

Table IV.3. **North Atlantic air traffic in 1984 in both directions**
IATA and non-IATA

Number of passengers transported in 1984 : 22 142 000	Relative share (%)			Variation 1984/83 (%)		
	Total	Scheduled flights	Non-scheduled flights	Total	Scheduled flights	Non-scheduled flights
January	5.0	5.5	1.7	9.3	8.7	28.3
February	3.9	4.3	1.0	15.1	14.3	52.2
March	5.5	6.0	1.6	7.4	7.8	−3.5
April	6.7	7.1	3.4	12.8	14.0	−2.7
May	8.7	8.9	7.7	14.0	15.5	3.2
June	11.7	11.1	15.8	14.9	15.0	14.3
July	13.5	12.3	21.9	11.5	10.6	14.9
August	13.6	12.5	21.7	14.8	13.4	21.1
September	11.6	11.3	14.2	14.8	15.4	11.7
October	8.6	8.8	7.1	6.2	5.7	10.7
November	5.4	5.9	1.8	16.0	16.1	13.7
December	5.8	6.3	2.1	12.6	12.8	8.2
TOTAL	100.0	100.0	100.0	12.6	12.5	13.6

Source: International Air Transport Association (IATA), Geneva.

Table IV.4. **Pattern of air traffic between the United States and European countries**

To and from	Passengers carried in 1984 in both directions: 17 644 416							
	Change 1984/1983 %			Breakdown in 1984				
				Among countries by flight category			Between flight categories	
	S	NS	Total	S	NS	Total	S	NS
Austria	33.2	−47.7	26.7	0.8	0.2	0.7	97	3
Belgium	−3.5	−13.1	−4.0	2.7	1.1	2.6	96	4
Denmark	5.8	−11.0	5.5	2.9	0.3	2.7	99	1
Finland	10.7	−11.6	9.9	0.7	0.2	0.6	97	3
France	10.0	41.2	13.4	8.3	12.9	8.7	86	14
Germany	15.4	16.7	15.6	15.1	24.5	16.1	86	14
Greece	12.9	−11.5	9.5	2.8	3.3	2.8	89	11
Iceland	20.7	79.4	21.1	1.0	0.1	0.9	99	1
Ireland	13.1	4.8	12.1	2.6	3.1	2.7	89	11
Italy	16.4	−7.1	14.5	7.6	4.9	7.3	94	6
Luxembourg	27.5	18.6	27.3	0.6	0.1	0.5	97	3
Netherlands	11.5	72.4	15.8	6.0	6.8	6.1	89	11
Norway	3.5	199.0	11.4	0.6	0.7	0.6	89	11
Portugal	17.8	4.4	14.1	1.2	3.9	1.5	75	25
Spain	8.4	21.6	9.8	4.4	5.5	4.5	88	12
Sweden	1.0	2.1	1.0	0.8	0.4	0.8	95	5
Switzerland	26.5	54.9	30.3	4.4	8.0	4.7	84	16
Turkey[1]	138.7		138.7	0.0		0.0	100	
United Kingdom	15.2	5.6	14.6	36.9	23.8	35.7	94	6
Yugoslavia	15.9	81.6	17.6	0.6	0.2	0.5	96	4
TOTAL	13.8	17.4	14.1	100.0	100.0	100.0	91	9

S   Scheduled flights.
NS   Non-scheduled flights.
1.   No non-scheduled flights in 1984.
Source: U.S. International Air Travel Statistics, U.S. Department of Transportation, Transportation Systems Center, Cambridge, Massachussetts.

65 per cent were US citizens. This marks a change in the situation since the start of deregulation in 1979 when United States travellers represented only 53 per cent of total passengers on this network.

The increases were particularly marked in traffic between the United States and Turkey (+ 139 per cent), Switzerland (+ 30 per cent), Luxembourg (+ 27 per cent), Austria (+ 27 per cent) and Iceland (+ 21 per cent). The breakdown in passenger traffic between categories of flight was marked by some changes such as the decrease in the number of passengers carried on non-scheduled flights between the United States and

Austria, which represented 3 per cent of total traffic in 1984 as against 8 per cent in 1983, while the opposite occurred in the case of Norway whose non-scheduled traffic represented 11 per cent of the total in 1984 against 4 per cent in 1983.

A new Memorandum of Understanding on North Atlantic pricing, which had been signed for a two-year period on 1st November 1984, was extended to 30th April 1987. It was signed by the aeronautical authorities of 16 Member States of the European Civil Aviation Conference (ECAC) and the United States. Like earlier similar arrangements between ECAC States and the United States, the first of which came into force on 1st August 1982, the new Memorandum provides for the aeronautical authorities of the States concerned to grant automatic approval to North Atlantic fares filed by airlines within specified pricing zones. These authorities also undertake not to prevent any carrier from participating in multilateral tariff co-ordination while the arrangement is in force. This applies to the IATA Traffic Conferences on United States–Europe routes in which some non-IATA airlines, as well as IATA carriers, have taken part.

The ECAC parties to this new Understanding are: Belgium, Denmark, Finland, France, Germany, Greece, Ireland, Italy, the Netherlands, Norway, Portugal, Spain, Sweden, Switzerland, the United Kingdom and Yugoslavia. This list includes all signatories of one or more of the earlier arrangements.

The pricing zone system in the new Memorandum is based on an agreed reference fare level for each route. A zone of automatic approval is then established within an agreed percentage range of that reference level for each of the five main fare types (first class, business class, economy, "discount" and "deep discount").

Compared with previous arrangements, some pricing zones have been widened on several main North Atlantic routes. Twenty-three new city air routes (involving France, Germany, Italy and Switzerland) have also been added to the previous total of 121 routes covered by the last agreement.

d) Air traffic in Europe

According to available data, the 19 Members of the Association of European Airlines (AEA) carried 109 million scheduled passengers in 1984, or 6 per cent more than in the previous year, which was the first increase since 1981. Through better management of capacity and a commercial policy geared more closely to the needs of the various market segments, the load factors of AEA airlines as a whole rose by 3 points from the previous year to a record level of 66 per cent in 1984. The main kinds of action taken by the airlines included: the improvement of in-flight services for passengers travelling on the full economy fare, an increase in the number of operators providing a separate "business" class (from 10 to 14 in 1984) and the development of a wider range of "low fares" intended particularly for tourists. In the latter case, promotional fares represented 62 per cent of total capacity, 36 per cent on intra-European routes and 50 per cent on the North Atlantic network. On the financial side, the preliminary data for 1984 show positive results of around $650 million after interest, or a 3 per cent improvement on the previous year.

Civil Aviation Memorandum No. 2 ("Progress towards the development of a Community Air Transport Policy") presented by the Commission of the European Communities in February 1984 has given rise to many reactions, particularly from the industry.

The European Council of Ministers of Transport examined the proposals in the Memorandum at a meeting in May 1984. In view of the range of opinions expressed by the civil aviation authorities of Member States, the Council decided to submit all the material concerning the question to a working group consisting of high-level representatives of the States and the Commission. The group was instructed to review the situation in the light of the initial observations made, to sum them up and to submit a report to the Council containing proposed guidelines. In this connection the Council recalled that the objective was to make the present system more flexible so as to permit increased efficiency from the economic and social viewpoints.

In December the Council adopted the group's report which contained guidelines for a Community air transport policy and instructed the group to define standards on which the Council could give a ruling before the end of 1985. In the meantime, the European Parliament and the Economic and Social Committee are to give their opinions.

The compromise submitted by the group concern economic issues that are by far the most important. They relate to: *fares* (for example, the possibility of a compromise between the principles of multilateral agreements and bilateral commitments through a zone system subject to dual approval and the "country of origin" rule); *competition,* with the objective of protecting the sovereignty of States and the financial balance of airlines (in certain circumstances, consultations among airlines might not be considered contrary to the rules of competition under the Treaty of Rome or a "group exemption" could be granted for them; *capacity* (objective: not preventing new carriers from entering the market, avoiding over-capacity and maintaining a "reasonable" load factor); and *market access* conditions, which were also referred to in connection with fares and capacity. Other proposals concern government aid, for which precise criteria are to be decided by the Council; the social aspect and its consequences on employment; and the effects on outside States, in terms of compatibility with the world aviation system in force, the respect of certain rights held by certain airlines on intra-Community routes, etc.

IATA studied the proposals made by the Commission, following an invitation to this effect. As was to be expected, the Association is concerned that the efforts made by the Common Market might affect the multilateral characteristics specific to the international air transport system in which the IATA Traffic Conferences are one of the main features. Moreover, IATA considers it difficult to assess the effects of some of the proposals in the Memorandum on the international system as a whole as it now stands since the Commission has not examined closely enough the difficulties confronting the European countries not belonging to the EEC and since 70 per cent of IATA's scheduled international air traffic is carried from, to or within Europe, while under 10 per cent of this traffic exclusively concerns EEC countries. Over and above these policy problems, IATA's observations concern fares, competition, facilitation and charges. In co-ordination with IATA, AEA also presented its observations in 1984.

In November 1984, the Directors General of Civil Aviation of the Member States of ECAC and the Presidents of airlines members of the AEA met in Paris to review jointly recent developments in international air transport. Views were exchanged on a wide range of issues. Some of the conclusions which emerged included:

i) Confirmation that the present system of regulating air traffic in Europe (i.e. on the basis of intergovernmental bilateral and multilateral agreements) continues to be the most appropriate for Europe;

ii) Recognition, nevertheless, that there is a need for more flexibility in the present regulatory system in order to increase its general efficiency; and

iii) Agreement, in the light of developments within the European Economic Community, that it is essential to maintain the coherence of the air transport system throughout ECAC's 22 Member States.

A meeting on the same subject attended by ECAC representatives and the chief executives of 17 members of the European Air Carrier Assembly (EURACA) was held in March 1985. No official statement on the contents of their discussions was issued following the talks. In 1984 EURACA airlines carried 23.9 million passengers mainly on charter flights.

Among the events marking the trend in European aviation policy in 1984, reference should also be made to the very liberal bilateral agreement concluded by the United Kingdom and the Netherlands. The provisions of this agreement include full freedom of access to the market for the airlines of the two countries, as well as greater pricing freedom even on routes outside the United Kingdom-Netherlands network. The four airlines serving the Amsterdam-London route have thus been able to offer fares with 50 per cent reductions outside peak periods.

Another development is affecting airline organisation at a time when the trend towards privatisation is becoming increasingly marked. This is the case of Alitalia, where a study is being conducted on increasing the private stake in the airline, and of Lufthansa where a reduction in the German Government's shareholding from 80 per cent to 51/55 per cent is being discussed. In addition, Sabena's chairman has announced that the State's interest in the carrier has been cut from 98 to 56 per cent and is to be further reduced to give the airline increased flexibility on the money market. The privatisation of British Airways which was announced some time ago by the United Kingdom Government is expected in the near future.

e) Air traffic to and from Australia

Passenger data for 1984 shows that the total increased by 10 per cent over 1983 results.

There were no major fluctuations in the distribution of total traffic between the major regional groupings as identified in Table IV.5. However, results for 1984 show that traffic between Australia and Asian nations has continued to increase as a percentage of total traffic, while the proportion of passengers travelling between Australia and the traditional destinations of United Kingdom/Europe has continued to decline.

Traffic to both Africa and North America has increased slightly in relation to total departures and traffic between Australia and its Pacific neighbours (Oceania) has decreased in overall importance.

1984 saw the introduction of services between Australia and China, and the resumption of services to Australia by Olympic Airways after a break of some seven years.

B. RAIL AND ROAD TRANSPORT

In the international rail and road transport sector, the European Conference of Ministers of Transport (ECMT) is the body which, while its activities are concentrated on European problems, brings together the greater part of OECD Member countries. It may be noted that Australia, Canada, Japan and the United States are associated with the ECMT's work.

Table IV.5. **International air traffic to and from Australia**

Country/Region	Overseas visitors (Arrivals)			Australians residents (Departures)		
	1982 %	1983 %	1984 %	1982 %	1983 %	1984 %
Africa	1.3	0.8	1.1	1.2	0.9	1.1
United States/Canada	9.9	10.2	10.2	9.7	9.9	10.1
Asia/Orient	38.1	40.1	40.7	37.0	38.0	38.8
United Kingdom/Ireland	8.5	7.1	6.7	8.6	7.6	7.3
Other Europe	6.7	5.8	5.6	6.4	6.2	5.9
Total Europe	13.2	12.9	12.3	15.0	13.8	13.2
Oceania[1]	35.4	35.6	35.3	37.0	37.1	36.4
Other countries	0.1	0.4	0.4	0.1	0.3	0.4
TOTAL (%)	100.0	100.0	100.0	100.0	100.0	100.0
TOTAL (in thousands of passengers)	2 234.7	2 147.6	2 368.7	2 123.8	2 104.8	2 318.8

1. New-Zealand included.
Source: Australian Bureau of Statistics, MIG 008.

After having suspended its activities in the railway sector for several years, the ECMT decided in 1983 to bring together some general consideration on the role and position of railways in overall transport economies with a view to placing its work in a more concrete and definite framework. With this in mind, two Ad Hoc Groups were set up to cover commercial action concerning railways and the improvement of international rail links. During 1984 the first of these Groups concentrated on questions of international freight traffic while the second directed its efforts towards the passenger sector.

As the 31st Annual Report of the ECMT points out, it was noted that at present only relatively low average speeds can be achieved in international rail traffic. These low speeds have largely accounted for the fact that travellers are turning away from rail particularly where long distances are involved, in favour of competitive modes with higher performance factors. Among the practical recommendations which the Ad Hoc Group put forward which are of importance for European tourist travel, the ECMT Council of Ministers gave its approval to a series of proposals for action concerning the improvement of "journey time" and the quality of the services offered, including cutting out "unnecessary" stops, raising the standard of equipment, increasing the punctuality, improving the frequency of services and connections, and speeding up frontier formalities (passports, customs and currency controls).

With reference to frontier formalities which are often the source of delay and difficulty to tourists in both rail and road, the efforts which have been made within the European Communities during the last few years have certainly contributed to making the situation easier. In this connection the European Parliament received in April 1985, a report by its Committee on Legal Affairs and Citizens' Rights on the proposal by the CEC to the

Council for a directive on the easing of controls and formalities applicable to nationals of the Member States when crossing intra-Community borders (document A2-18/85). This report includes a proposed Directive laying down conditions for the progressive elimination before 1992 of the controls and formalities which affect nationals of Member states at frontiers within the Community regardless of the means of transport concerned.

The two main commercial railway travel groupings in Europe, "Eurail" and "BritRail" have gained considerably from the increase in tourists from North America which they have encouraged by keeping their prices competitive, by improving the quality of services provided and by adapting their products and special terms to meet the demand better. Among these marketing innovations, the stability of the price of the "Eurail pass" and the "Eurail Youth pass" on sale in the United States is notable as well as the provision of a large number of free bonuses (ferries, lake and river cruises and tourist coach tours in certain regions, etc.). To make it easier for tourists arriving by air to gain access to the railway system, "Eurail" aims over the coming years to increase the rail links between airports and cities including Stuttgart (1985), Rome (1986), Munich (1987) and Geneva (1987). BritRail's marketing efforts have included making it possible to issue the "BritRail Pass" at the time of making reservations with British Airways, improving the access to BritRail products for American travel agencies via computerised information systems and reducing the travel time for a number of intercity services.

With regard to international road transport of particular concern to tourists, the International Road Transport Union (IRU) adopted in November 1984 an international "star" system of classification for tourists coaches. After three years of effort, the IRU now classifies coaches in the following way: * for standard coaches, ** for excursion coaches, *** for tourist coaches and **** for de luxe tourist coaches.

To illustrate the effects upon travellers using their private cars, which a majority of European tourists do,

Table IV.6 shows the price of premium gasoline in OECD Member countries on 1st January and 1st July 1984 and how they have changed since the corresponding dates in 1982 and 1983.

Table IV.6. **Changes in the prices of premium gasoline**

Country		1984 (Price per litre)		% variation over previous year for corresponding dates			
				1984/1983		1983/1982	
		1st January	1st July	1st January	1st July	1st January	1st July
Austria	S	11.3	..	2.7	..	−3.5	−3.5
Belgium	FB	31.1	31.1	4.4	−5.2	15.1	2.2
Denmark	KrD	5.52	6.27	−8.3	0.0	9.3	−0.2
Finland	mkF	3.72	3.79	−3.4	5.3	9.7	6.5
France	FF	4.99	5.24	7.2	7.6	0.2	−4.8
Germany	DM	1.41	1.38	1.3	0.9	16.3	14.2
Greece	Dr	50.0	57.0	0.0	14.0	10.1	17.4
Ireland	£Ir	0.62	0.63	13.7	4.8	17.1	14.2
Italia	L	1 300.00	1 280.00	11.6	−9.9	6.4	1.5
Luxembourg	Flux	26.9	26.6	7.6	−0.7	1.9	1.5
Netherlands	fl.	1.80	1.78	7.3	3.5	−11.3	5.4
Norway	KrN	5.19	5.20	3.1	6.8	27.6	34.4
Portugal	Esc	84.0	99.0	13.5	17.9	21.1	21.1
Spain	Ptas	93.3	93.3	8.1	8.1	11.4	5.8
Sweden	FrS	4.34	4.15	3.1	−1.2	2.5	3.9
Switzerland	FS	1.21	1.21	−1.6	1.6	16.0	17.0
Turkey	LT	..	..	..	..	4.9	8.9
United Kingdom	£	0.40	0.41	8.7	0.5	4.9	8.9
Canada	$Can	0.51	0.52	11.5	2.8	9.2	12.6
United States	$US	0.32	0.32	0.0	−3.3	−10.6	−5.7
Australia	$A	0.46	0.48	6.5	9.0	21.4	6.5
New Zealand	$NZ	0.71	0.88	0.0	23.2	10.9	0.0
Japan	Y	150.00	150.00	−15.3	−2.7	5.4	−11.8

Source: OECD, International Energy Agency.

NOTE

We would like to express our thanks to the following organisations which have provided us with a certain amount of information and statistical data which has helped in the drafting of this chapter:

International Air Transport Association (IATA)

Association of European Airlines (AEA)

European Civil Aviation Conference (ECAC)

European Conference of Ministers of Transport (ECMT)

Institute of Air Transport (ITA)

International Civil Aviation Organisation (ICAO)

International Road Transport Union (IRU)

Statistical Annexes

Annex I.   *FOREIGN TOURISM IN THE OECD AREA*

Annex II.   *DATA CONCERNING INTERNATIONAL TOURIST FLOWS*

Annex III.   *DATA CONCERNING INTERNATIONAL TOURIST RECEIPTS AND EXPENDITURE*

Annex IV.   *DATA CONCERNING TRANSPORT*

Annex V.   *DATA CONCERNING TOURIST ACCOMMODATION*

A.I.1   TOURISM FROM EUROPEAN MEMBER COUNTRIES[1]

	Arrivals at frontiers[2]			Arrivals at all means of accommodation[3]			Nights spent in all means of accommodation[4]		
	Volume 1984 ('000)	% 84/83	% 83/82	Volume 1984 ('000)	% 84/83	% 83/82	Volume 1984 ('000)	% 84/83	% 83/82
Austria				13 042.7	1.9	− 0.1	81 474.4	− 1.8	− 3.4
Belgium									4.6
Denmark							7 600.6	− 7.5	2.5
Finland							1 439.2	2.6	− 5.1
France[5]			− 4.4	3 377.4	0.6	− 6.7	9 170.0	3.8	− 3.7
Germany						− 1.0			− 0.2
Greece	3 982.1	13.4	2.5						
Iceland	54.5	10.9	2.3						
Ireland	9 379.0	0.6	0.5						
Italy	42 163.8	4.4	− 1.0			− 2.9			− 5.0
Luxembourg						1.7			6.8
Netherlands						− 4.4			− 3.6
Norway			1.1				2 321.5		
Portugal	3 667.2	10.0	20.2	2 221.2	8.0	4.7	10 863.7	3.9	− 1.1
Spain	37 759.3	2.9	− 2.1				81 446.8	11.7	4.0
Sweden							6 237.6	1.6	18.6
Switzerland				6 437.0	− 2.2	− 3.5	27 716.4	− 6.1	− 4.3
Turkey	881.8	17.5	14.8			47.4			53.9
United Kingdom	7 520.4	5.9	1.4				67 623.0	3.3	2.2
Canada	944.4	6.2	−12.9						−14.6
United States	1 796.0	− 4.7	− 2.3						
Australia			−11.1						
New Zealand	69.7	4.0	4.4						
Japan	351.7	1.8	9.9						
Yugoslavia				5 726.3	21.9	− 0.9	35 133.9	18.0	− 2.0

1. Derived from tables of series II.1 (see corresponding notes).
2. *Tourist* or *visitor arrivals*. When both available *tourist arrivals*.
3. Arrivals *in all means of accommodation* or *in hotels and similar establishments*. When both available : arrivals *in all means of accommodation*.
4. Nights spent *in all means of accommodation* or *in hotels and similar establishments*. When both available : nights spent *in all means of accommodation*.
5. Data concerns Ile-de-France region only.

A.I.2   TOURISM FROM CANADA AND THE UNITED STATES[1]

	Arrivals at frontiers[2]			Arrivals at all means of accommodation[3]			Nights spent in all means of accommodation[4]		
	Volume 1984 ('000)	% 84/83	% 83/82	Volume 1984 ('000)	% 84/83	% 83/82	Volume 1984 ('000)	% 84/83	% 83/82
Austria				1 012.2	34.7	27.0	2 412.8	25.8	19.3
Belgium									7.4
Denmark							553.4	5.5	19.2
Finland							185.0	4.8	29.6
France[5]			41.3	1 447.4	33.5	16.8	3 864.7	29.4	24.0
Germany						25.0			23.7
Greece	557.1	16.2	20.5						
Iceland	28.3	9.0	18.9						
Ireland	324.0	12.1	− 9.2						
Italy	2 111.0	3.0	7.2			27.9			20.5
Luxembourg						44.2			46.7
Netherlands						12.4			7.3
Norway			6.8				561.0		
Portugal	217.7	39.2	− 5.4	353.1	18.9	29.3	994.2	17.9	25.9
Spain	1 091.5	14.9	6.5				2 880.9	18.3	25.5
Sweden							463.9	6.7	31.2
Switzerland				1 685.9	27.9	17.4	3 635.4	25.6	13.3
Turkey	231.4	13.8	79.5			43.5			27.1
United Kingdom	3 330.5	17.4	32.8				35 118.0	12.5	18.6
Canada	11 706.5	7.3	4.3						0.6
United States	10 982.0	− 8.0	14.4						
Australia			9.0						
New Zealand	124.1	15.8	13.6						
Japan	564.1	9.5	12.2						
Yugoslavia				260.1	35.9	22.4	710.0	37.2	21.3

1. Derived from tables of series II.1 (see corresponding notes).
2. *Tourist* or *visitor arrivals*. When both available *tourist arrivals*.
3. Arrivals *in all means of accommodation* or *in hotels and similar establishments*. When both available : arrivals *in all means of accommodation*.
4. Nights spent *in all means of accommodation* or *in hotels and similar establishments*. When both available : nights spent *in all means of accommodation*.
5. Data concerns Ile-de-France region only.

A.I.3 TOURISM FROM AUSTRALIA, NEW ZEALAND AND JAPAN[1]

	Arrivals at frontiers[2]			Arrivals at all means of accommodation[3]			Nights spent in all means of accommodation[4]		
	Volume 1984 ('000)	% 84/83	% 83/82	Volume 1984 ('000)	% 84/83	% 83/82	Volume 1984 ('000)	% 84/83	% 83/82
Austria				179.0	20.0	5.0	375.3	13.2	6.2
Belgium									− 7.6
Denmark							79.5	− 3.2	10.5
Finland							41.9	13.8	52.9
France[5]				528.2	− 4.9	4.3	1 301.3	− 8.3	9.3
Germany						− 0.2			− 0.1
Greece	183.4	11.0	2.8						
Iceland	1.0	8.1	−11.0						
Ireland	34.0	25.9							
Italy	702.1	0.4	7.8			8.1			7.2
Luxembourg									
Netherlands						−15.2	63.0		−10.5
Norway			− 3.5						
Portugal	30.9	25.7	1.8	41.9	29.2	7.6	105.2	17.4	5.6
Spain	179.1	11.9	1.0				339.0	8.2	1.6
Sweden							60.1	10.7	− 4.7
Switzerland				449.0	9.7	7.6	842.0	6.9	6.9
Turkey	30.8	66.3	16.3			63.6			44.0
United Kingdom	751.7	30.2	− 1.4				15 456.0	23.1	11.3
Canada	222.6	19.5	− 1.5						−13.2
United States	1 407.0	10.0	4.8						
Australia			1.1						
New Zealand	293.8	14.0	4.9						
Japan	68.4	20.0	− 1.8						
Yugoslavia				9.3	6.8	− 6.7	26.4	− 3.9	0.2

1. Derived from tables of series II.1 (see corresponding notes).
2. *Tourist* or *visitor arrivals.* When both available *tourist arrivals.*
3. Arrivals *in all means of accommodation* or *in hotels and similar establishments.* When both available : arrivals *in all means of accommodation.*
4. Nights spent *in all means of accommodation* or *in hotels and similar establishments.* When both available : nights spent *in all means of accommodation.*
5. Data concerns Ile-de-France region only.

A.I.4 TOURISM FROM ALL OECD COUNTRIES[1]

	Arrivals at frontiers[2]			Arrivals at all means of accommodation[3]			Nights spent in all means of accommodation[4]		
	Volume 1984 ('000)	% 84/83	% 83/82	Volume 1984 ('000)	% 84/83	% 83/82	Volume 1984 ('000)	% 84/83	% 83/82
Austria				14 233.9	3.9	1.2	84 262.6	− 1.1	− 2.9
Belgium									4.7
Denmark							8 154.0	− 6.7	3.3
Finland							1 666.1	3.1	− 1.3
France[5]			− 2.0	5 352.9	7.1	− 1.2	14 336.0	8.3	2.8
Germany						3.9			3.9
Greece	4 722.6	13.6	4.3						
Iceland	83.7	10.2	7.2						
Ireland	9 737.0	1.0	0.4						
Italy	44 977.0	4.3	− 0.5			1.1			− 3.3
Luxembourg						6.0			8.1
Netherlands						− 2.5			− 2.8
Norway			2.1				2 945.4		
Portugal	3 915.9	11.4	18.6	2 616.2	9.7	7.3	11 963.1	5.0	0.6
Spain	39 029.9	3.3	− 1.9				84 666.6	11.9	4.5
Sweden							6 761.6	2.0	19.1
Switzerland				8 571.9	3.2	− 0.2	32 193.8	− 3.0	− 2.7
Turkey	1 144.0	17.6	24.2			47.5			50.5
United Kingdom	11 602.6	10.3	8.2				118 197.0	8.2	7.4
Canada	12 873.5	7.4	2.7						− 3.4
United States	14 185.0	− 6.1	11.2						
Australia			− 2.0						
New Zealand	487.6	12.9	6.8						
Japan	984.2	7.3	10.3						
Yugoslavia				5 995.7	22.4	− 0.2	35 870.3	18.4	− 1.7

1. Derived from tables of series II.1 (see corresponding notes).
2. *Tourist* or *visitor arrivals.* When both available *tourist arrivals.*
3. Arrivals *in all means of accommodation* or *in hotels and similar establishments.* When both available : arrivals *in all means of accommodation.*
4. Nights spent *in all means of accommodation* or *in hotels and similar establishments.* When both available : nights spent *in all means of accommodation.*
5. Data concerns Ile-de-France region only.

A.I.5 TOURISM FROM NON-MEMBER COUNTRIES[1]

	Arrivals at frontiers[2]			Arrivals at all means of accommodation[3]			Nights spent in all means of accommodation[4]		
	Volume 1984 ('000)	% 84/83	% 83/82	Volume 1984 ('000)	% 84/83	% 83/82	Volume 1984 ('000)	% 84/83	% 83/82
Austria				876.4	12.9	9.8	2 450.7	10.5	2.8
Belgium									2.3
Denmark							958.2	22.1	3.3
Finland							446.4	0.5	15.0
France[5]			26.6	1 078.9	7.8	-2.8	3 313.1	8.7	-1.9
Germany						4.0			1.3
Greece	800.5	28.9	-40.7						
Iceland	1.6	-1.1	-6.5						
Ireland	29.0	-21.6	-35.4						
Italy	4 173.8	21.4	-30.8			-7.1			-5.6
Luxembourg						-83.8			-80.2
Netherlands						-1.4			-1.4
Norway			-7.8				514.4		
Portugal	202.8	1.2	-1.3	189.4	12.3	-1.0	569.1	6.3	1.3
Spain	3 745.4	7.9	-0.1				3 094.0	8.5	-34.1
Sweden							788.4	23.3	10.1
Switzerland				909.7	2.0	3.5	2 764.2	-0.8	6.0
Turkey	973.1	49.1	7.2			42.3			49.7
United Kingdom	2 108.3	6.3	3.6				37 131.0	2.5	3.2
Canada	543.1	8.1	-1.7						-9.7
United States	6 625.0	0.7	-10.3						
Australia			2.0						
New Zealand	78.5	2.5	-1.2						
Japan	1 126.2	7.2	9.3						
Yugoslavia				1 228.1	16.9	0.2	6 399.6	26.8	6.1

1. Derived from tables of series II.1 (see corresponding notes).
2. *Tourist* or *visitor arrivals*. When both available *tourist arrivals*.
3. Arrivals *in all means of accommodation* or *in hotels and similar establishments*. When both available : arrivals *in all means of accommodation*.
4. Nights spent *in all means of accommodation* or *in hotels and similar establishments*. When both available : nights spent *in all means of accommodation*.
5. Data concerns Ile-de-France region only.

A.I.6 TOURISM FROM ALL COUNTRIES[1]

	Arrivals at frontiers[2]			Arrivals at all means of accommodation[3]			Nights spent in all means of accommodation[4]		
	Volume 1984 ('000)	% 84/83	% 83/82	Volume 1984 ('000)	% 84/83	% 83/82	Volume 1984 ('000)	% 84/83	% 83/82
Austria[5]	129 330.0	0.1	0.4	15 110.2	4.3	1.6	86 713.3	-0.8	-2.8
Belgium									4.5
Denmark							9 112.3	-4.4	3.3
Finland							2 112.5	2.5	1.8
France[6]			0.0	6 523.6	6.6	0.5	17 942.4	7.8	4.2
Germany[7]			-1.8			3.9			3.5
Greece	5 523.2	15.6	-5.1				32 425.2	17.2	-7.6
Iceland	85.3	10.0	6.9						
Ireland	9 891.0	1.0	0.1	1 838.0	7.2	-0.3	19 254.6	2.9	8.6
Italy	49 150.7	5.5	-3.6			0.1			-3.5
Luxembourg[8]						-9.7			9.3
Netherlands						-2.4			-2.7
Norway			1.4	1 347.1	5.9	4.9	3 459.8		
Portugal	4 118.6	10.9	17.4	2 805.6	9.8	6.7	12 532.2	5.1	0.6
Spain	42 931.7	4.0	-1.8	13 040.5	11.2	4.9	89 064.1	11.7	4.0
Sweden							7 550.0	3.9	18.3
Switzerland[9]	11 850.0	3.0	0.0	9 481.6	3.1	0.2	34 958.0	-2.8	-2.1
Turkey	2 117.1	30.3	16.8			45.9			50.2
United Kingdom	13 710.9	9.7	7.4				155 328.0	6.8	6.3
Canada	13 416.6	7.4	2.5						-4.1
United States	20 810.0	-4.0	3.7						
Australia			-1.1						
New Zealand	566.1	11.3	5.6						
Japan	2 110.3	7.2	9.8						
Yugoslavia	19 716.6	5.3	4.6	7 223.8	21.5	-0.1	42 269.8	19.6	-0.6

1. Derived from tables of series II.1. See corresponding notes, except for the countries memtioned in notes 5 and 7 to 9 below.
2. *Tourist* or *visitor arrivals*. When both available *tourist arrivals*.
3. Arrivals *in all means of accommodation* or *in hotels and similar establishments*. When both available : arrivals *in all means of accommodation*.
4. Nights spent *in all means of accommodation* or *in hotels and similar establishments*. When both available : nights spent *in all means of accommodation*.
5. Austria : *visitor* arrivals at frontiers.
6. France : data concerns Ile-de-France region only.
7. Germany : *visitor* arrivals at frontiers.
8. Luxembourg : arrivals and nights *in all means of accommodation*.
9. Switzerland : *tourist* arrivals at frontiers: estimates.

Tables A.II.1

STATISTICS OF FOREIGN TOURISM
BY RECEIVING COUNTRY

(Breakdown by month and by country)

ARRIVALS OF FOREIGN VISITORS OR TOURISTS AT FRONTIERS

Canada	Italy	Turkey
France	Japan	United Kingdom
Greece	New Zealand	United States
Iceland	Portugal	Yugoslavia
Ireland	Spain	

ARRIVALS OF FOREIGN TOURISTS AT HOTELS

Austria	Italy	Switzerland
France	Portugal	Yugoslavia

ARRIVALS OF FOREIGN TOURISTS AT REGISTERED TOURIST ACCOMMODATION

Austria	Portugal	Yugoslavia
Italy	Switzerland	

NIGHTS SPENT BY FOREIGN TOURISTS IN HOTELS

Austria	Italy	Sweden
Denmark	Norway	Switzerland
Finland	Portugal	Yugoslavia
France	Spain	

NIGHTS SPENT BY FOREIGN TOURISTS IN REGISTERED TOURIST ACCOMMODATION

Austria	Portugal	United Kingdom
Denmark	Sweden	Yugoslavia
Italy	Switzerland	

The corresponding statistical tables are grouped by country listed in alphabetical order.
Data concerning 1984 are very often provisional.

AUSTRIA

ARRIVALS OF FOREIGN TOURISTS IN HOTELS
(by month)

	Total number 1984	% Variation over 1983	% of 1984 total	From Germany	% Variation over 1983	From United States	% Variation over 1983
January	775 564	2.1	7.1	471 691	2.1	21 031	15.2
February	790 250	− 2.0	7.3	414 217	1.4	22 089	28.2
March	809 835	9.4	7.5	460 493	− 7.4	25 580	20.5
April	691 501	26.7	6.4	379 076	34.2	30 394	4.9
May	752 111	− 8.0	6.9	343 165	−22.0	77 379	38.8
June	1 183 586	13.0	10.9	559 399	3.3	147 686	65.7
July	1 511 649	1.7	13.9	609 415	−11.0	167 137	31.4
August	1 591 982	9.3	14.6	725 551	0.4	120 868	50.3
September	1 212 316	7.5	11.2	583 181	− 2.6	147 001	43.6
October	630 856	2.6	5.8	327 611	− 6.1	67 696	10.9
November	279 125	19.8	2.6	139 950	15.3	21 933	30.4
December	638 374	6.5	5.9	357 237	0.6	28 216	30.5
Total	10 867 149	6.2	100.0	5 370 986	− 1.7	877 010	37.0

(by country of residence)

	1983	Relative share	1984	Relative share	% Variation over 1983
Austria					
Belgium [1]	239 840	2.3	242 799	2.2	1.2
Denmark	120 795	1.2	119 569	1.1	−1.0
Finland	32 509	0.3	36 160	0.3	11.2
France	392 871	3.8	498 797	4.6	27.0
Germany (F.R.)	5 463 033	53.4	5 370 986	49.4	−1.7
Greece	40 794	0.4	46 097	0.4	13.0
Iceland [2]					
Ireland	6 854	0.1	7 144	0.1	4.2
Italy	375 530	3.7	451 187	4.2	20.1
Luxembourg [1]					
Netherlands	733 440	7.2	754 410	6.9	2.9
Norway	38 550	0.4	41 260	0.4	7.0
Portugal	10 182	0.1	9 068	0.1	−10.9
Spain	86 722	0.8	91 386	0.8	5.4
Sweden	194 312	1.9	205 429	1.9	5.7
Switzerland	383 621	3.7	414 279	3.8	8.0
Turkey	19 592	0.2	24 277	0.2	23.9
United Kingdom	662 194	6.5	732 403	6.7	10.6
Other OECD-Europe					
Total Europe	8 800 839	86.0	9 045 251	83.2	2.8
Canada	53 503	0.5	66 384	0.6	24.1
United States	639 947	6.3	877 010	8.1	37.0
Total North America	693 450	6.8	943 394	8.7	36.0
Australia [3]	58 341	0.6	72 596	0.7	24.4
New Zealand [3]					
Japan	90 755	0.9	106 355	1.0	17.2
Total Australasia and Japan	149 096	1.5	178 951	1.6	20.0
Total OECD Countries	9 643 385	94.2	10 167 596	93.6	5.4
Yugoslavia (S.F.R.)	72 454	0.7	80 388	0.7	11.0
Other European countries	210 052	2.1	251 717	2.3	19.8
of which: Bulgaria	6 784	0.1	9 183	0.1	35.4
Czechoslovakia	27 544	0.3	27 718	0.3	0.6
Hungary	140 722	1.4	177 312	1.6	26.0
Poland	21 759	0.2	22 762	0.2	4.6
Rumania	5 047	0.0	4 622	0.0	−8.4
USSR	8 196	0.1	10 120	0.1	23.5
Latin America	58 050	0.6	79 049	0.7	36.2
Asia-Oceania	111 719	1.1	122 543	1.1	9.7
Africa	30 213	0.3	37 326	0.3	23.5
Origin country undetermined	108 422	1.1	128 530	1.2	18.5
Total Non-OECD Countries	590 910	5.8	699 553	6.4	18.4
TOTAL	10 234 295	100.0	10 867 149	100.0	6.2

1. Luxembourg included in Belgium.
2. Iceland included in "Other European countries".
3. New Zealand included in Australia.
Source: Austrian Central Statistical Office - Vienna.

AUSTRIA

ARRIVALS OF FOREIGN TOURISTS IN REGISTERED TOURIST ACCOMMODATION
(by month)

	Total number 1984	% Variation over 1983	% of 1984 total	From Germany	% Variation over 1983	From United States	% Variation over 1983
January	1 079 438	2.1	7.1	714 177	1.8	23 691	17.0
February	1 116 404	−4.8	7.4	649 485	−0.5	24 315	27.0
March	1 139 573	11.2	7.5	700 730	−6.3	27 195	19.1
April	879 320	28.0	5.8	533 511	36.0	32 293	5.4
May	865 933	−12.6	5.7	426 558	−26.2	80 352	38.1
June	1 542 330	11.3	10.2	816 942	3.2	154 936	63.1
July	2 445 569	−1.9	16.2	1 112 238	−13.7	181 012	29.7
August	2 544 205	7.8	16.8	1 337 607	0.4	131 627	46.7
September	1 510 089	5.2	10.0	815 898	−3.0	151 565	42.5
October	750 827	0.5	5.0	421 211	−4.4	70 465	11.9
November	314 615	21.5	2.1	167 205	18.9	23 183	28.5
December	921 930	6.1	6.1	578 909	1.9	30 871	26.6
Total	15 110 233	4.3	100.0	8 274 471	−2.4	931 505	35.6

(by country of residence)

	1983	Relative share	1984	Relative share	% Variation over 1983
Austria	344 675	2.4	350 720	2.3	1.8
Belgium [1]	167 556	1.2	169 333	1.1	1.1
Denmark	32 509	0.2	36 160	0.2	11.2
Finland	491 816	3.4	639 070	4.2	29.9
France	8 475 052	58.5	8 274 471	54.8	−2.4
Germany (F.R.)	44 332	0.3	50 135	0.3	13.1
Greece					
Iceland [2]	6 854	0.0	7 144	0.0	4.2
Ireland	434 179	3.0	540 344	3.6	24.5
Italy					
Luxembourg [1]	1 203 495	8.3	1 251 737	8.3	4.0
Netherlands	38 550	0.3	41 260	0.3	7.0
Norway	10 182	0.1	9 068	0.1	−10.9
Portugal	86 722	0.6	91 386	0.6	5.4
Spain	249 661	1.7	259 634	1.7	4.0
Sweden	443 856	3.1	475 978	3.2	7.2
Switzerland	19 592	0.1	24 277	0.2	23.9
Turkey	755 518	5.2	821 998	5.4	8.8
United Kingdom					
Other OECD-Europe					
Total Europe	12 804 549	88.4	13 042 715	86.3	1.9
Canada	64 339	0.4	80 695	0.5	25.4
United States	687 116	4.7	931 505	6.2	35.6
Total North America	751 455	5.2	1 012 200	6.7	34.7
Australia [3]	58 341	0.4	72 596	0.5	24.4
New Zealand [3]	90 755	0.6	106 355	0.7	17.2
Japan					
Total Australasia and Japan	149 096	1.0	178 951	1.2	20.0
Total OECD Countries	13 705 100	94.6	14 233 866	94.2	3.9
Yugoslavia (S.F.R.)	83 256	0.6	92 912	0.6	11.6
Other European countries	259 183	1.8	307 150	2.0	18.5
of which: Bulgaria	8 625	0.1	10 901	0.1	26.4
Czechoslovakia	34 276	0.2	35 414	0.2	3.3
Hungary	175 790	1.2	218 619	1.4	24.4
Poland	25 660	0.2	26 207	0.2	2.1
Rumania	6 636	0.0	5 889	0.0	−11.3
USSR	8 196	0.1	10 120	0.1	23.5
Latin America	58 050	0.4	79 049	0.5	36.2
Asia-Oceania	122 383	0.8	134 100	0.9	9.6
Africa	30 213	0.2	37 326	0.2	23.5
Origin country undetermined	223 346	1.5	225 830	1.5	1.1
Total Non-OECD Countries	776 431	5.4	876 367	5.8	12.9
TOTAL	14 481 531	100.0	15 110 233	100.0	4.3

1. Luxembourg included in Belgium.
2. Iceland included in "Other European countries".
3. New Zealand included in Australia.
Source: Austrian Central Statistical Office - Vienna.

AUSTRIA

NIGHTS SPENT BY FOREIGN TOURISTS IN HOTELS
(by month)

	Total number 1984	% Variation over 1983	% of 1984 total	From Germany	% Variation over 1983	From United States	% Variation over 1983
January	5 359 405	4.3	9.7	3 391 954	3.2	91 770	14.1
February	5 484 885	− 0.6	9.9	3 014 939	6.2	97 009	20.3
March	5 269 068	1.3	9.5	3 275 250	−15.2	94 000	16.5
April	2 910 941	13.6	5.2	1 989 181	19.4	63 332	− 8.4
May	2 469 303	−15.4	4.4	1 380 286	−25.7	153 028	27.4
June	5 171 781	3.9	9.3	3 143 654	− 2.2	290 001	66.9
July	8 168 305	− 5.1	14.7	4 709 319	−12.5	355 147	14.3
August	9 034 692	2.2	16.3	5 768 282	− 2.0	286 121	42.6
September	5 475 836	− 0.7	9.9	3 527 533	− 5.8	291 109	34.4
October	1 988 724	0.8	3.6	1 182 957	− 7.4	147 353	15.1
November	781 243	21.8	1.4	427 078	19.4	55 446	22.8
December	3 409 723	10.3	6.1	2 092 969	7.7	100 604	26.0
Total	55 523 906	1.0	100.0	33 903 402	− 4.0	2 024 920	27.7

(by country of residence)

	1983	Relative share	1984	Relative share	% Variation over 1983
Austria					
Belgium [1]	1 495 336	2.7	1 509 715	2.7	1.0
Denmark	603 742	1.1	587 598	1.1	−2.7
Finland	123 220	0.2	139 867	0.3	13.5
France	1 388 688	2.5	1 791 041	3.2	29.0
Germany (F.R.)	35 319 470	64.2	33 903 402	61.1	−4.0
Greece	106 856	0.2	122 764	0.2	14.9
Iceland [2]					
Ireland	33 117	0.1	32 748	0.1	−1.1
Italy	849 266	1.5	1 018 728	1.8	20.0
Luxembourg [1]					
Netherlands	5 169 166	9.4	5 306 708	9.6	2.7
Norway	132 003	0.2	143 741	0.3	8.9
Portugal	20 510	0.0	17 744	0.0	−13.5
Spain	184 906	0.3	182 082	0.3	−1.5
Sweden	891 596	1.6	907 062	1.6	1.7
Switzerland	1 287 135	2.3	1 426 872	2.6	10.9
Turkey	43 661	0.1	52 598	0.1	20.5
United Kingdom	3 612 169	6.6	3 907 860	7.0	8.2
Other OECD-Europe					
Total Europe	51 260 841	93.2	51 050 530	91.9	−0.4
Canada	135 619	0.2	163 894	0.3	20.8
United States	1 585 808	2.9	2 024 920	3.6	27.7
Total North America	1 721 427	3.1	2 188 814	3.9	27.2
Australia [3]	149 836	0.3	177 648	0.3	18.6
New Zealand [3]					
Japan	181 703	0.3	197 654	0.4	8.8
Total Australasia and Japan	331 539	0.6	375 302	0.7	13.2
Total OECD Countries	53 313 807	96.9	53 614 646	96.6	0.6
Yugoslavia (S.F.R.)	198 390	0.4	201 879	0.4	1.8
Other European countries	511 268	0.9	594 105	1.1	16.2
of which: Bulgaria	22 073	0.0	29 128	0.1	32.0
Czechoslovakia	63 597	0.1	64 434	0.1	1.3
Hungary	314 304	0.6	366 164	0.7	16.5
Poland	67 044	0.1	82 576	0.1	23.2
Rumania	15 608	0.0	12 590	0.0	−19.3
USSR	28 642	0.1	39 213	0.1	36.9
Latin America	134 317	0.2	167 868	0.3	25.0
Asia-Oceania	372 487	0.7	404 421	0.7	8.6
Africa	126 942	0.2	158 807	0.3	25.1
Origin country undetermined	336 005	0.6	382 181	0.7	13.7
Total Non-OECD Countries	1 679 409	3.1	1 909 261	3.4	13.7
TOTAL	54 993 216	100.0	55 523 907	100.0	1.0

1. Luxembourg included in Belgium.
2. Iceland included in "Other European countries".
3. New Zealand included in Australia.
Source: Austrian Central Statistical Office - Vienna.

AUSTRIA

NIGHTS SPENT BY FOREIGN TOURISTS IN REGISTERED TOURIST ACCOMMODATION
(by month)

	Total number 1984	% Variation over 1983	% of 1984 total	From Germany	% Variation over 1983	From United States	% Variation over 1983
January	7 842 131	5.1	9.0	5 353 671	3.7	104 136	14.9
February	7 920 920	−1.9	9.1	4 741 779	5.7	109 857	21.1
March	7 690 952	1.6	8.9	5 040 182	−15.4	102 611	16.4
April	4 131 566	11.3	4.8	3 045 783	16.5	68 618	−8.7
May	3 073 172	−19.5	3.5	1 874 328	−28.5	160 794	25.8
June	7 408 261	0.6	8.5	4 953 739	−4.9	307 312	63.0
July	15 459 655	−7.8	17.8	9 458 664	−15.2	397 677	15.1
August	16 668 970	0.4	19.2	11 714 475	−1.8	317 965	39.9
September	7 834 577	−2.7	9.0	5 578 496	−6.3	306 929	32.0
October	2 536 523	−1.5	2.9	1 635 804	−7.6	154 745	15.8
November	923 159	22.1	1.1	537 938	20.3	59 815	22.5
December	5 223 368	11.7	6.0	3 472 069	9.7	112 568	22.2
Total	86 713 254	−0.8	100.0	57 406 928	−5.1	2 203 027	26.6

(by country of residence)

	1983	Relative share	1984	Relative share	% Variation over 1983
Austria					
Belgium [1]	2 317 479	2.7	2 346 770	2.7	1.3
Denmark	796 586	0.9	803 177	0.9	0.8
Finland	123 220	0.1	139 867	0.2	13.5
France	1 835 328	2.1	2 362 341	2.7	28.7
Germany (F.R.)	60 463 785	69.1	57 406 928	66.2	−5.1
Greece	119 184	0.1	136 391	0.2	14.4
Iceland [2]					
Ireland	33 117	0.0	32 748	0.0	−1.1
Italy	1 051 332	1.2	1 245 719	1.4	18.5
Luxembourg [1]					
Netherlands	9 047 356	10.3	9 354 457	10.8	3.4
Norway	132 003	0.2	143 741	0.2	8.9
Portugal	20 510	0.0	17 744	0.0	−13.5
Spain	184 906	0.2	182 082	0.2	−1.5
Sweden	1 140 276	1.3	1 149 513	1.3	0.8
Switzerland	1 609 514	1.8	1 761 806	2.0	9.5
Turkey	43 661	0.0	52 598	0.1	20.5
United Kingdom	4 059 757	4.6	4 338 545	5.0	6.9
Other OECD-Europe					
Total Europe	82 978 014	94.9	81 474 427	94.0	−1.8
Canada	176 853	0.2	209 823	0.2	18.6
United States	1 740 612	2.0	2 203 027	2.5	26.6
Total North America	1 917 465	2.2	2 412 850	2.8	25.8
Australia [3]	149 836	0.2	177 648	0.2	18.6
New Zealand [3]					
Japan	181 703	0.2	197 654	0.2	8.8
Total Australasia and Japan	331 539	0.4	375 302	0.4	13.2
Total OECD Countries	85 227 018	97.5	84 262 579	97.2	−1.1
Yugoslavia (S.F.R.)	259 776	0.3	271 446	0.3	4.5
Other European countries	645 530	0.7	746 928	0.9	15.7
of which: Bulgaria	31 787	0.0	35 413	0.0	11.4
Czechoslovakia	83 325	0.1	83 406	0.1	0.1
Hungary	398 057	0.5	468 735	0.5	17.8
Poland	83 932	0.1	104 058	0.1	24.0
Rumania	19 787	0.0	16 103	0.0	−18.6
USSR	28 642	0.0	39 213	0.0	36.9
Latin America	134 317	0.2	167 868	0.2	25.0
Asia-Oceania	407 313	0.5	444 105	0.5	9.0
Africa	126 942	0.1	158 807	0.2	25.1
Origin country undetermined	643 585	0.7	661 521	0.8	2.8
Total Non-OECD Countries	2 217 463	2.5	2 450 675	2.8	10.5
TOTAL	87 444 481	100.0	86 713 254	100.0	−0.8

1. Luxembourg included in Belgium.
2. Iceland included in "Other European countries".
3. New Zealand included in Australia.
Source: Austrian Central Statistical Office - Vienna.

CANADA

ARRIVALS OF FOREIGN VISITORS AT FRONTIERS
(by month)

	Total number 1984	% Variation over 1983	% of 1984 total	From United Kingdom	% Variation over 1983	From United States	% Variation over 1983
January	1 429 700	− 4.6	4.1	10 300	10.8	1 372 900	− 5.2
February	1 576 300	2.6	4.5	9 000	13.9	1 521 300	2.4
March	1 759 400	− 4.4	5.0	12 300	−19.6	1 690 300	− 4.4
April	2 143 800	− 0.7	6.1	22 500	− 8.2	2 032 000	− 1.5
May	2 862 800	− 0.2	8.2	37 500	− 5.1	2 697 300	− 0.5
June	4 055 700	5.4	11.6	54 900	− 2.0	3 799 800	5.6
July	5 664 800	− 1.6	16.2	64 300	− 5.4	5 326 400	− 2.0
August	5 640 900	3.8	16.2	70 200	− 1.0	5 311 300	3.4
September	3 359 200	− 1.5	9.6	47 000	− 5.4	3 154 100	− 1.8
October	2 470 300	1.5	7.1	21 400	−12.3	2 348 500	1.4
November	1 992 400	11.3	5.7	16 000	8.1	1 910 300	11.1
December	1 909 700	13.7	5.5	19 900	− 3.4	1 813 500	14.2
Total	34 865 000	1.8	100.0	385 300	− 3.9	32 977 700	1.5

(by country of residence)

	1983	Relative share	1984	Relative share	% Variation over 1983
Austria	15 400	0.0	16 500	0.0	7.1
Belgium	16 700	0.0	17 700	0.1	6.0
Denmark	14 900	0.0	17 700	0.1	18.8
Finland	9 500	0.0	11 300	0.0	18.9
France	100 000	0.3	121 300	0.3	21.3
Germany (F.R.)	191 000	0.6	200 200	0.6	4.8
Greece	12 900	0.0	15 500	0.0	20.2
Iceland	1 000	0.0	1 600	0.0	60.0
Ireland	13 900	0.0	14 400	0.0	3.6
Italy	57 600	0.2	65 500	0.2	13.7
Luxembourg	700	0.0	1 000	0.0	42.9
Netherlands	68 900	0.2	66 800	0.2	−3.0
Norway	11 100	0.0	11 700	0.0	5.4
Portugal	9 400	0.0	10 300	0.0	9.6
Spain	11 700	0.0	13 200	0.0	12.8
Sweden	19 000	0.1	23 700	0.1	24.7
Switzerland	46 600	0.1	51 300	0.1	10.1
Turkey	2 900	0.0	3 300	0.0	13.8
United Kingdom	400 900	1.2	385 400	1.1	−3.9
Other OECD-Europe					
Total Europe	1 004 100	2.9	1 048 400	3.0	4.4
Canada					
United States	32 479 800	94.8	32 977 800	94.6	1.5
Total North America	32 479 800	94.8	32 977 800	94.6	1.5
Australia	62 700	0.2	74 900	0.2	19.5
New Zealand	14 600	0.0	16 900	0.0	15.8
Japan	138 700	0.4	162 200	0.5	16.9
Total Australasia and Japan	216 000	0.6	254 000	0.7	17.6
Total OECD Countries	33 699 900	98.4	34 280 200	98.3	1.7
Yugoslavia (S.F.R.)	9 800	0.0	10 900	0.0	11.2
Other European countries	43 300	0.1	47 700	0.1	10.2
of which: Bulgaria	400	0.0	400	0.0	0.0
Czechoslovakia	4 200	0.0	4 600	0.0	9.5
Hungary	5 300	0.0	5 800	0.0	9.4
Poland	22 600	0.1	27 700	0.1	22.6
Rumania	1 200	0.0	1 300	0.0	8.3
USSR	9 600	0.0	7 900	0.0	−17.7
Latin America [1]	102 100	0.3	107 200	0.3	5.0
Asia-Oceania	247 100	0.7	268 800	0.8	8.8
Africa	50 600	0.1	48 300	0.1	−4.5
Origin country undetermined	102 700	0.3	101 900	0.3	−0.8
Total Non-OECD Countries	555 600	1.6	584 800	1.7	5.3
TOTAL	34 255 500	100.0	34 865 000	100.0	1.8

1. Including Mexico.
Source: Statistics Canada - International Travel section - Ottawa.

CANADA

ARRIVALS OF FOREIGN TOURISTS AT FRONTIERS
(by month)

	Total number 1984	% Variation over 1983	% of 1984 total	From United Kingdom	% Variation over 1983	From United States	% Variation over 1983
January	345 100	2.9	2.6	9 400	8.0	292 200	1.4
February	435 000	13.3	3.2	8 400	13.5	383 700	13.9
March	482 600	− 1.1	3.6	11 600	−20.0	417 800	− 1.0
April	661 100	5.9	4.9	20 900	− 9.9	560 500	4.6
May	1 076 100	1.8	8.0	35 500	− 4.8	925 500	1.1
June	1 827 300	10.6	13.6	51 100	− 1.5	1 594 300	11.8
July	2 566 600	− 1.5	19.1	59 100	− 4.8	2 262 300	− 2.1
August	2 694 900	9.4	20.1	63 200	− 3.2	2 402 800	9.3
September	1 386 800	− 1.8	10.3	42 700	− 6.6	1 202 300	− 2.6
October	849 400	2.3	6.3	19 500	−11.8	740 000	1.9
November	548 200	8.8	4.1	14 900	14.6	473 300	7.9
December	543 400	9.0	4.1	19 100	− 3.5	451 800	10.4
Total [1]	13 416 500	4.4	100.0	355 400	− 4.2	11 706 500	4.1

(by country of residence)

	1983	Relative share	1984	Relative share	% Variation over 1983
Austria	13 300	0.1	14 200	0.1	6.8
Belgium	15 800	0.1	16 000	0.1	1.3
Denmark	12 600	0.1	15 900	0.1	26.2
Finland	8 200	0.1	9 900	0.1	20.7
France	90 700	0.7	111 100	0.8	22.5
Germany (F.R.)	163 000	1.3	174 000	1.3	6.7
Greece	11 200	0.1	14 200	0.1	26.8
Iceland	800	0.0	1 400	0.0	75.0
Ireland	11 800	0.1	12 300	0.1	4.2
Italy	45 700	0.4	54 900	0.4	20.1
Luxembourg	600	0.0	800	0.0	33.3
Netherlands	63 300	0.5	61 900	0.5	−2.2
Norway	9 800	0.1	10 500	0.1	7.1
Portugal	9 000	0.1	9 800	0.1	8.9
Spain	9 300	0.1	11 200	0.1	20.4
Sweden	15 800	0.1	20 900	0.2	32.3
Switzerland	42 500	0.3	47 000	0.4	10.6
Turkey	2 600	0.0	3 000	0.0	15.4
United Kingdom	363 400	2.9	355 400	2.6	−2.2
Other OECD-Europe					
Total Europe	889 400	7.1	944 400	7.0	6.2
Canada					
United States	10 912 700	87.4	11 706 500	87.3	7.3
Total North America	10 912 700	87.4	11 706 500	87.3	7.3
Australia	56 400	0.5	68 300	0.5	21.1
New Zealand	13 100	0.1	15 200	0.1	16.0
Japan	116 700	0.9	139 100	1.0	19.2
Total Australasia and Japan	186 200	1.5	222 600	1.7	19.5
Total OECD Countries	11 988 300	96.0	12 873 500	96.0	7.4
Yugoslavia (S.F.R.)	9 500	0.1	10 600	0.1	11.6
Other European countries	35 000	0.3	46 100	0.3	31.7
of which: Bulgaria	400	0.0	400	0.0	0.0
Czechoslovakia	4 000	0.0	4 400	0.0	10.0
Hungary	5 000	0.0	5 600	0.0	12.0
Poland	15 800	0.1	26 700	0.2	69.0
Rumania	1 200	0.0	1 200	0.0	0.0
USSR	8 600	0.1	7 800	0.1	−9.3
Latin America [2]	90 500	0.7	96 500	0.7	6.6
Asia-Oceania	222 600	1.8	244 200	1.8	9.7
Africa	48 100	0.4	46 400	0.3	−3.5
Origin country undetermined	96 700	0.8	99 300	0.7	2.7
Total Non-OECD Countries	502 400	4.0	543 100	4.0	8.1
TOTAL [1]	12 490 700	100.0	13 416 600	100.0	7.4

1. Discrepancies between data by month and by country of origin arise because monthly figures are estimates.
2. Including Mexico.
Source: Statistics Canada - International Travel section - Ottawa.

DENMARK

NIGHTS SPENT BY FOREIGN TOURISTS IN HOTELS
(by month)

	Total number 1984	% Variation over 1983	% of 1984 total	From Germany	% Variation over 1983	From United States	% Variation over 1983
January	127 400	8.1	2.8	18 700	13.3	13 100	2.3
February	133 900	10.4	2.9	16 200	14.9	14 200	15.4
March	184 800	−16.2	4.0	25 300	−38.9	20 700	−16.2
April	281 900	14.9	6.1	65 200	47.5	21 900	−16.1
May	375 600	− 9.3	8.2	71 200	−27.5	52 300	13.0
June	605 100	0.6	13.1	148 100	−13.1	80 400	21.3
July	1 013 400	− 1.6	22.0	247 600	−17.1	100 700	− 0.7
August	815 900	2.3	17.7	267 600	4.0	97 800	4.3
September	413 900	6.5	9.0	109 900	− 3.3	60 300	4.1
October	267 700	3.8	5.8	48 500	−16.1	31 900	10.8
November	215 900	25.7	4.7	22 600	16.5	23 200	25.4
December	172 800	28.0	3.7	29 800	20.6	14 100	6.0
Total	4 608 300	2.4	100.0	1 070 700	− 7.4	530 600	5.7

(by country of nationality)

	1983	Relative share	1984	Relative share	% Variation over 1983
Austria [1]					
Belgium [1]					
Denmark					
Finland	110 500	2.5	107 500	2.3	−2.7
France	72 200	1.6	80 900	1.8	12.0
Germany (F.R.)	1 156 200	25.7	1 070 700	23.2	−7.4
Greece [1]					
Iceland [1]					
Ireland [1]					
Italy	82 100	1.8	81 200	1.8	−1.1
Luxembourg [1]					
Netherlands	120 500	2.7	108 300	2.4	−10.1
Norway	600 700	13.3	657 700	14.3	9.5
Portugal [1]					
Spain [1]					
Sweden	860 800	19.1	851 600	18.5	−1.1
Switzerland [1]					
Turkey [1]					
United Kingdom	340 800	7.6	300 500	6.5	−11.8
Other OECD-Europe					
Total Europe	3 343 800	74.3	3 258 400	70.7	−2.6
Canada					
United States	502 200	11.2	530 600	11.5	5.7
Total North America	502 200	11.2	530 600	11.5	5.7
Australia					
New Zealand					
Japan	82 100	1.8	79 500	1.7	−3.2
Total Australasia and Japan	82 100	1.8	79 500	1.7	−3.2
Total OECD Countries	3 928 100	87.3	3 868 500	83.9	−1.5
Yugoslavia (S.F.R.)					
Other European countries	247 800	5.5	257 900	5.6	4.1
of which: Bulgaria					
Czechoslovakia					
Hungary					
Poland					
Rumania					
USSR					
Latin America					
Asia-Oceania					
Africa					
Origin country undetermined	325 200	7.2	481 900	10.5	48.2
Total Non-OECD Countries	573 000	12.7	739 800	16.1	29.1
TOTAL	4 501 100	100.0	4 608 300	100.0	2.4

1. Included in "Other European countries".
Source: Danmarks Statistik - Copenhagen.

DENMARK

NIGHTS SPENT BY FOREIGN TOURISTS IN REGISTERED TOURIST ACCOMMODATION[1]
(by month)

	Total number 1984	% Variation over 1983	% of 1984 total	From Germany	% Variation over 1983	From United States	% Variation over 1983
January	127 400	8.1	1.5	18 700	13.3	13 100	2.3
February	133 900	10.4	1.5	16 200	14.9	14 200	15.4
March	184 800	−16.2	2.1	25 300	−38.9	20 700	−16.2
April	348 800	21.7	4.0	126 700	55.1	22 000	−15.7
May	499 400	−13.9	5.7	173 100	−26.3	52 800	13.3
June	1 068 800	−1.4	12.3	452 400	−8.6	81 900	20.4
July	3 054 900	−12.8	35.0	1 277 900	−25.5	104 000	−1.0
August	2 109 400	−2.6	24.2	1 156 400	7.9	100 500	3.7
September	536 900	5.1	6.2	214 900	−1.3	60 800	4.3
October	267 700	3.8	3.1	48 500	−16.1	31 900	10.8
November	215 900	25.7	2.5	22 600	16.5	23 200	25.4
December	172 800	27.9	2.0	29 800	20.6	14 100	6.0
TOTAL[1]	8 720 700	−4.7	100.0	3 562 500	−10.8	539 200	5.5

(by country of nationality)

	1983	Relative share	1984	Relative share	% Variation over 1983
Austria					
Belgium					
Denmark					
Finland	209 868	2.2	198 958	2.2	−5.2
France	113 797	1.2	149 341	1.6	31.2
Germany (F.R.)	4 115 659	43.2	3 677 135	40.4	−10.7
Greece					
Iceland					
Ireland					
Italy	120 925	1.3	119 973	1.3	−0.8
Luxembourg					
Netherlands	888 410	9.3	724 805	8.0	−18.4
Norway	999 441	10.5	1 055 181	11.6	5.6
Portugal					
Spain					
Sweden	1 341 726	14.1	1 294 624	14.2	−3.5
Switzerland					
Turkey					
United Kingdom	429 650	4.5	380 574	4.2	−11.4
Other OECD-Europe					
Total Europe	8 219 476	86.3	7 600 591	83.4	−7.5
Canada					
United States	524 641	5.5	553 435	6.1	5.5
Total North America	524 641	5.5	553 435	6.1	5.5
Australia					
New Zealand					
Japan					
Total Australasia and Japan					
Total OECD Countries	8 744 117	91.8	8 154 026	89.5	−6.7
Yugoslavia (S.F.R.)					
Other European countries					
of which: Bulgaria					
Czechoslovakia					
Hungary					
Poland					
Rumania					
USSR					
Latin America					
Asia-Oceania					
Africa					
Origin country undetermined	784 791	8.2	958 245	10.5	22.1
Total non-OECD Countries[2]	784 791	8.2	958 245	10.5	22.1
TOTAL[3]	9 528 908	100.0	9 112 271	100.0	−4.4

1. Monthly figures includes nights at hotels for the whole year and nights in camping sites from April to September.
2. Includes nights spent by foreign tourists from a number of Member countries.
3. Annual figures include nights at hotels and at youth hostels for the whole year, and nights in camping sites from April to September. Youth hostels represent 377 171 nights in 1984 and 357 508 nights in 1983. Camping sites represent from October to March 14 400 nights for 1984 and 16 700 nights for 1983.
Source: Danmarks Statistik - Copenhagen.

FINLAND

NIGHTS SPENT BY FOREIGN TOURISTS IN HOTELS
(by month)

	Total number 1984	% Variation over 1983	% of 1984 total	From Sweden	% Variation over 1983	From United States	% Variation over 1983
January	94 357	11.2	4.5	24 942	7.6	6 007	34.1
February	100 321	− 1.2	4.7	26 142	− 7.5	5 984	7.2
March	113 023	−11.8	5.4	31 548	− 3.8	8 405	− 8.7
April	107 195	− 9.6	5.1	34 392	− 5.1	5 890	−13.9
May	177 415	11.0	8.4	54 367	2.3	12 671	24.3
June	289 222	10.1	13.7	62 324	− 5.8	25 914	31.9
July	381 981	0.3	18.1	91 222	−10.9	27 300	− 2.4
August	340 390	0.6	16.1	66 453	−13.0	30 263	− 3.7
September	180 951	9.2	8.6	46 268	1.5	15 986	2.4
October	136 558	8.4	6.5	40 097	4.1	9 722	8.6
November	111 542	− 0.7	5.3	37 144	3.8	5 128	−17.1
December	79 553	− 2.5	3.8	25 962	3.4	4 207	7.3
Total	2 112 508	2.5	100.0	540 861	− 4.0	157 477	5.0

(by country of residence)

	1983	Relative share	1984	Relative share	% Variation over 1983
Austria	22 665	1.1	24 457	1.2	7.9
Belgium	13 154	0.6	12 876	0.6	−2.1
Denmark	51 499	2.5	55 017	2.6	6.8
Finland					
France	46 481	2.3	58 842	2.8	26.6
Germany (F.R.)	255 136	12.4	277 889	13.2	8.9
Greece [1]					
Iceland	5 518	0.3	7 154	0.3	29.6
Ireland [2]					
Italy	39 723	1.9	44 950	2.1	13.2
Luxembourg [1]					
Netherlands	36 767	1.8	44 140	2.1	20.1
Norway	169 833	8.2	166 007	7.9	−2.3
Portugal [3]					
Spain [3]	19 508	0.9	19 119	0.9	−2.0
Sweden	563 497	27.3	540 861	25.6	−4.0
Switzerland	75 024	3.6	79 824	3.8	6.4
Turkey [1]					
United Kingdom [2]	104 067	5.1	108 073	5.1	3.8
Other OECD-Europe					
Total Europe	1 402 872	68.1	1 439 209	68.1	2.6
Canada	26 552	1.3	27 559	1.3	3.8
United States	150 011	7.3	157 477	7.5	5.0
Total North America	176 563	8.6	185 036	8.8	4.8
Australia					
New Zealand					
Japan	36 807	1.8	41 872	2.0	13.8
Total Australasia and Japan	36 807	1.8	41 872	2.0	13.8
Total OECD Countries	1 616 242	78.4	1 666 117	78.9	3.1
Yugoslavia (S.F.R.)					
Other European countries	335 752	16.3	331 192	15.7	−1.4
Bulgaria [4]	8 294	0.4	5 207	0.2	−37.2
Czechoslovakia	14 279	0.7	12 781	0.6	−10.5
Hungary	20 360	1.0	20 206	1.0	−0.8
Poland	17 229	0.8	16 015	0.8	−7.0
Rumania [4]					
USSR	245 001	11.9	245 766	11.6	0.3
Latin America [5]					
Asia-Oceania [5]					
Africa [5]					
Origin country undetermined	108 568	5.3	115 199	5.5	6.1
Total Non-OECD Countries	444 320	21.6	446 391	21.1	0.5
TOTAL	2 060 562	100.0	2 112 508	100.0	2.5

1. Greece, Luxembourg and Turkey included in "Other European countries".
2. Ireland included in United Kingdom.
3. Portugal included in Spain.
4. Rumania included in Bulgaria.
5. Latin America, Asia-Oceania and Africa included in "Origin country undetermined".
Source: Central Statistical Office - Helsinki.

FRANCE

ARRIVALS OF FOREIGN TOURISTS AT FRONTIERS[1]
(by month)

	Total number 1984	% Variation over 1983	% of 1984 total			
January						
February						
March						
April						
May						
June						
July						
August						
September						
October						
November						
December						
Total						

(by country of residence)

	1983	Relative share	1984	Relative share	% Variation over 1983
Austria	513 000	1.5			
Belgium [4]	2 658 000	8.0			
Denmark [2]					
Finland [2]					
France					
Germany (F.R.)	8 059 000	24.3			
Greece [3]					
Iceland [3]					
Ireland [5]					
Italy	2 193 000	6.6			
Luxembourg [4]					
Netherlands	3 806 000	11.5			
Norway [2]	698 000	2.1			
Portugal [3]					
Spain	813 000	2.4			
Sweden [2]					
Switzerland	3 267 000	9.8			
Turkey [3]					
United Kingdom	5 934 000	17.9			
Other OECD-Europe					
Total Europe	27 941 000	84.2			
Canada	283 000	0.9			
United States	2 050 000	6.2			
Total North America	2 333 000	7.0			
Australia					
New Zealand					
Japan					
Total Australasia and Japan					
Total OECD Countries	30 274 000	91.2			
Yugoslavia (S.F.R.)					
Other European countries	130 000	0.4			
of which: Bulgaria					
Czechoslovakia					
Hungary					
Poland					
Rumania					
USSR					
Latin America	414 000	1.2			
Asia-Oceania					
Africa	1 207 000	3.6			
Origin country undetermined	1 159 000	3.5			
Total Non-OECD Countries	2 910 000	8.8			
TOTAL	33 184 000	100.0			

1. Estimates of number of "trips", the same person coming perhaps several times in one year.
2. Finland, Norway, Sweden included in Denmark.
3. Included in "Origin country undetermined".
4. Luxembourg included in Belgium.
5. Ireland included in United Kingdom.
Source: Secrétariat d'État chargé du Tourisme - Paris.

FRANCE

ARRIVALS OF FOREIGN TOURISTS IN HOTELS[1]
(quarterly)

	Total number 1984	% Variation over 1983	% of 1984 total	From Germany	% Variation over 1983	From United States	% Variation over 1983
January February March	1 089 932	−2.8	16.7	103 796		140 912	
April May June	1 928 534	7.0	29.6	278 682		397 783	
July August September	2 107 028	13.4	32.3	207 670		504 725	
October November December	1 398 104	4.5	21.4	149 812		240 329	
Total	6 523 598	6.6	100.0	739 960	−14.0	1 283 749	34.9

(by country of residence)

	1983	Relative share	1984	Relative share	% Variation over 1983
Austria	47 567	0.8	41 531	0.6	−12.7
Belgium[3]	233 710	3.8	230 973	3.5	−1.2
Denmark	59 890	1.0	81 450	1.2	36.0
Finland[2]	230 782	3.8	202 925	3.1	−12.1
France					
Germany (F.R.)	812 869	13.3	739 960	11.3	−9.0
Greece					
Iceland[2]					
Ireland[4]					
Italy	444 508	7.3	476 743	7.3	7.3
Luxembourg[3]					
Netherlands	316 971	5.2	313 282	4.8	−1.2
Norway[2]					
Portugal					
Spain	194 250	3.2	196 230	3.0	1.0
Sweden[2]					
Switzerland	226 358	3.7	282 227	4.3	24.7
Turkey					
United Kingdom[4]	790 472	12.9	812 045	12.4	2.7
Other OECD-Europe	122 196	2.0	91 823	1.4	−24.9
Total Europe	3 479 573	56.9	3 469 189	53.2	−0.3
Canada	132 561	2.2	163 634	2.5	23.4
United States	951 811	15.6	1 283 749	19.7	34.9
Total North America	1 084 372	17.7	1 447 383	22.2	33.5
Australia	90 541	1.5	68 993	1.1	−23.8
New Zealand	7 418	0.1	11 323	0.2	52.6
Japan	457 159	7.5	447 843	6.9	−2.0
Total Australasia and Japan	555 118	9.1	528 159	8.1	−4.9
Total OECD Countries	5 119 063	83.6	5 444 731	83.5	6.4
Yugoslavia (S.F.R.) Other European countries of which: Bulgaria Czechoslovakia Hungary Poland Rumania USSR	48 418	0.8	52 900	0.8	9.3
Latin America	155 279	2.5	168 010	2.6	8.2
Asia-Oceania	320 947	5.2	312 624	4.8	−2.6
Africa	353 403	5.8	370 829	5.7	4.9
Origin country undetermined	122 559	2.0	174 504	2.7	42.4
Total Non-OECD Countries	1 000 606	16.4	1 078 867	16.5	7.8
TOTAL	6 119 669	100.0	6 523 598	100.0	6.6

1. Data concerns Ile-de-France region only.
2. Iceland, Norway, Sweden included in Finland.
3. Luxembourg included in Belgium.
4. Ireland included in United Kingdom.
Source: Secrétariat d'État Chargé du Tourisme - Paris.

FRANCE

NIGHTS SPENT BY FOREIGN TOURISTS IN HOTELS[1]
(quarterly)

	Total number 1984	% Variation over 1983	% of 1984 total	From Germany	% Variation over 1983	From United States	% Variation over 1983
January February March	2 824 325	– 4.0	15.7	260 896		360 200	
April May June	5 400 248	8.1	30.1	776 175		1 028 014	
July August September	5 889 128	14.9	32.8	532 585		1 357 776	
October November December	3 828 690	6.7	21.3	380 889		653 716	
Total	17 942 391	7.8	100.0	1 950 545	–12.1	3 399 706	31.2

(by country of residence)

	1983	Relative share	1984	Relative share	% Variation over 1983
Austria	126 758	0.8	119 603	0.7	–5.6
Belgium[3]	505 121	3.0	507 272	2.8	0.4
Denmark	195 208	1.2	318 398	1.8	63.1
Finland[2]	732 961	4.4	644 534	3.6	–12.1
France					
Germany (F.R.)	2 093 247	12.6	1 950 545	10.9	–6.8
Greece					
Iceland[2]					
Ireland[4]					
Italy	1 284 566	7.7	1 365 991	7.6	6.3
Luxembourg[3]					
Netherlands	798 432	4.8	843 017	4.7	5.6
Norway[2]					
Portugal					
Spain	548 311	3.3	551 864	3.1	0.6
Sweden[2]					
Switzerland	605 873	3.6	770 204	4.3	27.1
Turkey					
United Kingdom[4]	1 940 170	11.7	2 098 601	11.7	8.2
Other OECD-Europe	368 066	2.2	293 228	1.6	–20.3
Total Europe	9 198 713	55.2	9 463 257	52.7	2.9
Canada	396 673	2.4	465 016	2.6	17.2
United States	2 590 584	15.6	3 399 706	18.9	31.2
Total North America	2 987 257	17.9	3 864 722	21.5	29.4
Australia	248 644	1.5	196 680	1.1	–20.9
New Zealand	24 105	0.1	30 871	0.2	28.1
Japan	1 145 566	6.9	1 073 741	6.0	–6.3
Total Australasia and Japan	1 418 315	8.5	1 301 292	7.3	–8.3
Total OECD Countries	13 604 285	81.7	14 629 271	81.5	7.5
Yugoslavia (S.F.R.)					
Other European countries	186 319	1.1	197 613	1.1	6.1
of which: Bulgaria					
Czechoslovakia					
Hungary					
Poland					
Rumania					
USSR					
Latin America	489 367	2.9	530 964	3.0	8.5
Asia-Oceania	996 443	6.0	968 136	5.4	–2.8
Africa	1 094 391	6.6	1 145 590	6.4	4.7
Origin country undetermined	280 404	1.7	470 817	2.6	67.9
Total Non-OECD Countries	3 046 924	18.3	3 313 120	18.5	8.7
TOTAL	16 651 209	100.0	17 942 391	100.0	7.8

1. Data concerns Ile-de-France region only.
2. Iceland, Norway, Sweden included in Finland.
3. Luxembourg included in Belgium.
4. Ireland included in United Kingdom.
Source: Secrétariat d'État Chargé du Tourisme - Paris.

GREECE

ARRIVALS OF FOREIGN TOURISTS AT FRONTIERS[1]
(by month)

	Total number 1984	% Variation over 1983	% of 1984 total	From United Kingdom	% Variation over 1983	From United States	% Variation over 1983
January	85 839	11.6	1.6	7 694	7.5	12 223	11.1
February	83 437	13.1	1.5	7 357	9.7	10 940	24.7
March	158 381	−16.2	2.9	14 381	−32.3	23 457	15.5
April	459 966	47.4	8.3	60 389	23.1	39 240	33.8
May	582 767	1.4	10.6	132 290	5.2	49 414	14.3
June	697 207	14.3	12.6	153 797	4.8	71 241	26.1
July	1 060 118	11.9	19.2	191 582	19.0	71 995	4.6
August	995 569	16.5	18.0	191 816	21.9	52 805	5.7
September	751 218	21.2	13.6	179 220	32.7	59 361	20.4
October	408 567	25.0	7.4	84 921	48.0	48 325	16.0
November	126 118	25.5	2.3	11 793	−8.8	20 983	37.2
December	114 005	23.3	2.1	8 123	−5.4	14 901	17.2
Total	5 523 192	15.6	100.0	1 043 363	17.4	474 885	16.7

(by country of nationality)

	1983	Relative share	1984	Relative share	% Variation over 1983
Austria	195 381	4.1	237 918	4.3	21.8
Belgium	76 442	1.6	76 825	1.4	0.5
Denmark	148 626	3.1	124 037	2.2	−16.5
Finland	92 711	1.9	134 164	2.4	44.7
France	299 506	6.3	405 907	7.3	35.5
Germany (F.R.)	728 478	15.2	864 000	15.6	18.6
Greece					
Iceland [2]					
Ireland	27 245	0.6	30 515	0.6	12.0
Italy	327 610	6.9	328 598	5.9	0.3
Luxembourg					
Netherlands	153 672	3.2	192 879	3.5	25.5
Norway	130 608	2.7	106 608	1.9	−18.4
Portugal	5 204	0.1	6 119	0.1	17.6
Spain	31 021	0.6	37 091	0.7	19.6
Sweden	189 921	4.0	194 356	3.5	2.3
Switzerland	173 830	3.6	156 995	2.8	−9.7
Turkey	43 427	0.9	42 770	0.8	−1.5
United Kingdom	888 991	18.6	1 043 363	18.9	17.4
Other OECD-Europe					
Total Europe	3 512 673	73.5	3 982 145	72.1	13.4
Canada	72 540	1.5	82 226	1.5	13.4
United States	406 887	8.5	474 845	8.6	16.7
Total North America	479 427	10.0	557 071	10.1	16.2
Australia	83 230	1.7	96 953	1.8	16.5
New Zealand [3]					
Japan	82 029	1.7	86 476	1.6	5.4
Total Australasia and Japan	165 259	3.5	183 429	3.3	11.0
Total OECD Countries	4 157 359	87.0	4 722 645	85.5	13.6
Yugoslavia (S.F.R.)	55 375	1.2	263 209	4.8	375.3
Other European countries	107 227	2.2	107 871	2.0	0.6
of which: Bulgaria	43 123	0.9	37 036	0.7	−14.1
Czechoslovakia	12 685	0.3	10 400	0.2	−18.0
Hungary	21 280	0.4	17 821	0.3	−16.3
Poland	15 915	0.3	27 874	0.5	75.1
Rumania	7 454	0.2	7 333	0.1	−1.6
USSR	6 770	0.1	7 407	0.1	9.4
Latin America	25 159	0.5	26 001	0.5	3.3
Asia-Oceania	211 727	4.4	183 148	3.3	−13.5
Africa	96 219	2.0	101 274	1.8	5.3
Origin country undetermined	125 411	2.6	119 044	2.2	−5.1
Total Non-OECD Countries	621 118	13.0	800 547	14.5	28.9
TOTAL	4 778 477	100.0	5 523 192	100.0	15.6

1. Excluding Greek nationals residing abroad, and including cruise passengers who numbered 479 897 (+11.3%) in 1983.
2. Included in "Other European countries".
3. Included in "Asia-Oceania".
Source: National Statistical Service of Greece - Athens.

ICELAND

ARRIVALS OF FOREIGN VISITORS AT FRONTIERS[1]
(by month)

	Total number 1984	% Variation over 1983	% of 1984 total	From Germany	% Variation over 1983	From United States	% Variation over 1983
January	2 166	− 0.2	2.5	111	50.0	1 065	5.1
February	2 325	12.8	2.7	109	18.5	1 014	31.9
March	3 311	13.3	3.9	107	−33.1	1 508	39.8
April	4 507	19.8	5.3	388	83.0	1 680	22.4
May	7 307	16.1	8.6	841	32.4	2 347	4.9
June	12 768	8.8	15.0	1 310	−20.5	4 072	21.0
July	22 359	13.2	26.2	3 845	12.6	5 235	16.9
August	14 615	11.0	17.2	2 121	34.3	4 187	12.5
September	7 635	16.0	9.0	471	−10.5	2 715	3.7
October	2 128	−49.3	2.5	73	−64.7	929	−53.0
November	3 220	14.7	3.8	118	− 6.3	1 390	2.1
December	2 849	32.9	3.3	121	31.5	1 151	24.6
Total	85 190	9.8	100.0	9 615	9.7	27 293	9.5

(by country of nationality)

	1983	Relative share	1984	Relative share	% Variation over 1983
Austria	1 252	1.6	1 473	1.7	17.7
Belgium	624	0.8	499	0.6	−20.0
Denmark	6 665	8.6	7 759	9.1	16.4
Finland	1 821	2.3	2 003	2.3	10.0
France	3 922	5.1	4 846	5.7	23.6
Germany (F.R.)	8 765	11.3	9 615	11.3	9.7
Greece	48	0.1	66	0.1	37.5
Iceland					
Ireland	413	0.5	266	0.3	−35.6
Italy	1 053	1.4	1 037	1.2	−1.5
Luxembourg	157	0.2	88	0.1	−43.9
Netherlands	1 506	1.9	1 610	1.9	6.9
Norway	5 345	6.9	6 055	7.1	13.3
Portugal	79	0.1	65	0.1	−17.7
Spain	440	0.6	277	0.3	−37.0
Sweden	5 554	7.2	6 699	7.9	20.6
Switzerland	2 600	3.4	2 689	3.2	3.4
Turkey	17	0.0	27	0.0	58.8
United Kingdom	8 868	11.4	9 398	11.0	6.0
Other OECD-Europe					
Total Europe	49 129	63.3	54 472	63.8	10.9
Canada	1 038	1.3	1 001	1.2	−3.6
United States	24 915	32.1	27 293	32.0	9.5
Total North America	25 953	33.4	28 294	33.2	9.0
Australia	315	0.4	329	0.4	4.4
New Zealand	123	0.2	95	0.1	−22.8
Japan	453	0.6	539	0.6	19.0
Total Australasia and Japan	891	1.1	963	1.1	8.1
Total OECD Countries	75 973	97.9	83 729	98.1	10.2
Yugoslavia (S.F.R.)	65	0.1	105	0.1	61.5
Other European countries	406	0.5	511	0.6	25.9
of which: Bulgaria	2	0.0	15	0.0	650.0
Czechoslovakia	76	0.1	76	0.1	0.0
Hungary	45	0.1	62	0.1	37.8
Poland	74	0.1	140	0.2	89.2
Rumania	13	0.0	7	0.0	−46.2
USSR	196	0.3	211	0.2	7.7
Latin America	270	0.3	261	0.3	−3.3
Asia-Oceania	511	0.7	324	0.4	−36.6
Africa	243	0.3	192	0.2	−21.0
Origin country undetermined	124	0.2	208	0.2	67.7
Total Non-OECD Countries	1 619	2.1	1 601	1.9	−1.1
TOTAL	77 592	100.0	85 330	100.0	10.0

1. Excluding shore excursionists.
Source: Iceland Immigration Office - Reykjavik.

IRELAND

ARRIVALS OF FOREIGN VISITORS AT FRONTIERS
(by month)

	Total number 1984	% Variation over 1983	% of 1984 total	From United Kingdom	% Variation over 1983	From United States	% Variation over 1983
January							
February							
March							
April							
May							
June							
July							
August							
September							
October							
November							
December							
Total	9 891 000	1.0	100.0	9 206 000	0.6	303 000	13.1

(by country of nationality)

	1983	Relative share	1984	Relative share	% Variation over 1983
Austria					
Belgium					
Denmark					
Finland					
France	81 000	0.8	82 000	0.8	1.2
Germany (F.R.)	93 000	0.9	91 000	0.9	−2.2
Greece					
Iceland					
Ireland					
Italy					
Luxembourg					
Netherlands					
Norway					
Portugal					
Spain					
Sweden					
Switzerland					
Turkey					
United-Kingdom [1]	9 149 000	93.4	9 206 000	93.1	0.6
Other OECD-Europe	121 000	1.2	125 000	1.3	3.3
Total Europe	9 444 000	96.4	9 504 000	96.1	0.6
Canada	21 000	0.2	21 000	0.2	0.0
United States	268 000	2.7	303 000	3.1	13.1
Total North America	289 000	2.9	324 000	3.3	12.1
Australia [2]	27 000	0.3	34 000	0.3	25.9
New Zealand [2]					
Japan [3]					
Total Australasia and Japan	27 000	0.3	34 000	0.3	25.9
Total OECD Countries	9 760 000	99.6	9 862 000	99.7	1.0
Yugoslavia (S.F.R.)					
Other European countries					
of which: Bulgaria					
Czechoslovakia					
Hungary					
Poland					
Rumania					
USSR					
Latin America					
Asia-Oceania					
Africa					
Origin country unspecified [3]	37 000	0.4	29 000	0.3	−21.6
Total Non-OECD Countries	37 000	0.4	29 000	0.3	−21.6
TOTAL	9 797 000	100.0	9 891 000	100.0	1.0

1. Figures includes visitors arriving via Northern Ireland.
2. New Zealand included in Australia.
3. Origin country unspecified includes Japan.
Source: Central Statistics Office - Dublin.

ITALY

ARRIVALS OF FOREIGN VISITORS AT FRONTIERS[1]
(by month)

	Total number 1984	% Variation over 1983	% of 1984 total	From Germany	% Variation over 1983	From United States	% Variation over 1983
January	2 500 661	9.2	5.1	345 779	7.8	88 370	13.4
February	2 165 786	4.0	4.4	320 040	– 1.4	77 660	8.0
March	2 695 719	– 5.6	5.5	463 166	–21.9	105 097	5.8
April	3 706 085	17.6	7.5	752 831	25.8	122 100	19.9
May	3 429 554	–10.9	7.0	637 091	–34.3	140 095	0.7
June	5 040 524	14.9	10.3	1 362 969	22.3	197 367	8.0
July	6 925 260	– 3.0	14.1	1 705 580	– 6.2	282 072	1.4
August	8 196 426	10.1	16.7	2 215 400	11.5	265 474	5.1
September	5 216 400	11.7	10.6	1 331 124	23.5	184 998	– 2.2
October	3 447 221	– 3.9	7.0	703 338	–10.3	135 010	– 5.9
November	2 795 812	16.0	5.7	462 599	24.5	90 441	0.6
December	3 031 288	12.1	6.2	512 495	26.3	86 137	– 5.4
Total	49 150 736	5.5	100.0	10 812 412	4.3	1 774 821	3.3

(by country of nationality)

	1983	Relative share	1984	Relative share	% Variation over 1983
Austria	4 621 911	9.9	4 981 180	10.1	7.8
Belgium	854 965	1.8	880 558	1.8	3.0
Denmark	394 501	0.8	369 821	0.8	–6.3
Finland	223 748	0.5	226 764	0.5	1.3
France	7 891 903	16.9	8 462 438	17.2	7.2
Germany (F.R.)	10 366 053	22.3	10 812 412	22.0	4.3
Greece	436 869	0.9	405 273	0.8	–7.2
Iceland [2]					
Ireland	114 368	0.2	96 955	0.2	–15.2
Italy					
Luxembourg	165 214	0.4	137 883	0.3	–16.5
Netherlands	1 704 467	3.7	1 763 087	3.6	3.4
Norway	210 456	0.5	209 356	0.4	–0.5
Portugal	200 079	0.4	187 751	0.4	–6.2
Spain	663 455	1.4	486 569	1.0	–26.7
Sweden	406 849	0.9	404 819	0.8	–0.5
Switzerland	10 022 872	21.5	10 750 203	21.9	7.3
Turkey	223 815	0.5	200 362	0.4	–10.5
United Kingdom	1 890 159	4.1	1 788 371	3.6	–5.4
Other OECD-Europe					
Total Europe	40 391 684	86.7	42 163 802	85.8	4.4
Canada	331 506	0.7	336 205	0.7	1.4
United States	1 717 411	3.7	1 774 821	3.6	3.3
Total North America	2 048 917	4.4	2 111 026	4.3	3.0
Australia	279 929	0.6	281 358	0.6	0.5
New Zealand	92 269	0.2	80 560	0.2	–12.7
Japan	327 133	0.7	340 209	0.7	4.0
Total Australasia and Japan	699 331	1.5	702 127	1.4	0.4
Total OECD Countries	43 139 932	92.6	44 976 955	91.5	4.3
Yugoslavia (S.F.R.)	1 147 018	2.5	1 820 682	3.7	58.7
Other European countries	647 976	1.4	611 629	1.2	–5.6
of which: Bulgaria					
Czechoslovakia					
Hungary					
Poland					
Rumania					
USSR	27 893	0.1	31 808	0.1	14.0
Latin America	504 016	1.1	491 442	1.0	–2.5
Asia-Oceania	203 127	0.4	192 823	0.4	–5.1
Africa	130 490	0.3	143 701	0.3	10.1
Origin country undetermined	804 242	1.7	913 504	1.9	13.6
Total Non-OECD Countries	3 436 869	7.4	4 173 781	8.5	21.4
TOTAL	46 576 801	100.0	49 150 736	100.0	5.5

1. Includes excursionists.
2. Included in "Other European countries".
Source: Istituto Centrale di Statistica - Rome.

ITALY

ARRIVALS OF FOREIGN TOURISTS IN HOTELS
(by month)

	Total number 1984	% Variation over 1983	% of 1984 total		
January	466 715	− 0.3	3.0		
February	521 409	− 0.4	3.3		
March	803 712	−12.0	5.1		
April	1 568 070	33.6	9.9		
May	1 570 442	− 6.3	10.0		
June	1 971 357	16.5	12.5		
July	2 175 314	− 0.5	13.8		
August	2 124 979	4.6	13.5		
September	2 137 393	9.6	13.6		
October	1 407 133	− 0.5	8.9		
November	547 317	12.2	3.5		
December	478 228	9.9	3.0		
Total	15 772 069	5.5	100.0		

(by country of nationality)

	1983	Relative share	1984	Relative share	% Variation over 1983
Austria	808 832	5.4			
Belgium	337 698	2.3			
Denmark	101 767	0.7			
Finland	83 543	0.6			
France	1 465 922	9.8			
Germany (F.R.)	4 032 436	27.0			
Greece	149 314	1.0			
Iceland [1]					
Ireland	46 879	0.3			
Italy					
Luxembourg	26 197	0.2			
Netherlands	270 749	1.8			
Norway	66 275	0.4			
Portugal	52 395	0.4			
Spain	471 600	3.2			
Sweden	161 469	1.1			
Switzerland	901 593	6.0			
Turkey	48 471	0.3			
United Kingdom	1 176 289	7.9			
Other OECD-Europe					
Total Europe	10 201 429	68.2			
Canada	206 278	1.4			
United States	2 180 196	14.6			
Total North America	2 386 474	16.0			
Australia	202 221	1.4			
New Zealand					
Japan	262 390	1.8			
Total Australasia and Japan	464 611	3.1			
Total OECD Countries	13 052 514	87.3			
Yugoslavia (S.F.R.)	123 052	0.8			
Other European countries	223 710	1.5			
of which: Bulgaria					
Czechoslovakia					
Hungary					
Poland					
Rumania					
USSR	23 426	0.2			
Latin America	297 126	2.0			
Asia-Oceania	211 735	1.4			
Africa	97 166	0.6			
Origin country undetermined	948 229	6.3			
Total Non-OECD Countries	1 901 018	12.7			
TOTAL	14 953 532	100.0	15 772 069		5.5

1. Included in "Other European countries".
Source: Istituto Centrale di Statistica - Rome.

ITALY

ARRIVALS OF FOREIGN TOURISTS IN REGISTERED TOURIST ACCOMMODATION
(by month)

	Total number 1984	% Variation over 1983	% of 1984 total		
January	512 388	− 0.2	2.7		
February	578 531	− 0.2	3.0		
March	870 526	−13.3	4.5		
April	1 750 929	36.2	9.1		
May	1 721 874	−10.8	8.9		
June	2 459 196	16.6	12.8		
July	3 129 562	− 2.8	16.2		
August	3 078 469	3.2	16.0		
September	2 549 922	8.6	13.2		
October	1 518 429	− 0.4	7.9		
November	576 142	12.9	3.0		
December	519 333	9.3	2.7		
Total	19 265 301	4.2	100.0		

(by country of nationality)

	1983	Relative share	1984	Relative share	% Variation over 1983
Austria	1 124 624	6.1			
Belgium	431 997	2.3			
Denmark	155 647	0.8			
Finland	97 822	0.5			
France	1 760 083	9.5			
Germany (F.R.)	5 781 707	31.3			
Greece	157 233	0.9			
Iceland [1]					
Ireland	54 161	0.3			
Italy					
Luxembourg	31 574	0.2			
Netherlands	490 437	2.7			
Norway	81 200	0.4			
Portugal	61 888	0.3			
Spain	541 944	2.9			
Sweden	206 892	1.1			
Switzerland	1 081 424	5.9			
Turkey	51 688	0.3			
United Kingdom	1 338 690	7.2			
Other OECD-Europe					
Total Europe	13 449 011	72.8			
Canada	229 361	1.2			
United States	2 262 230	12.2			
Total North America	2 491 591	13.5			
Australia	235 975	1.3			
New Zealand					
Japan	268 279	1.5			
Total Australasia and Japan	504 254	2.7			
Total OECD Countries	16 444 856	89.0			
Yugoslavia (S.F.R.)	138 202	0.7			
Other European countries	270 514	1.5			
of which: Bulgaria					
Czechoslovakia					
Hungary					
Poland					
Rumania					
USSR	24 212	0.1			
Latin America	312 485	1.7			
Asia-Oceania	220 677	1.2			
Africa	104 171	0.6			
Origin country undetermined	992 420	5.4			
Total Non-OECD Countries	2 038 469	11.0			
TOTAL	18 483 325	100.0	19 265 301		4.2

1. Included in "Other European countries".
Source: Istituto Centrale di Statistica - Rome.

ITALY

NIGHTS SPENT BY FOREIGN TOURISTS IN HOTELS
(by month)

	Total number 1984	% Variation over 1983	% of 1984 total		
January	1 994 635	0.5	3.2		
February	2 227 893	0.1	3.5		
March	2 945 248	−13.7	4.7		
April	5 046 541	23.7	8.0		
May	5 250 372	−12.2	8.3		
June	8 492 506	5.9	13.5		
July	10 262 630	−8.0	16.3		
August	10 270 991	−2.0	16.3		
September	8 802 695	4.4	14.0		
October	4 579 484	−3.7	7.3		
November	1 556 567	11.6	2.5		
December	1 604 406	8.8	2.5		
Total	63 033 968	−0.6	100.0		

(by country of nationality)

	1983	Relative share	1984	Relative share	% Variation over 1983
Austria	3 899 050	6.2			
Belgium	1 714 055	2.7			
Denmark	487 017	0.8			
Finland	463 114	0.7			
France	4 770 553	7.5			
Germany (F.R.)	25 421 833	40.1			
Greece	362 234	0.6			
Iceland [1]					
Ireland	172 806	0.3			
Italy					
Luxembourg	178 827	0.3			
Netherlands	1 275 387	2.0			
Norway	310 375	0.5			
Portugal	126 304	0.2			
Spain	914 706	1.4			
Sweden	714 890	1.1			
Switzerland	4 167 307	6.6			
Turkey	135 923	0.2			
United Kingdom	5 889 738	9.3			
Other OECD-Europe					
Total Europe	51 004 119	80.5			
Canada	526 937	0.8			
United States	5 222 524	8.2			
Total North America	5 749 461	9.1			
Australia	493 397	0.8			
New Zealand					
Japan	578 209	0.9			
Total Australasia and Japan	1 071 606	1.7			
Total OECD Countries	57 825 186	91.2			
Yugoslavia (S.F.R.)	319 272	0.5			
Other European countries	717 249	1.1			
of which: Bulgaria					
Czechoslovakia					
Hungary					
Poland					
Rumania					
USSR					
Latin America	65 457	0.1			
Asia-Oceania	840 844	1.3			
Africa	459 549	0.7			
Origin country undetermined	303 549	0.5			
	2 917 849	4.6			
Total Non-OECD Countries	5 558 312	8.8			
TOTAL	63 383 498	100.0	63 033 968		−0.6

1. Included in "Other European countries".
Source: Istituto Centrale di Statistica - Rome.

ITALY

NIGHTS SPENT BY FOREIGN TOURISTS IN REGISTERED TOURIST ACCOMMODATION
(by month)

	Total number 1984	% Variation over 1983	% of 1984 total		
January	2 511 155	0.9	2.6		
February	2 804 877	1.1	2.9		
March	3 565 167	−14.5	3.7		
April	6 143 789	26.1	6.5		
May	6 306 552	−17.9	6.6		
June	12 530 384	7.1	13.2		
July	19 254 273	− 9.1	20.2		
August	20 238 517	− 3.5	21.3		
September	12 664 547	2.9	13.3		
October	5 353 632	− 3.4	5.6		
November	1 814 998	7.9	1.9		
December	1 974 479	5.5	2.1		
Total	95 162 370	− 2.1	100.0		

(by country of nationality)

	1983	Relative share	1984	Relative share	% Variation over 1983
Austria	7 520 970	7.7			
Belgium	2 734 222	2.8			
Denmark	940 502	1.0			
Finland	553 097	0.6			
France	6 737 231	6.9			
Germany (F.R.)	42 704 778	43.9			
Greece	591 984	0.6			
Iceland [1]					
Ireland	218 518	0.2			
Italy					
Luxembourg	243 945	0.3			
Netherlands	3 562 466	3.7			
Norway	448 115	0.5			
Portugal	168 806	0.2			
Spain	1 126 977	1.2			
Sweden	1 155 603	1.2			
Switzerland	6 145 862	6.3			
Turkey	164 715	0.2			
United Kingdom	7 219 971	7.4			
Other OECD-Europe					
Total Europe	82 237 762	84.6			
Canada	674 423	0.7			
United States	6 035 756	6.2			
Total North America	6 710 179	6.9			
Australia	655 927	0.7			
New Zealand					
Japan	618 537	0.6			
Total Australasia and Japan	1 274 464	1.3			
Total OECD Countries	90 222 405	92.8			
Yugoslavia (S.F.R.)	495 704	0.5			
Other European countries	1 087 266	1.1			
of which: Bulgaria					
Czechoslovakia					
Hungary					
Poland					
Rumania					
USSR	72 130	0.1			
Latin America	967 071	1.0			
Asia-Oceania	491 942	0.5			
Africa	380 865	0.4			
Origin country undetermined	3 603 579	3.7			
Total Non-OECD Countries	7 026 427	7.2			
TOTAL	97 248 832	100.0	95 162 170		−2.1

1. Included in "Other European countries".
Source: Istituto Centrale di Statistica - Rome.

JAPAN

ARRIVALS OF FOREIGN VISITORS AT FRONTIERS[1]
(by month)

	Total number 1984	% Variation over 1983	% of 1984 total	From United Kingdom	% Variation over 1983	From United States	% Variation over 1983
January	126 065	5.5	6.0	12 903	32.8	28 785	19.2
February	147 770	11.4	7.0	16 569	−9.2	25 154	19.3
March	151 720	5.3	7.2	13 187	−9.6	39 565	23.9
April	201 784	12.1	9.6	16 037	19.4	45 197	14.8
May	195 142	10.6	9.2	12 093	−1.8	49 874	14.0
June	175 534	9.9	8.3	10 911	−17.5	47 686	12.4
July	197 351	− 0.3	9.4	15 149	−21.9	45 229	2.6
August	184 484	− 1.8	8.7	16 121	−21.7	41 170	1.7
September	190 804	15.9	9.0	13 236	8.9	49 042	15.5
October	220 610	7.2	10.5	13 095	−4.2	64 254	1.7
November	168 085	3.3	8.0	13 117	6.0	42 086	7.1
December	150 997	9.9	7.2	14 652	−1.3	33 083	13.7
Total	2 110 346	7.2	100.0	167 070	−4.3	511 125	10.8

(by country of nationality)

	1983	Relative share	1984	Relative share	% Variation over 1983
Austria	5 878	0.3	5 435	0.3	−7.5
Belgium	4 975	0.3	5 205	0.2	4.6
Denmark	6 295	0.3	7 007	0.3	11.3
Finland	5 686	0.3	6 554	0.3	15.3
France	28 813	1.5	34 109	1.6	18.4
Germany (F.R.)	43 417	2.2	48 978	2.3	12.8
Greece	2 457	0.1	2 682	0.1	9.2
Iceland	188	0.0	238	0.0	26.6
Ireland	1 843	0.1	1 647	0.1	−10.6
Italy	14 231	0.7	15 706	0.7	10.4
Luxembourg	211	0.0	180	0.0	−14.7
Netherlands	12 812	0.7	14 162	0.7	10.5
Norway	6 324	0.3	5 963	0.3	−5.7
Portugal	4 775	0.2	3 904	0.2	−18.2
Spain	7 411	0.4	5 687	0.3	−23.3
Sweden	12 740	0.6	13 278	0.6	4.2
Switzerland	11 093	0.6	12 130	0.6	9.3
Turkey	1 891	0.1	1 735	0.1	−8.2
United Kingdom	174 563	8.9	167 070	7.9	−4.3
Other OECD-Europe					
Total Europe	345 603	17.6	351 670	16.7	1.8
Canada	53 618	2.7	52 989	2.5	−1.2
United States	461 325	23.4	511 125	24.2	10.8
Total North America	514 943	26.2	564 114	26.7	9.5
Australia	42 178	2.1	52 040	2.5	23.4
New Zealand	14 813	0.8	16 366	0.8	10.5
Japan					
Total Australasia and Japan	56 991	2.9	68 406	3.2	20.0
Total OECD Countries	917 537	46.6	984 190	46.6	7.3
Yugoslavia (S.F.R.)	1 151	0.1	1 147	0.1	−0.3
Other European countries	18 432	0.9	19 755	0.9	7.2
of which: Bulgaria	783	0.0	596	0.0	−23.9
Czechoslovakia	1 284	0.1	913	0.0	−28.9
Hungary	1 031	0.1	1 484	0.1	43.9
Poland	875	0.0	1 015	0.0	16.0
Rumania	280	0.0	230	0.0	−17.9
USSR	8 561	0.4	7 397	0.4	−13.6
Latin America	30 276	1.5	37 847	1.8	25.0
Asia-Oceania	978 047	49.7	1 044 067	49.5	6.8
Africa	18 876	1.0	18 780	0.9	−0.5
Origin country undetermined	4 142	0.2	4 560	0.2	10.1
Total Non-OECD Countries	1 050 924	53.4	1 126 156	53.4	7.2
TOTAL	1 968 461	100.0	2 110 346	100.0	7.2

1. Includes excursionists.
Source: Ministry of Justice, Immigration Bureau - Tokyo.

NEW ZEALAND

ARRIVALS OF FOREIGN VISITORS AT FRONTIERS
(by month)

	Total number 1984	% Variation over 1983	% of 1984 total	From Australia	% Variation over 1983	From United States	% Variation over 1983
January	50 805	1.4	9.0	18 624	− 4.6	7 844	15.5
February	52 441	8.2	9.2	19 531	9.3	10 844	16.5
March	51 860	11.4	9.1	20 676	− 4.3	12 216	62.4
April	45 661	27.2	8.0	20 553	30.8	10 184	30.0
May	34 516	17.6	6.1	17 700	25.3	5 360	11.5
June	31 611	18.4	5.6	16 737	17.6	5 476	25.5
July	35 560	2.8	6.3	17 892	2.5	5 940	6.5
August	39 301	8.0	6.9	20 764	18.1	6 880	−13.6
September	37 164	10.0	6.5	18 784	13.8	5 860	− 7.2
October	47 088	11.0	8.3	17 608	11.6	11 124	7.0
November	56 558	18.9	10.0	19 181	21.7	11 438	32.1
December	85 046	11.0	15.0	48 289	27.2	7 866	9.7
Total	**567 611**	**11.6**	**100.0**	**256 339**	**14.4**	**101 032**	**16.5**

(by country of residence)

	1983	Relative share	1984	Relative share	% Variation over 1983
Austria	964	0.2	996	0.2	3.3
Belgium	428	0.1	360	0.1	−15.9
Denmark	1 096	0.2	1 220	0.2	11.3
Finland	188	0.0	316	0.1	68.1
France	1 928	0.4	2 216	0.4	14.9
Germany (F.R.)	9 528	1.9	9 511	1.7	−0.2
Greece	296	0.1	196	0.0	−33.8
Iceland	32	0.0	24	0.0	−25.0
Ireland	628	0.1	540	0.1	−14.0
Italy	864	0.2	956	0.2	10.6
Luxembourg	56	0.0	4	0.0	−92.9
Netherlands	4 824	0.9	5 164	0.9	7.0
Norway	620	0.1	604	0.1	−2.6
Portugal	44	0.0	32	0.0	−27.3
Spain	308	0.1	324	0.1	5.2
Sweden	1 812	0.4	2 416	0.4	33.3
Switzerland	4 224	0.8	4 552	0.8	7.8
Turkey	32	0.0	40	0.0	25.0
United Kingdom	39 096	7.7	40 209	7.1	2.8
Other OECD-Europe					
Total Europe	**66 968**	**13.2**	**69 680**	**12.3**	**4.0**
Canada	20 464	4.0	23 041	4.1	12.6
United States	86 716	17.1	101 032	17.8	16.5
Total North America	**107 180**	**21.1**	**124 073**	**21.9**	**15.8**
Australia	224 100	44.1	250 879	44.3	11.9
New Zealand [1]	1 108	0.2	1 032	0.2	−6.9
Japan	32 481	6.4	41 888	7.4	29.0
Total Australasia and Japan	**257 689**	**50.7**	**293 799**	**51.9**	**14.0**
Total OECD Countries	**431 837**	**84.9**	**487 552**	**86.1**	**12.9**
Yugoslavia (S.F.R.)	48	0.0	72	0.0	50.0
Other European countries	1 672	0.3	1 572	0.3	−6.0
of which: Bulgaria	8	0.0	4	0.0	−50.0
Czechoslovakia	24	0.0	36	0.0	50.0
Hungary	76	0.0	44	0.0	−42.1
Poland	20	0.0	104	0.0	420.0
Rumania	36	0.0	24	0.0	−33.3
USSR	1 448	0.3	1 292	0.2	−10.8
Latin America	1 964	0.4	1 580	0.3	−19.6
Asia-Oceania	45 963	9.0	52 830	9.3	14.9
Africa	3 199	0.6	3 005	0.5	−6.1
Origin country undetermined	23 782	4.7	19 480	3.4	−18.1
Total Non-OECD Countries	**76 628**	**15.1**	**78 539**	**13.9**	**2.5**
TOTAL	**508 465**	**100.0**	**566 091**	**100.0**	**11.3**

1. New Zealanders, who have lived abroad for less than 12 months, returning for a short stay.
Source: Tourist and Publicity Department - Wellington.

NEW ZEALAND

ARRIVALS OF FOREIGN TOURISTS AT FRONTIERS
(by month)

	Total number 1984	% Variation over 1983	% of 1984 total	From Australia	% Variation over 1983	From United States	% Variation over 1983
January	41 480	4.5	9.4	14 984	− 5.1	6 376	31.5
February	40 705	10.4	9.2	15 103	8.0	8 344	24.4
March	40 740	10.3	9.2	16 252	− 7.8	10 324	65.6
April	35 821	31.0	8.1	16 145	34.1	8 328	28.8
May	24 308	16.1	5.5	12 756	22.4	3 888	7.3
June	22 521	23.6	5.1	12 457	21.9	4 028	39.9
July	25 984	1.5	5.9	13 568	− 0.6	3 976	− 3.2
August	29 254	9.9	6.6	16 108	18.9	5 180	−11.2
September	27 532	11.1	6.2	14 524	14.1	4 292	− 9.6
October	35 220	12.9	7.9	12 732	9.8	8 752	9.6
November	44 517	17.8	10.0	14 225	19.1	9 514	34.1
December	75 129	11.7	17.0	39 184	12.5	6 410	11.7
Total	443 211	12.7	100.0	198 038	11.0	79 412	19.8

(by country of residence)

	1983	Relative share	1984	Relative share	% Variation over 1983
Austria					
Belgium					
Denmark					
Finland					
France					
Germany (F.R.)					
Greece					
Iceland					
Ireland					
Italy					
Luxembourg					
Netherlands					
Norway					
Portugal					
Spain					
Sweden					
Switzerland					
Turkey					
United Kingdom					
Other OECD-Europe					
Total Europe					
Canada					
United States					
Total North America					
Australia					
New Zealand					
Japan					
Total Australasia and Japan					
Total OECD Countries					
Yugoslavia (S.F.R.)					
Other European countries					
of which: Bulgaria					
Czechoslovakia					
Hungary					
Poland					
Rumania					
USSR					
Latin America					
Asia-Oceania					
Africa					
Origin country undetermined					
Total Non-OECD Countries					
TOTAL					

Source: Tourist and Publicity Department - Wellington.

NORWAY

NIGHTS SPENT BY FOREIGN TOURISTS IN HOTELS[1]
(by month)

	Total number 1984	% Variation over 1983	% of 1984 total	From Germany	% Variation over 1983	From United States	% Variation over 1983
January	107 496	14.0	4.3	8 269	26.0	4 999	−14.5
February	188 146	17.2	7.5	9 813	17.0	8 877	20.3
March	165 020	15.1	6.6	15 204	10.9	16 298	68.1
April	94 318	−12.1	3.8	7 827	− 2.6	8 637	− 5.8
May	154 032	4.4	6.1	16 496	−11.1	33 973	6.6
June	385 759	4.6	15.4	81 554	4.6	91 521	20.8
July	527 743	5.3	21.0	114 877	3.6	127 002	4.3
August	449 611	8.4	17.9	85 021	20.6	120 993	7.5
September	190 708	7.0	7.6	15 903	− 7.1	58 260	22.3
October	95 214	3.3	3.8	8 024	− 5.6	13 005	−21.3
November	78 083	13.4	3.1	8 211	32.9	8 080	38.3
December	75 484	19.9	3.0	7 655	53.8	4 607	7.0
Total	2 511 614	7.3	100.0	378 854	7.8	496 252	10.7

(by country of nationality)

	1983	Relative share	1984	Relative share	% Variation over 1983
Austria [2]					
Belgium [2]					
Denmark	246 297	10.5	288 144	11.5	17.0
Finland	63 799	2.7	62 679	2.5	−1.8
France	73 666	3.1	81 496	3.2	10.6
Germany (F.R.)	351 376	15.0	378 854	15.1	7.8
Greece [2]					
Iceland [2]					
Ireland [2]					
Italy [2]					
Luxembourg [2]					
Netherlands	109 082	4.7	85 228	3.4	−21.9
Norway					
Portugal [2]					
Spain [2]					
Sweden	327 302	14.0	319 702	12.7	−2.3
Switzerland [2]					
Turkey [2]					
United Kingdom	298 932	12.8	310 995	12.4	4.0
Other OECD-Europe					
Total Europe	1 470 454	62.8	1 527 098	60.8	3.9
Canada [2]					
United States	448 329	19.2	496 252	19.8	10.7
Total North America	448 329	19.2	496 252	19.8	10.7
Australia [2]					
New Zealand [2]					
Japan	52 997	2.3	57 447	2.3	8.4
Total Australasia and Japan	52 997	2.3	57 447	2.3	8.4
Total OECD Countries	1 971 780	84.3	2 080 797	82.8	5.5
Yugoslavia (S.F.R.) [2]					
Other European countries					
of which: Bulgaria					
Czechoslovakia					
Hungary					
Poland					
Rumania					
USSR					
Latin America [2]					
Asia-Oceania [2]					
Africa [2]					
Origin country undetermined	368 370	15.7	430 817	17.2	17.0
Total Non-OECD Countries	368 370	15.7	430 817	17.2	17.0
TOTAL	2 340 150	100.0	2 511 614	100.0	7.3

1. Nights spent at approved hotels (establishments licensed to use the designation "hotel"). And as from 1st of July 1983 the system of approval of hotels was discontinued, so no new hotels have been approved since that date.
2. Included in "Origin country undetermined".
Source: Central Bureau of Statistics - Oslo.

PORTUGAL

ARRIVALS OF FOREIGN VISITORS AT FRONTIERS
(by month)

	Total number 1984	% Variation over 1983	% of 1984 total	From Spain	% Variation over 1983	From United States	% Variation over 1983
January	351 262	8.4	3.6	266 382	7.9	6 037	16.1
February	318 332	– 3.5	3.2	227 316	– 6.8	7 680	22.3
March	455 195	– 9.3	4.6	318 210	–12.3	14 034	13.0
April	633 822	11.2	6.5	445 270	7.2	15 780	29.3
May	566 011	– 5.4	5.8	340 532	–10.5	22 973	23.0
June	716 353	3.5	7.3	485 457	5.1	25 458	23.2
July	1 588 332	19.6	16.2	1 086 615	27.0	30 934	5.0
August	1 899 169	1.0	19.4	1 541 897	2.3	21 297	10.3
September	1 224 054	7.2	12.5	958 703	6.9	23 707	– 2.1
October	850 110	13.1	8.7	657 652	15.3	22 316	0.4
November	617 026	75.9	6.3	504 508	95.3	10 167	18.3
December	591 346	45.4	6.0	476 269	52.1	9 015	18.8
Total	9 811 012	10.5	100.0	7 308 811	12.2	209 398	12.1

(by country of nationality)

	1983	Relative share	1984	Relative share	% Variation over 1983
Austria	22 422	0.3	22 911	0.2	2.2
Belgium	61 360	0.7	59 137	0.6	–3.6
Denmark	41 332	0.5	45 668	0.5	10.5
Finland	13 809	0.2	15 417	0.2	11.6
France	327 895	3.7	326 646	3.3	–0.4
Germany (F.R.)	355 268	4.0	344 020	3.5	–3.2
Greece	10 632	0.1	10 546	0.1	–0.8
Iceland	1 583	0.0	2 258	0.0	42.6
Ireland	24 589	0.3	23 389	0.2	–4.9
Italy	66 056	0.7	71 760	0.7	8.6
Luxembourg	1 796	0.0	1 894	0.0	5.5
Netherlands	156 241	1.8	151 887	1.5	–2.8
Norway	24 834	0.3	28 464	0.3	14.6
Portugal					
Spain	6 512 569	73.7	7 308 811	74.5	12.2
Sweden	65 513	0.7	71 486	0.7	9.1
Switzerland	46 071	0.5	53 185	0.5	15.4
Turkey	1 756	0.0	1 832	0.0	4.3
United Kingdom	629 527	7.1	709 724	7.2	12.7
Other OECD-Europe					
Total Europe	8 363 253	94.6	9 249 035	94.3	10.6
Canada	46 781	0.5	56 116	0.6	20.0
United States	186 828	2.1	208 398	2.1	11.5
Total North America	233 609	2.6	264 514	2.7	13.2
Australia	11 303	0.1	12 135	0.1	7.4
New Zealand [1]	2 360	0.0	3 029	0.0	28.3
Japan	14 354	0.2	19 514	0.2	35.9
Total Australasia and Japan	28 017	0.3	34 678	0.4	23.8
Total OECD Countries	8 624 879	97.5	9 548 227	97.3	10.7
Yugoslavia (S.F.R.)	3 885	0.0	4 172	0.0	7.4
Other European countries	34 441	0.4	36 796	0.4	6.8
of which: Bulgaria	1 451	0.0	2 422	0.0	66.9
Czechoslovakia	1 618	0.0	1 793	0.0	10.8
Hungary	1 353	0.0	1 421	0.0	5.0
Poland	4 615	0.1	5 804	0.1	25.8
Rumania	832	0.0	896	0.0	7.7
USSR	23 062	0.3	22 763	0.2	–1.3
Latin America	15 020	0.2	105 769	1.1	604.2
Asia-Oceania	30 078	0.3	29 106	0.3	–3.2
Africa	83 922	0.9	84 835	0.9	1.1
Origin country undetermined	49 859	0.6	2 107	0.0	–95.8
Total Non-OECD Countries	217 205	2.5	262 785	2.7	21.0
TOTAL	8 842 084	100.0	9 811 012	100.0	11.0

1. New Zealand included in Australia.
Source: Direccao-Geral do Turismo - Lisbon.

PORTUGAL

ARRIVALS OF FOREIGN TOURISTS AT FRONTIERS
(by month)

	Total number 1984	% Variation over 1983	% of 1984 total	From Spain	% Variation over 1983	From United States	% Variation over 1983
January	135 952	19.0	3.3	66 659	29.2	3 992	−22.7
February	136 099	7.7	3.3	56 858	− 6.0	7 627	113.8
March	204 621	− 8.2	5.0	91 805	−17.3	10 497	57.4
April	288 645	23.1	7.0	128 797	16.0	10 084	51.5
May	284 167	0.7	6.9	90 827	− 4.7	16 667	14.4
June	354 739	5.0	8.6	151 719	11.6	19 625	47.2
July	792 212	16.4	19.2	332 630	40.3	24 191	32.9
August	758 950	− 5.2	18.4	441 094	− 3.0	19 045	27.6
September	465 474	18.3	11.3	217 845	17.5	22 704	168.9
October	330 326	24.5	8.0	162 301	44.0	19 166	42.1
November	184 197	47.9	4.5	91 574	85.7	4 321	− 3.3
December	183 244	39.9	4.4	92 452	51.9	7 480	36.3
Total	4 118 626	10.9	100.0	1 924 561	15.5	165 399	43.9

(by country of nationality)

	1983	Relative share	1984	Relative share	% Variation over 1983
Austria	20 638	0.6	19 052	0.5	−7.7
Belgium	59 618	1.6	53 999	1.3	−9.4
Denmark	39 568	1.1	41 099	1.0	3.9
Finland	13 312	0.4	14 964	0.4	12.4
France	315 579	8.5	312 783	7.6	−0.9
Germany (F.R.)	311 963	8.4	294 636	7.2	−5.6
Greece [1]					
Iceland [1]	23 136	0.6	22 578	0.5	−2.4
Ireland	53 953	1.5	59 443	1.4	10.2
Italy	1 666	0.0	1 871	0.0	12.3
Luxembourg	146 128	3.9	142 619	3.5	−2.4
Netherlands	21 006	0.6	26 333	0.6	25.4
Norway					
Portugal	1 665 748	44.9	1 924 561	46.7	15.5
Spain	64 001	1.7	69 456	1.7	8.5
Sweden	42 724	1.2	45 150	1.1	5.7
Switzerland					
Turkey [1]					
United Kingdom	553 489	14.9	638 641	15.5	15.4
Other OECD-Europe					
Total Europe	3 332 529	89.7	3 667 185	89.0	10.0
Canada	41 445	1.1	52 331	1.3	26.3
United States	114 978	3.1	165 399	4.0	43.9
Total North America	156 423	4.2	217 730	5.3	39.2
Australia	11 491	0.3	14 836	0.4	29.1
New-Zealand [2]					
Japan	13 126	0.4	16 100	0.4	22.7
Total Australasia and Japan	24 617	0.7	30 936	0.8	25.7
Total OECD Countries	3 513 569	94.6	3 915 851	95.1	11.4
Yugoslavia (S.F.R.) [1]					
Other European countries	15 244	0.4	18 151	0.4	19.1
of which: Bulgaria					
Czechoslovakia					
Hungary					
Poland					
Rumania					
USSR					
Latin America					
Asia-Oceania	80 165	2.2	79 042	1.9	−1.4
Africa	104 962	2.8	105 582	2.6	0.6
Origin country undetermined					
Total Non-OECD Countries	200 371	5.4	202 775	4.9	1.2
TOTAL	3 713 940	100.0	4 118 626	100.0	10.9

1. Included in "Other European countries".
2. New Zealand included in Australia.
Source: Direccao-Geral do Turismo - Lisbon.

PORTUGAL

ARRIVALS OF FOREIGN TOURISTS IN HOTELS[1]
(by month)

	Total number 1984	% Variation over 1983	% of 1984 total	From Spain	% Variation over 1983	From United States	% Variation over 1983
January	81 330	8.1	3.4	10 399	10.5	7 651	14.4
February	95 748	7.4	4.0	10 958	24.7	10 863	26.8
March	145 433	−11.4	6.1	17 152	−49.2	18 630	26.4
April	216 935	28.1	9.1	45 103	78.6	19 403	15.7
May	242 597	14.6	10.2	21 381	35.9	31 847	23.9
June	232 928	15.0	9.8	27 617	4.6	31 912	35.4
July	271 708	15.6	11.4	42 205	3.6	29 431	27.1
August	327 283	17.1	13.8	80 818	10.8	27 976	33.3
September	293 598	17.4	12.4	46 881	14.3	34 641	10.6
October	237 617	11.1	10.0	38 255	25.5	33 406	− 5.3
November	129 194	28.9	5.4	22 619	94.6	14 452	18.6
December	102 743	28.7	4.3	15 625	23.2	9 430	17.8
Total	2 377 114	14.8	100.0	379 013	15.3	269 642	18.8

(by country of residence)

	1983	Relative share	1984	Relative share	% Variation over 1983
Austria	19 101	0.9	21 924	0.9	14.8
Belgium	47 695	2.3	47 581	2.0	−0.2
Denmark	34 650	1.7	42 520	1.8	22.7
Finland	14 786	0.7	16 704	0.7	13.0
France	169 049	8.2	212 536	8.9	25.7
Germany (F.R.)	201 939	9.8	214 104	9.0	6.0
Greece	4 168	0.2	4 494	0.2	7.8
Iceland	1 367	0.1	2 685	0.1	96.4
Ireland	17 433	0.8	18 454	0.8	5.9
Italy	57 453	2.8	64 342	2.7	12.0
Luxembourg	2 145	0.1	1 853	0.1	−13.6
Netherlands	94 887	4.6	102 719	4.3	8.3
Norway	23 957	1.2	28 535	1.2	19.1
Portugal					
Spain	328 838	15.9	379 013	15.9	15.3
Sweden	69 482	3.4	77 319	3.3	11.3
Switzerland	63 368	3.1	74 266	3.1	17.2
Turkey	980	0.0	816	0.0	−16.7
United Kingdom	448 171	21.6	510 246	21.5	13.9
Other OECD-Europe					
Total Europe	1 599 469	77.2	1 820 111	76.6	13.8
Canada	61 458	3.0	75 318	3.2	22.6
United States	226 985	11.0	269 672	11.3	18.8
Total North America	288 443	13.9	344 990	14.5	19.6
Australia	5 919	0.3	7 956	0.3	34.4
New Zealand	989	0.0	1 370	0.1	38.5
Japan	15 904	0.8	22 991	1.0	44.6
Total Australasia and Japan	22 812	1.1	32 317	1.4	41.7
Total OECD Countries	1 910 724	92.3	2 197 418	92.4	15.0
Yugoslavia (S.F.R.)	1 223	0.1	1 741	0.1	42.4
Other European countries	6 866	0.3	7 497	0.3	9.2
of which: Bulgaria	424	0.0	517	0.0	21.9
Czechoslovakia	659	0.0	1 318	0.1	100.0
Hungary	1 132	0.1	1 157	0.0	2.2
Poland	955	0.0	728	0.0	−23.8
Rumania	181	0.0	384	0.0	112.2
USSR	3 515	0.2	3 393	0.1	−3.5
Latin America	81 738	3.9	87 915	3.7	7.6
Asia-Oceania	21 131	1.0	21 698	0.9	2.7
Africa	48 370	2.3	60 006	2.5	24.1
Origin country undetermined	800	0.0	839	0.0	4.9
Total Non-OECD Countries	160 128	7.7	179 696	7.6	12.2
TOTAL	2 070 852	100.0	2 377 114	100.0	14.8

1. Includes arrivals at hotels, studio-hotels, holiday-flats, villages, motels, inns and boarding-houses.
Source: National Institute of Statistics (I.N.E.) - Lisbon.

PORTUGAL

ARRIVALS OF FOREIGN TOURISTS IN REGISTERED TOURIST ACCOMMODATION[1]
(by month)

	Total number 1984	% Variation over 1983	% of 1984 total	From Spain	% Variation over 1983	From United States	% Variation over 1983
January	84 555	8.4	3.0	10 596	11.2	7 817	15.1
February	99 155	7.5	3.5	11 399	27.4	10 994	26.2
March	151 893	−12.3	5.4	17 947	−50.2	18 860	25.2
April	238 980	28.1	8.5	51 313	68.4	19 835	16.2
May	262 135	13.0	9.3	24 259	32.5	32 199	23.5
June	268 975	11.7	9.6	31 140	2.6	32 507	35.0
July	355 995	− 6.8	12.7	57 811	−14.3	30 006	23.6
August	501 891	12.3	17.9	120 697	7.7	28 694	31.9
September	351 179	14.4	12.5	55 906	12.2	35 136	10.3
October	250 788	9.8	8.9	40 700	25.0	33 730	− 5.4
November	134 021	26.7	4.8	23 334	94.8	14 664	17.5
December	106 011	27.3	3.8	15 978	22.8	9 594	17.7
Total	2 805 578	9.8	100.0	461 080	9.6	274 036	18.1

(by country of residence)

	1983	Relative share	1984	Relative share	% Variation over 1983
Austria	24 566	1.0	26 821	1.0	9.2
Belgium	62 411	2.4	59 321	2.1	−5.0
Denmark	43 532	1.7	51 251	1.8	17.7
Finland	16 090	0.6	17 419	0.6	8.3
France	282 375	11.1	312 657	11.1	10.7
Germany (F.R.)	317 944	12.4	317 757	11.3	−0.1
Greece	4 324	0.2	4 670	0.2	8.0
Iceland	1 373	0.1	2 698	0.1	96.5
Ireland	18 298	0.7	19 502	0.7	6.6
Italy	71 247	2.8	75 261	2.7	5.6
Luxembourg	2 735	0.1	2 549	0.1	−6.8
Netherlands	144 790	5.7	144 535	5.2	−0.2
Norway	25 163	1.0	29 702	1.1	18.0
Portugal					
Spain	420 524	16.5	461 080	16.4	9.6
Sweden	72 503	2.8	80 306	2.9	10.8
Switzerland	71 443	2.8	80 877	2.9	13.2
Turkey	1 016	0.0	872	0.0	−14.2
United Kingdom	475 678	18.6	533 945	19.0	12.2
Other OECD-Europe					
Total Europe	2 056 012	80.5	2 221 223	79.2	8.0
Canada	65 057	2.5	79 034	2.8	21.5
United States	231 941	9.1	274 036	9.8	18.1
Total North America	296 998	11.6	353 070	12.6	18.9
Australia	12 239	0.5	14 193	0.5	16.0
New Zealand	3 914	0.2	4 348	0.2	11.1
Japan	16 277	0.6	23 374	0.8	43.6
Total Australasia and Japan	32 430	1.3	41 915	1.5	29.2
Total OECD Countries	2 385 440	93.4	2 616 208	93.3	9.7
Yugoslavia (S.F.R.)	1 534	0.1	2 067	0.1	34.7
Other European countries	7 702	0.3	8 590	0.3	11.5
of which: Bulgaria	476	0.0	637	0.0	33.8
Czechoslovakia	702	0.0	1 405	0.1	100.1
Hungary	1 282	0.1	1 586	0.1	23.7
Poland	1 219	0.0	979	0.0	−19.7
Rumania	405	0.0	587	0.0	44.9
USSR	3 618	0.1	3 396	0.1	−6.1
Latin America	84 279	3.3	91 288	3.3	8.3
Asia-Oceania	21 706	0.8	22 403	0.8	3.2
Africa	52 552	2.1	64 123	2.3	22.0
Origin country undetermined	842	0.0	899	0.0	6.8
Total Non-OECD Countries	168 615	6.6	189 370	6.7	12.3
TOTAL	2 554 055	100.0	2 805 578	100.0	9.8

1. Includes arrivals at hotels, studio-hotels, holiday-flats, villages, motels, inns, boarding-houses, recreation centres for children and camping-sites.
Source: National Institute of Statistics (I.N.E.) - Lisbon.

PORTUGAL

NIGHTS SPENT BY FOREIGN TOURISTS IN HOTELS[1]
(by month)

	Total number 1984	% Variation over 1983	% of 1984 total	From Spain	% Variation over 1983	From United States	% Variation over 1983
January	438 867	7.5	4.0	22 153	10.6	26 329	16.9
February	514 649	5.6	4.7	24 995	43.4	39 108	24.8
March	716 197	– 4.6	6.5	34 296	–48.6	59 253	21.1
April	885 847	15.8	8.0	98 954	55.4	49 882	19.1
May	1 033 527	9.8	9.4	44 312	20.7	74 237	16.1
June	1 168 373	15.6	10.6	59 459	1.0	77 260	32.4
July	1 342 092	9.8	12.2	103 686	6.3	74 647	19.6
August	1 469 713	7.3	13.3	198 789	4.8	68 734	21.9
September	1 323 848	16.0	12.0	102 396	12.6	88 470	14.9
October	1 012 593	11.9	9.2	77 032	27.5	87 314	7.4
November	612 349	20.8	5.6	47 954	88.1	36 962	11.2
December	507 184	32.4	4.6	33 177	31.7	28 031	25.9
Total	11 025 239	11.5	100.0	847 203	12.6	710 227	18.5

(by country of residence)

	1983	Relative share	1984	Relative share	% Variation over 1983
Austria	95 327	1.0	97 283	0.9	2.1
Belgium	214 430	2.1	220 998	2.0	3.1
Denmark	226 911	2.3	271 559	2.5	19.7
Finland	97 299	1.0	106 202	1.0	9.2
France	515 971	5.2	652 463	5.9	26.5
Germany (F.R.)	1 143 324	11.5	1 237 364	11.2	8.2
Greece	13 178	0.1	13 041	0.1	–1.0
Iceland	19 333	0.2	30 796	0.3	59.3
Ireland	152 587	1.5	171 776	1.6	12.6
Italy	151 226	1.5	168 860	1.5	11.7
Luxembourg	9 211	0.1	8 916	0.1	–3.2
Netherlands	644 423	6.5	725 530	6.6	12.6
Norway	183 326	1.8	218 956	2.0	19.4
Portugal					
Spain	752 614	7.5	847 203	7.7	12.6
Sweden	506 818	5.1	513 893	4.7	1.4
Switzerland	221 116	2.2	251 495	2.3	13.7
Turkey	33 240	0.3	3 042	0.0	–90.8
United Kingdom	3 580 124	35.9	3 915 939	35.5	9.4
Other OECD-Europe					
Total Europe	8 560 458	85.8	9 455 316	85.8	10.5
Canada	215 396	2.2	258 803	2.3	20.2
United States	599 581	6.0	710 227	6.4	18.5
Total North America	814 977	8.2	969 030	8.8	18.9
Australia	15 974	0.2	21 602	0.2	35.2
New Zealand	2 650	0.0	4 002	0.0	51.0
Japan	36 131	0.4	50 000	0.5	38.4
Total Australasia and Japan	54 755	0.5	75 604	0.7	38.1
Total OECD Countries	9 430 190	94.5	10 499 950	95.2	11.3
Yugoslavia (S.F.R.)	4 742	0.0	5 173	0.0	9.1
Other European countries	21 634	0.2	22 654	0.2	4.7
of which: Bulgaria	1 548	0.0	1 422	0.0	–8.1
Czechoslovakia	1 938	0.0	3 659	0.0	88.8
Hungary	3 885	0.0	3 571	0.0	–8.1
Poland	3 944	0.0	3 397	0.0	–13.9
Rumania	892	0.0	1 273	0.0	42.7
USSR	9 427	0.1	9 332	0.1	–1.0
Latin America	261 073	2.6	214 094	1.9	–18.0
Asia-Oceania	72 993	0.7	62 406	0.6	–14.5
Africa	189 369	1.9	218 317	2.0	15.3
Origin country undetermined	2 249	0.0	2 645	0.0	17.6
Total Non-OECD Countries	552 060	5.5	525 289	4.8	–4.8
TOTAL	9 982 250	100.0	11 025 239	100.0	10.4

1. Includes nights spent at hotels, studio-hotels, holiday-flats, villages, motels, inns and boarding-houses.
Source: National Institute of Statistics (I.N.E.) - Lisbon.

PORTUGAL

NIGHTS SPENT BY FOREIGN TOURISTS IN REGISTERED TOURIST ACCOMMODATION[1]
(by month)

	Total number 1984	% Variation over 1983	% of 1984 total	From Spain	% Variation over 1983	From United States	% Variation over 1983
January	472 604	7.4	3.8	23 153	11.2	27 198	16.5
February	544 634	7.6	4.3	26 361	46.2	39 432	23.9
March	755 801	− 5.6	6.0	37 895	−48.7	60 300	19.9
April	956 491	14.8	7.6	116 281	45.8	51 206	18.9
May	1 089 945	7.1	8.7	51 071	11.9	75 065	15.1
June	1 281 568	12.5	10.2	69 672	0.3	78 584	31.5
July	1 602 643	− 7.5	12.8	150 149	−20.5	76 097	16.7
August	2 074 245	− 5.9	16.6	334 910	−16.4	71 388	19.4
September	1 509 775	12.4	12.0	133 110	7.3	89 932	14.3
October	1 065 561	10.2	8.5	85 036	25.2	88 438	6.8
November	642 320	19.5	5.1	50 299	89.7	37 484	10.6
December	536 639	30.5	4.3	34 251	31.1	28 531	25.5
Total	12 532 226	5.0	100.0	1 112 188	− 2.6	723 655	17.3

(by country of residence)

	1983	Relative share	1984	Relative share	% Variation over 1983
Austria	111 019	0.9	110 770	0.9	−0.2
Belgium	267 094	2.2	262 511	2.1	−1.7
Denmark	272 850	2.3	307 085	2.5	12.5
Finland	102 568	0.9	108 717	0.9	6.0
France	937 082	7.9	948 530	7.6	1.2
Germany (F.R.)	1 663 256	13.9	1 609 271	12.8	−3.2
Greece	13 565	0.1	13 461	0.1	−0.8
Iceland	19 342	0.2	30 821	0.2	59.3
Ireland	156 413	1.3	176 057	1.4	12.6
Italy	197 982	1.7	199 223	1.6	0.6
Luxembourg	11 673	0.1	11 279	0.1	−3.4
Netherlands	879 579	7.4	914 844	7.3	4.0
Norway	188 506	1.6	223 097	1.8	18.4
Portugal					
Spain	1 141 439	9.6	1 112 188	8.9	−2.6
Sweden	518 270	4.3	524 180	4.2	1.1
Switzerland	246 984	2.1	271 691	2.2	10.0
Turkey	3 488	0.0	3 292	0.0	−5.6
United Kingdom	3 728 299	31.3	4 036 694	32.2	8.3
Other OECD-Europe					
Total Europe	10 459 409	87.7	10 863 711	86.7	3.9
Canada	226 596	1.9	270 522	2.2	19.4
United States	616 671	5.2	723 655	5.8	17.3
Total North America	843 267	7.1	994 177	7.9	17.9
Australia	38 441	0.3	41 852	0.3	8.9
New Zealand	14 159	0.1	12 549	0.1	−11.4
Japan	37 035	0.3	50 838	0.4	37.3
Total Australasia and Japan	89 635	0.8	105 239	0.8	17.4
Total OECD Countries	11 392 311	95.5	11 963 127	95.5	5.0
Yugoslavia (S.F.R.)	5 976	0.1	6 022	0.0	0.8
Other European countries	25 078	0.2	27 339	0.2	9.0
of which: Bulgaria	1 722	0.0	1 879	0.0	9.1
Czechoslovakia	2 185	0.0	3 819	0.0	74.8
Hungary	4 286	0.0	5 709	0.0	33.2
Poland	4 743	0.0	4 030	0.0	−15.0
Rumania	2 226	0.0	2 556	0.0	14.8
USSR	9 916	0.1	9 346	0.1	−5.7
Latin America	210 619	1.8	226 597	1.8	7.6
Asia-Oceania	75 720	0.6	65 020	0.5	−14.1
Africa	215 433	1.8	241 248	1.9	12.0
Origin country undetermined	2 482	0.0	2 873	0.0	15.8
Total Non-OECD Countries	535 308	4.5	569 099	4.5	6.3
TOTAL	11 927 619	100.0	12 532 226	100.0	5.1

1. Includes nights spent at hotels, studio-hotels, holiday-flats, villages, motels, inns, boarding-houses, recreation centres for children and camping-sites.
Source: National Institute of Statistics (I.N.E.) - Lisbon.

SPAIN

ARRIVALS OF FOREIGN VISITORS AT FRONTIERS
(by month)

	Total number 1984	% Variation over 1983	% of 1984 total	From France	% Variation over 1983	From United States	% Variation over 1983
January	1 893 032	1.7	4.4	409 854	8.8	29 067	−27.5
February	1 727 653	4.0	4.0	435 270	11.0	42 161	20.6
March	2 057 087	− 6.5	4.8	509 831	− 8.4	58 888	22.1
April	3 124 812	17.0	7.3	804 430	23.9	78 833	33.4
May	3 197 066	8.6	7.4	760 852	10.6	84 996	21.9
June	3 966 746	4.5	9.2	900 772	4.4	102 870	15.9
July	7 365 809	10.8	17.2	1 545 326	− 8.1	108 592	−13.3
August	7 262 045	− 5.4	16.9	2 012 913	−14.2	118 859	28.5
September	4 765 686	3.8	11.1	917 643	−16.7	107 373	26.9
October	3 129 638	5.3	7.3	701 635	− 4.3	108 463	31.4
November	2 028 559	4.6	4.7	480 225	1.5	44 012	−19.5
December	2 413 525	4.6	5.6	502 922	7.0	51 772	66.5
Total	42 931 658	4.0	100.0	9 981 673	− 3.4	935 886	15.3

(by country of nationality)

	1983	Relative share	1984	Relative share	% Variation over 1983
Austria	227 834	0.6	244 881	0.6	7.5
Belgium	1 022 800	2.5	1 001 983	2.3	−2.0
Denmark	395 823	1.0	418 268	1.0	5.7
Finland	164 054	0.4	204 002	0.5	24.4
France	10 330 750	25.0	9 981 673	23.3	−3.4
Germany (F.R.)	4 970 190	12.0	5 250 065	12.2	5.6
Greece	45 239	0.1	47 879	0.1	5.8
Iceland	11 788	0.0	15 684	0.0	33.1
Ireland	235 703	0.6	239 751	0.6	1.7
Italy	669 493	1.6	814 303	1.9	21.6
Luxembourg	55 669	0.1	58 758	0.1	5.5
Netherlands	1 315 227	3.2	1 385 031	3.2	5.3
Norway	280 130	0.7	354 886	0.8	26.7
Portugal	8 465 604	20.5	8 351 752	19.5	−1.3
Spain [1]	2 054 485	5.0	2 020 526	4.7	−1.7
Sweden	464 981	1.1	511 873	1.2	10.1
Switzerland	770 895	1.9	817 780	1.9	6.1
Turkey	12 356	0.0	13 561	0.0	9.8
United Kingdom	5 188 291	12.6	6 026 612	14.0	16.2
Other OECD-Europe	0	0.0	156 421	0.4	
Total Europe	36 681 312	88.9	37 915 689	88.3	3.4
Canada	138 471	0.3	155 570	0.4	12.3
United States	811 543	2.0	935 886	2.2	15.3
Total North America	950 014	2.3	1 091 456	2.5	14.9
Australia	47 089	0.1	52 331	0.1	11.1
New Zealand	17 978	0.0	18 247	0.0	1.5
Japan	94 963	0.2	108 563	0.3	14.3
Total Australasia and Japan	160 030	0.4	179 141	0.4	11.9
Total OECD Countries	37 791 356	91.6	39 186 286	91.3	3.7
Yugoslavia (S.F.R.)	30 446	0.1	29 144	0.1	−4.3
Other European countries	405 037	1.0	243 120	0.6	−40.0
of which: Bulgaria	6 357	0.0	8 098	0.0	27.4
Czechoslovakia	9 037	0.0	8 940	0.0	−1.1
Hungary	20 908	0.1	21 322	0.0	2.0
Poland	28 791	0.1	30 677	0.1	6.6
Rumania	9 380	0.0	8 203	0.0	−12.5
USSR	160 040	0.4	165 880	0.4	3.6
Latin America	482 136	1.2	530 456	1.2	10.0
Asia-Oceania	198 364	0.5	205 628	0.5	3.7
Africa	2 343 481	5.7	2 723 899	6.3	16.2
Origin country undetermined	12 514	0.0	13 125	0.0	4.9
Total Non-OECD Countries	3 471 978	8.4	3 745 372	8.7	7.9
TOTAL	41 263 334	100.0	42 931 658	100.0	4.0

1. Spanish nationals residing abroad.
Source: Secretaria de Estado de Turismo - Madrid.

SPAIN

NIGHTS SPENT BY FOREIGN TOURISTS IN HOTELS[1]
(by month)

	Total number 1984	% Variation over 1983	% of 1984 total	From United Kingdom	% Variation over 1983	From United States	% Variation over 1983
January	3 441 903	10.3	3.9				
February	3 485 342	10.6	3.9				
March	4 214 560	14.0	4.7				
April	5 556 495	21.4	6.2				
May	9 150 827	15.1	10.3				
June	10 457 978	7.1	11.7				
July	12 495 040	7.0	14.0				
August	13 067 420	9.4	14.7				
September	11 665 327	8.9	13.1				
October	8 436 529	18.3	9.5				
November	3 674 990	15.9	4.1				
December	3 417 586	20.8	3.8				
Total	89 063 997	11.7	100.0				

(by country of nationality)

	1983	Relative share	1984	Relative share	% Variation over 1983
Austria					
Belgium[2]	6 206 461	7.8	6 914 238	7.8	11.4
Denmark[3]	3 302 748	4.1	3 571 977	4.0	8.2
Finland[3]					
France	6 021 210	7.6	6 363 778	7.1	5.7
Germany (F.R.)	22 390 953	28.1	23 159 596	26.0	3.4
Greece					
Iceland					
Ireland					
Italy	2 372 327	3.0	3 585 835	4.0	51.2
Luxembourg[2]					
Netherlands[2]					
Norway[3]					
Portugal	581 507	0.7	540 450	0.6	−7.1
Spain					
Sweden[3]					
Switzerland	2 009 935	2.5	2 151 469	2.4	7.0
Turkey					
United Kingdom	30 011 214	37.6	35 159 463	39.5	17.2
Other OECD-Europe	1 227 438	1.5	1 303 452	1.5	6.2
Total Europe	74 123 793	93.0	82 750 258	92.9	11.6
Canada[4]	2 435 473	3.1	2 880 857	3.2	18.3
United States[4]					
Total North America	2 435 473	3.1	2 880 857	3.2	18.3
Australia					
New Zealand					
Japan	313 286	0.4	338 978	0.4	8.2
Total Australasia and Japan	313 286	0.4	338 978	0.4	8.2
Total OECD Countries	76 872 552	96.4	85 970 093	96.5	11.8
Yugoslavia (S.F.R.)					
Other European countries					
of which: Bulgaria					
Czechoslovakia					
Hungary					
Poland					
Rumania					
USSR					
Latin America	1 205 483	1.5	1 512 363	1.7	25.5
Asia-Oceania					
Africa					
Origin country undetermined	1 647 312	2.1	1 581 604	1.8	−4.0
Total Non-OECD Countries	2 852 795	3.6	3 093 967	3.5	8.5
TOTAL	79 725 347	100.0	89 064 060	100.0	11.7

1. Nights recorded in hotels with "estrellas de oro" (golden stars) and "estrellas de plata" (silver stars).
2. Luxembourg and Netherlands included in Belgium.
3. Finland, Norway and Sweden included in Denmark.
4. United States included in Canada.
Source: Secretaria de Estado de Turismo - Madrid.

SWEDEN

NIGHTS SPENT BY FOREIGN TOURISTS IN HOTELS
(by month)

	Total number 1984	% Variation over 1983	% of 1984 total	From Norway	% Variation over 1983	From United States	% Variation over 1983
January	124 409	21.6	3.8	19 995	−4.3	10 932	43.2
February	147 276	17.6	4.5	25 258	5.3	10 522	35.7
March	162 127	14.0	4.9	28 788	−3.0	12 567	8.8
April	170 297	10.6	5.2	32 469	8.9	15 197	3.9
May	254 340	4.8	7.8	34 633	0.2	33 874	7.1
June	433 985	8.5	13.2	72 212	13.5	73 039	16.4
July	640 934	2.8	19.6	205 686	8.8	84 271	−2.3
August	494 456	0.8	15.1	91 331	0.1	83 467	−4.2
September	308 861	10.9	9.4	47 916	13.3	47 495	5.9
October	225 491	15.4	6.9	40 766	1.7	21 545	12.9
November	180 038	17.1	5.5	43 674	18.2	12 285	−1.3
December	133 434	14.2	4.1	27 191	4.9	10 455	8.6
Total	3 275 648	8.3	100.0	669 919	6.6	415 649	5.1

(by country of nationality)

	1983	Relative share	1984	Relative share	% Variation over 1983
Austria [1]					
Belgium [1]					
Denmark	177 364	5.9	192 806	5.9	8.7
Finland	319 635	10.6	348 117	10.6	8.9
France	73 058	2.4	83 257	2.5	14.0
Germany (F.R.)	381 445	12.6	413 625	12.6	8.4
Greece [1]					
Iceland [1]					
Ireland [1]					
Italy	62 703	2.1	70 115	2.1	11.8
Luxembourg [1]					
Netherlands	120 480	4.0	83 868	2.6	−30.4
Norway	628 203	20.8	669 919	20.5	6.6
Portugal [1]					
Spain [1]					
Sweden					
Switzerland	56 514	1.9	64 622	2.0	14.3
Turkey [1]					
United Kingdom	254 574	8.4	255 674	7.8	0.4
Other OECD-Europe					
Total Europe	2 073 976	68.6	2 182 003	66.6	5.2
Canada	23 139	0.8	28 707	0.9	24.1
United States	395 338	13.1	415 649	12.7	5.1
Total North America	418 477	13.8	444 356	13.6	6.2
Australia [2]					
New Zealand [2]					
Japan	52 121	1.7	58 480	1.8	12.2
Total Australasia and Japan	52 121	1.7	58 480	1.8	12.2
Total OECD Countries	2 544 574	84.1	2 684 839	82.0	5.5
Yugoslavia (S.F.R.)					
Other European countries	195 706	6.5	200 903	6.1	2.7
of which: Bulgaria					
Czechoslovakia					
Hungary					
Poland					
Rumania					
USSR					
Latin America [2]					
Asia-Oceania [2]					
Africa [2]					
Origin country undetermined	284 399	9.4	389 906	11.9	37.1
Total Non-OECD Countries	480 105	15.9	590 809	18.0	23.1
TOTAL	3 024 679	100.0	3 275 648	100.0	8.3

1. Included in "Other European countries".
2. Included in "Origin country undetermined".
Source: Central Bureau of Statistics - Stockholm.

SWEDEN

NIGHTS SPENT BY FOREIGN TOURISTS IN REGISTERED TOURIST ACCOMMODATION
(by month)

	Total number 1984	% Variation over 1983	% of 1984 total	From Norway	% Variation over 1983	From United States	% Variation over 1983
January	138 742	20.3	1.8	21 226	– 1.6	11 074	42.4
February	187 882	19.5	2.5	26 528	3.7	10 728	31.1
March	186 253	13.8	2.5	31 991	– 5.0	12 801	8.8
April	199 102	15.4	2.6	37 262	11.8	15 672	3.5
May	283 313	3.6	3.8	37 341	– 0.4	34 947	8.8
June	872 133	2.6	11.6	264 553	10.1	76 759	17.6
July	2 999 957	0.0	39.7	1 294 788	8.2	88 062	– 1.3
August	1 695 205	– 0.5	22.5	621 617	5.5	86 428	– 4.1
September	368 041	16.1	4.9	55 437	20.0	49 544	7.8
October	264 604	20.4	3.5	44 755	6.4	22 579	13.0
November	200 240	20.6	2.7	51 115	22.0	12 565	– 2.5
December	154 497	21.0	2.0	29 794	11.8	10 715	8.9
Total	7 549 969	3.9	100.0	2 516 407	7.8	431 874	5.8

(by country of nationality)

	1983	Relative share	1984	Relative share	% Variation over 1983
Austria [1]					
Belgium [1]	510 275	7.0	526 385	7.0	3.2
Denmark	511 240	7.0	549 832	7.3	7.5
Finland	118 820	1.6	150 698	2.0	26.8
France	1 460 811	20.1	1 453 152	19.2	–0.5
Germany (F.R.)					
Greece [1]					
Iceland [1]					
Ireland [1]	69 201	1.0	78 415	1.0	13.3
Italy					
Luxembourg [1]	716 840	9.9	538 424	7.1	–24.9
Netherlands	2 335 070	32.1	2 516 407	33.3	7.8
Norway					
Portugal [1]					
Spain [1]					
Sweden	63 638	0.9	73 103	1.0	14.9
Switzerland					
Turkey [1]	353 088	4.9	351 177	4.7	–0.5
United Kingdom					
Other OECD-Europe					
Total Europe	6 138 983	84.5	6 237 593	82.6	1.6
Canada	26 357	0.4	31 989	0.4	21.4
United States	408 293	5.6	431 874	5.7	5.8
Total North America	434 650	6.0	463 863	6.1	6.7
Australia [2]					
New Zealand [2]					
Japan	54 330	0.7	60 148	0.8	10.7
Total Australasia and Japan	54 330	0.7	60 148	0.8	10.7
Total OECD Countries	6 627 963	91.2	6 761 604	89.6	2.0
Yugoslavia (S.F.R.)					
Other European countries	272 049	3.7	278 040	3.7	2.2
of which: Bulgaria					
Czechoslovakia					
Hungary					
Poland					
Rumania					
USSR					
Latin America [2]					
Asia-Oceania [2]					
Africa [2]					
Origin country undetermined	367 364	5.1	510 325	6.8	38.9
Total Non-OECD Countries	639 413	8.8	788 365	10.4	23.3
TOTAL	7 267 376	100.0	7 549 969	100.0	3.9

1. Included in "Other European countries".
2. Included in "Origin country undetermined".
Source: Central Bureau of Statistics - Swedish Camping Sites Association - Swedish Tourist Board - Stockholm.

SWITZERLAND

ARRIVALS OF FOREIGN TOURISTS IN HOTELS
(by month)

	Total number 1984	% Variation over 1983	% of 1984 total	From Germany	% Variation over 1983	From United States	% Variation over 1983
January	356 817	– 0.7	4.9	105 566	– 3.4	35 604	11.4
February	384 790	– 0.4	5.3	108 921	– 6.4	36 873	26.5
March	494 324	– 2.6	6.8	173 084	–14.4	51 050	18.0
April	538 962	15.3	7.4	186 993	23.1	65 789	14.9
May	616 568	2.2	8.5	156 345	–16.5	134 998	29.8
June	834 291	15.3	11.5	196 722	– 0.4	232 059	55.7
July	968 974	5.9	13.3	182 119	– 8.8	257 194	32.7
August	1 033 828	7.0	14.2	226 719	– 4.2	210 186	36.5
September	875 321	6.6	12.0	220 651	– 7.3	229 413	35.1
October	538 859	– 2.0	7.4	132 178	–11.0	124 639	10.0
November	294 078	10.9	4.0	69 473	15.6	38 856	23.8
December	344 576	7.4	4.7	101 161	6.4	37 802	19.0
Total	7 281 388	5.8	100.0	1 859 932	– 4.3	1 454 463	31.2

(by country of residence)

	1983	Relative share	1984	Relative share	% Variation over 1983
Austria	141 742	2.1	141 659	1.9	–0.1
Belgium	201 190	2.9	196 794	2.7	–2.2
Denmark	41 084	0.6	42 707	0.6	4.0
Finland	24 766	0.4	25 846	0.4	4.4
France	484 822	7.0	531 541	7.3	9.6
Germany (F.R.)	1 942 505	28.2	1 859 932	25.5	–4.3
Greece	50 033	0.7	54 978	0.8	9.9
Iceland [1]					
Ireland	12 894	0.2	12 753	0.2	–1.1
Italy	417 033	6.1	442 321	6.1	6.1
Luxembourg	20 576	0.3	18 117	0.2	–12.0
Netherlands	276 389	4.0	248 906	3.4	–9.9
Norway	27 530	0.4	28 997	0.4	5.3
Portugal	31 640	0.5	33 255	0.5	5.1
Spain	147 471	2.1	154 571	2.1	4.8
Sweden	89 112	1.3	96 632	1.3	8.4
Switzerland					
Turkey	36 710	0.5	36 439	0.5	–0.7
United Kingdom	549 378	8.0	549 095	7.5	–0.1
Other OECD-Europe					
Total Europe	4 494 875	65.3	4 474 543	61.5	–0.5
Canada	104 090	1.5	125 876	1.7	20.9
United States	1 108 789	16.1	1 454 463	20.0	31.2
Total North America	1 212 879	17.6	1 580 339	21.7	30.3
Australia [2]	92 934	1.3	112 605	1.5	21.2
New Zealand [2]					
Japan	267 501	3.9	280 931	3.9	5.0
Total Australasia and Japan	360 435	5.2	393 536	5.4	9.2
Total OECD Countries	6 068 189	88.1	6 448 418	88.6	6.3
Yugoslavia (S.F.R.)	31 669	0.5	32 819	0.5	3.6
Other European countries	66 596	1.0	65 036	0.9	–2.3
of which: Bulgaria					
Czechoslovakia					
Hungary					
Poland					
Rumania					
USSR					
Latin America	7 950	0.1	5 857	0.1	–26.3
Asia-Oceania	139 765	2.0	157 890	2.2	13.0
Africa	423 943	6.2	425 134	5.8	0.3
Origin country undetermined	155 148	2.3	152 091	2.1	–2.0
Total Non-OECD Countries	817 121	11.9	832 970	11.4	1.9
TOTAL	6 885 310	100.0	7 281 388	100.0	5.8

1. Included in "Other European countries".
2. Australia includes New Zealand.
Source: Federal Statistical Office - Berne.

SWITZERLAND

ARRIVALS OF FOREIGN TOURISTS IN REGISTERED TOURIST ACCOMMODATION
(by month)

	Total number 1984	% Variation over 1983	% of 1984 total	From Germany	% Variation over 1983	From United States	% Variation over 1983
January	572 700	− 1.2	6.0	250 200	− 1.5	38 900	11.8
February	511 400	− 5.6	5.4	158 900	− 7.2	38 800	24.8
March	708 900	4.5	7.5	300 000	− 6.2	54 100	17.9
April	746 200	4.1	7.9	321 100	0.4	69 300	14.2
May	676 300	− 1.4	7.1	181 600	−22.3	140 000	28.7
June	1 004 700	14.4	10.6	276 800	2.6	245 200	50.8
July	1 381 200	1.1	14.6	296 500	−15.1	279 100	29.2
August	1 533 800	2.3	16.2	427 700	− 4.4	224 500	32.5
September	1 060 100	6.5	11.2	324 400	− 3.3	236 600	33.8
October	590 900	− 3.6	6.2	158 100	−14.0	128 900	9.2
November	311 400	10.0	3.3	76 100	13.4	41 100	21.6
December	384 000	5.6	4.0	119 700	8.3	40 300	17.5
Total	9 481 600	3.1	100.0	2 891 100	− 5.6	1 536 800	28.9

(by country of residence)

	1983	Relative share	1984	Relative share	% Variation over 1983
Austria	182 300	2.0	180 100	1.9	−1.2
Belgium	321 600	3.5	304 900	3.2	−5.2
Denmark	62 400	0.7	61 700	0.7	−1.1
Finland	34 700	0.4	36 400	0.4	4.9
France	642 000	7.0	700 200	7.4	9.1
Germany (F.R.)	3 062 200	33.3	2 891 100	30.5	−5.6
Greece	52 300	0.6	57 400	0.6	9.8
Iceland [1]					
Ireland	22 500	0.2	20 100	0.2	−10.7
Italy	485 300	5.3	516 700	5.4	6.5
Luxembourg	27 800	0.3	26 000	0.3	−6.5
Netherlands	575 500	6.3	519 400	5.5	−9.7
Norway	34 100	0.4	35 000	0.4	2.6
Portugal	37 600	0.4	39 200	0.4	4.3
Spain	187 500	2.0	197 200	2.1	5.2
Sweden	107 700	1.2	115 200	1.2	7.0
Switzerland					
Turkey	37 800	0.4	37 400	0.4	−1.1
United Kingdom	707 900	7.7	699 000	7.4	−1.3
Other OECD-Europe					
Total Europe	6 581 200	71.5	6 437 000	67.9	−2.2
Canada	126 100	1.4	149 100	1.6	18.2
United States	1 192 200	13.0	1 536 800	16.2	28.9
Total North America	1 318 300	14.3	1 685 900	17.8	27.9
Australia [2]	132 000	1.4	157 500	1.7	19.3
New Zealand [2]					
Japan	277 200	3.0	291 500	3.1	5.2
Total Australasia and Japan	409 200	4.4	449 000	4.7	9.7
Total OECD Countries	8 308 700	90.3	8 571 900	90.4	3.2
Yugoslavia (S.F.R.)	33 900	0.4	35 500	0.4	4.7
Other European countries	88 100	1.0	85 500	0.9	−3.0
of which: Bulgaria					
Czechoslovakia					
Hungary					
Poland					
Rumania					
USSR					
Latin America	147 200	1.6	167 600	1.8	13.9
Asia-Oceania	453 100	4.9	453 700	4.8	0.1
Africa	169 300	1.8	167 400	1.8	−1.1
Origin country undetermined					
Total Non-OECD Countries	891 600	9.7	909 700	9.6	2.0
TOTAL	9 200 300	100.0	9 481 600	100.0	3.1

1. Included in "Other European countries".
2. Australia includes New Zealand.
Source: Federal Statistical Office - Berne.

SWITZERLAND

NIGHTS SPENT BY FOREIGN TOURISTS IN HOTELS
(by month)

	Total number 1984	% Variation over 1983	% of 1984 total	From Germany	% Variation over 1983	From United States	% Variation over 1983
January	1 466 239	3.7	7.3	535 623	0.5	115 258	19.3
February	1 458 804	− 4.4	7.2	447 177	− 9.1	121 166	28.9
March	1 800 205	− 4.8	8.9	741 304	−19.5	147 631	28.3
April	1 532 514	11.8	7.6	626 816	16.2	140 597	17.4
May	1 363 717	− 3.4	6.8	367 153	−20.3	256 074	28.2
June	2 026 748	8.6	10.0	544 191	− 1.8	438 064	52.8
July	2 536 496	2.7	12.6	561 834	−11.5	519 264	30.8
August	2 817 877	1.3	14.0	722 800	− 7.9	435 418	27.9
September	2 141 904	0.3	10.6	641 077	− 8.7	434 600	29.5
October	1 192 728	− 6.8	5.9	301 891	−13.6	255 934	10.0
November	661 907	6.4	3.3	147 254	16.0	87 410	18.9
December	1 179 203	9.3	5.8	406 227	13.1	111 227	18.6
Total	20 178 342	1.7	100.0	6 043 347	− 6.4	3 062 643	28.4

(by country of residence)

	1983	Relative share	1984	Relative share	% Variation over 1983
Austria	329 739	1.7	327 817	1.6	−0.6
Belgium	837 774	4.2	839 942	4.2	0.3
Denmark	99 589	0.5	102 817	0.5	3.2
Finland	67 770	0.3	70 391	0.3	3.9
France	1 507 413	7.6	1 611 806	8.0	6.9
Germany (F.R.)	6 457 091	32.5	6 043 347	29.9	−6.4
Greece	137 980	0.7	146 525	0.7	6.2
Iceland [1]					
Ireland	37 318	0.2	37 708	0.2	1.0
Italy	841 670	4.2	892 055	4.4	6.0
Luxembourg	73 773	0.4	70 701	0.4	−4.2
Netherlands	943 363	4.8	822 955	4.1	−12.8
Norway	66 782	0.3	68 413	0.3	2.4
Portugal	71 361	0.4	74 455	0.4	4.3
Spain	280 962	1.4	295 853	1.5	5.3
Sweden	207 309	1.0	220 062	1.1	6.2
Switzerland					
Turkey	112 655	0.6	125 794	0.6	11.7
United Kingdom	2 018 989	10.2	1 954 476	9.7	−3.2
Other OECD-Europe					
Total Europe	14 091 538	71.0	13 705 117	67.9	−2.7
Canada	231 871	1.2	263 150	1.3	13.5
United States	2 384 870	12.0	3 062 643	15.2	28.4
Total North America	2 616 741	13.2	3 325 793	16.5	27.1
Australia [2]	203 575	1.0	236 023	1.2	15.9
New Zealand [2]					
Japan	486 302	2.4	496 904	2.5	2.2
Total Australasia and Japan	689 877	3.5	732 927	3.6	6.2
Total OECD Countries	17 398 156	87.6	17 763 837	88.0	2.1
Yugoslavia (S.F.R.)	68 311	0.3	69 718	0.3	2.1
Other European countries	221 484	1.1	196 699	1.0	−11.2
of which: Bulgaria					
Czechoslovakia					
Hungary					
Poland					
Rumania					
USSR	56 895	0.3	32 652	0.2	−42.6
Latin America	392 740	2.0	395 110	2.0	0.6
Asia-Oceania	1 201 046	6.1	1 231 194	6.1	2.5
Africa	568 121	2.9	521 784	2.6	−8.2
Origin country undetermined					
Total Non-OECD Countries	2 451 702	12.4	2 414 505	12.0	−1.5
TOTAL	19 849 858	100.0	20 178 342	100.0	1.7

1. Included in "Other European countries".
2. Australia includes New Zealand.
Source: Federal Statistical Office - Berne.

SWITZERLAND

NIGHTS SPENT BY FOREIGN TOURISTS IN REGISTERED TOURIST ACCOMMODATION
(by month)

	Total number 1984	% Variation over 1983	% of 1984 total	From Germany	% Variation over 1983	From United States	% Variation over 1983
January	3 564 600	0.9	10.2	1 933 000	1.9	141 400	21.4
February	2 476 900	−9.8	7.1	885 600	−6.3	132 300	27.2
March	3 665 900	7.0	10.5	1 949 000	−4.6	163 200	27.2
April	3 169 800	−16.2	9.1	1 840 800	−22.2	149 200	16.7
May	1 622 100	−5.8	4.6	519 900	−21.6	272 800	29.9
June	2 757 600	9.2	7.9	969 000	3.4	468 500	48.8
July	4 727 500	−5.6	13.5	1 359 000	−21.7	569 000	27.1
August	5 960 000	−4.9	17.0	2 240 600	−7.4	484 400	25.6
September	3 357 700	3.2	9.6	1 485 400	0.6	458 800	28.9
October	1 468 700	−9.0	4.2	485 300	−17.5	268 300	10.3
November	758 000	5.1	2.2	202 000	10.0	93 000	16.3
December	1 429 200	3.9	4.1	536 200	14.7	119 000	17.4
Total	34 958 000	−2.8	100.0	14 405 800	−8.4	3 319 900	26.9

(by country of residence)

	1983	Relative share	1984	Relative share	% Variation over 1983
Austria	513 600	1.4	489 100	1.4	−4.8
Belgium	1 916 200	5.3	1 769 500	5.1	−7.7
Denmark	189 000	0.5	181 900	0.5	−3.8
Finland	88 800	0.2	99 800	0.3	12.4
France	2 437 900	6.8	2 496 400	7.1	2.4
Germany (F.R.)	15 726 700	43.7	14 405 800	41.2	−8.4
Greece	151 400	0.4	159 700	0.5	5.5
Iceland [1]					
Ireland	70 100	0.2	58 000	0.2	−17.3
Italy	1 140 300	3.2	1 205 400	3.4	5.7
Luxembourg	147 300	0.4	148 400	0.4	0.7
Netherlands	3 350 100	9.3	2 961 300	8.5	−11.6
Norway	86 200	0.2	83 700	0.2	−2.9
Portugal	88 100	0.2	91 900	0.3	4.3
Spain	376 800	1.0	398 600	1.1	5.8
Sweden	295 400	0.8	297 300	0.9	0.6
Switzerland					
Turkey	121 000	0.3	134 700	0.4	11.3
United Kingdom	2 808 400	7.8	2 734 900	7.8	−2.6
Other OECD-Europe					
Total Europe	29 507 300	82.0	27 716 400	79.3	−6.1
Canada	279 700	0.8	315 500	0.9	12.8
United States	2 615 200	7.3	3 319 900	9.5	26.9
Total North America	2 894 900	8.0	3 635 400	10.4	25.6
Australia [2]	283 700	0.8	325 300	0.9	14.7
New Zealand [2]					
Japan	504 100	1.4	516 700	1.5	2.5
Total Australasia and Japan	787 800	2.2	842 000	2.4	6.9
Total OECD Countries	33 190 000	92.3	32 193 800	92.1	−3.0
Yugoslavia (S.F.R.)	77 600	0.2	81 100	0.2	4.5
Other European countries	282 900	0.8	255 400	0.7	−9.7
of which: Bulgaria					
Czechoslovakia					
Hungary					
Poland					
Rumania					
USSR					
Latin America	437 500	1.2	436 400	1.2	−0.3
Asia-Oceania	1 345 700	3.7	1 391 900	4.0	3.4
Africa	643 600	1.8	599 400	1.7	−6.9
Origin country undetermined					
Total Non-OECD Countries	2 787 300	7.7	2 764 200	7.9	−0.8
TOTAL	35 977 300	100.0	34 958 000	100.0	−2.8

1. Included in "Other European countries".
2. Australia includes New Zealand.
Source: Federal Statistical Office - Berne.

TURKEY

ARRIVALS OF FOREIGN TRAVELLERS AT FRONTIERS
(by month)

	Total number 1984	% Variation over 1983	% of 1984 total	From Germany	% Variation over 1983	From United States	% Variation over 1983
January	65 864	18.0	3.1	3 153	−9.2	3 004	−4.1
February	62 574	20.6	3.0	3 517	17.4	2 220	−25.4
March	90 783	6.9	4.3	7 805	−26.5	6 237	37.3
April	150 301	32.9	7.1	29 020	68.2	16 165	39.4
May	181 844	11.3	8.6	29 354	36.7	26 241	10.7
June	197 145	39.2	9.3	26 620	67.0	26 106	26.9
July	302 720	33.2	14.3	33 047	34.1	27 456	14.4
August	319 910	40.3	15.1	35 992	42.8	24 784	13.1
September	266 925	30.3	12.6	35 205	31.9	34 057	6.9
October	211 228	33.5	10.0	23 380	54.0	34 396	11.0
November	142 843	34.5	6.7	7 798	11.6	9 204	0.0
December	124 957	39.1	5.9	6 821	52.5	3 475	−20.8
Total	2 117 094	30.3	100.0	241 712	38.2	213 345	12.9

(by country of nationality)

	1983	Relative share	1984	Relative share	% Variation over 1983
Austria	73 793	4.5	71 151	3.4	−3.6
Belgium	16 912	1.0	21 707	1.0	28.4
Denmark	9 071	0.6	7 828	0.4	−13.7
Finland	10 049	0.6	10 225	0.5	1.8
France	88 209	5.4	103 359	4.9	17.2
Germany (F.R.)	174 936	10.8	241 712	11.4	38.2
Greece	138 676	8.5	179 284	8.5	29.3
Iceland [1]					
Ireland [1]					
Italy	57 583	3.5	65 856	3.1	14.4
Luxembourg [1]					
Netherlands	26 282	1.6	27 098	1.3	3.1
Norway	5 194	0.3	6 289	0.3	21.1
Portugal [1]					
Spain	16 196	1.0	19 386	0.9	19.7
Sweden	14 003	0.9	10 082	0.5	−28.0
Switzerland	35 472	2.2	28 143	1.3	−20.7
Turkey					
United Kingdom	84 434	5.2	89 709	4.2	6.2
Other OECD-Europe					
Total Europe	750 810	46.2	881 829	41.7	17.5
Canada	14 414	0.9	18 048	0.9	25.2
United States	188 887	11.6	213 345	10.1	12.9
Total North America	203 301	12.5	231 393	10.9	13.8
Australia	10 722	0.7	17 716	0.8	65.2
New-Zealand [1]					
Japan	7 782	0.5	13 060	0.6	67.8
Total Australasia and Japan	18 504	1.1	30 776	1.5	66.3
Total OECD Countries	972 615	59.8	1 143 998	54.0	17.6
Yugoslavia (S.F.R.)	60 315	3.7	179 705	8.5	197.9
Other European countries	178 860	11.0	195 577	9.2	9.3
of which: Bulgaria	75 338	4.6	59 800	2.8	−20.6
Czechoslovakia	10 727	0.7	9 873	0.5	−8.0
Hungary	41 552	2.6	44 070	2.1	6.1
Poland	17 246	1.1	46 301	2.2	168.5
Rumania	16 545	1.0	20 231	1.0	22.3
USSR	17 452	1.1	15 302	0.7	−12.3
Latin America	14 932	0.9	15 496	0.7	3.8
Asia-Oceania [2]			440 696	20.8	
Africa					
Origin country undetermined	398 377	24.5	141 622	6.7	−64.5
Total Non-OECD Countries	652 484	40.2	973 096	46.0	49.1
TOTAL	1 625 099	100.0	2 117 094	100.0	30.3

1. Included in "Origin country undetermined".
2. Includes Iraq, Kuwait, Libya, Lebanon, Egypt, Syria, Saudi Arabia, Jordan, Iran and Pakistan.
Source: Police Office - Ankara.

UNITED KINGDOM

ARRIVALS OF FOREIGN VISITORS AT FRONTIERS
(by month)

	Total number 1984	% Variation over 1983	% of 1984 total	From Germany	% Variation over 1983	From United States	% Variation over 1983
January	748 000	3.5	5.5	246 000	4.6	322 000	24.1
February	588 000	6.9	4.3				
March	831 000	12.3	6.1				
April	1 177 000	15.1	8.6	412 000	17.3	729 000	22.9
May	1 101 000	11.4	8.0				
June	1 320 000	11.0	9.6				
July	1 773 000	4.5	12.9	547 000	8.2	1 162 000	17.2
August	2 021 000	15.6	14.7				
September	1 413 000	11.3	10.3				
October	1 096 000	4.3	8.0	279 000	– 1.2	551 000	16.4
November	888 000	11.6	6.5				
December	756 000	9.6	5.5				
Total	13 712 000	10.0	100.0	1 484 000	8.0	2 764 000	19.3

(by country of residence)

	1983	Relative share	1984	Relative share	% Variation over 1983
Austria	88 400	0.7	111 200	0.8	25.8
Belgium	418 200	3.3	408 700	3.0	–2.3
Denmark	218 600	1.7	191 600	1.4	–12.4
Finland	61 700	0.5	72 100	0.5	16.9
France	1 516 000	12.1	1 631 700	11.9	7.6
Germany (F.R.)	1 374 200	11.0	1 484 000	10.8	8.0
Greece	84 900	0.7	81 000	0.6	–4.6
Iceland	14 500	0.1	27 900	0.2	92.4
Ireland	942 600	7.5	976 800	7.1	3.6
Italy	458 300	3.7	474 900	3.5	3.6
Luxembourg	12 200	0.1	17 300	0.1	41.8
Netherlands	734 600	5.9	740 900	5.4	0.9
Norway	194 000	1.6	215 500	1.6	11.1
Portugal	54 800	0.4	59 100	0.4	7.8
Spain	298 200	2.4	293 400	2.1	–1.6
Sweden	288 400	2.3	402 200	2.9	39.5
Switzerland	309 500	2.5	312 900	2.3	1.1
Turkey	32 500	0.3	18 500	0.1	–43.1
United Kingdom					
Other OECD-Europe					
Total Europe	7 101 600	56.8	7 520 400	54.8	5.9
Canada	518 800	4.2	566 700	4.1	9.2
United States	2 317 400	18.5	2 763 800	20.2	19.3
Total North America	2 836 200	22.7	3 330 500	24.3	17.4
Australia	330 700	2.6	456 300	3.3	38.0
New Zealand	76 200	0.6	94 800	0.7	24.4
Japan	170 300	1.4	200 600	1.5	17.8
Total Australasia and Japan	577 200	4.6	751 700	5.5	30.2
Total OECD Countries	10 515 000	84.1	11 602 600	84.6	10.3
Yugoslavia (S.F.R.)	24 000	0.2	23 700	0.2	–1.3
Other European countries	123 100	1.0	131 600	1.0	6.9
of which: Bulgaria					
Czechoslovakia					
Hungary[1]	50 000	0.4	56 700	0.4	13.4
Poland					
Rumania					
USSR					
Latin America	113 100	0.9	165 300	1.2	46.2
Asia-Oceania	1 027 600	8.2	1 097 900	8.0	6.8
Africa	648 000	5.2	639 100	4.7	–1.4
Origin country undetermined	48 007	0.4	50 700	0.4	5.6
Total Non-OECD Countries	1 983 807	15.9	2 108 300	15.4	6.3
TOTAL	12 498 807	100.0	13 710 900	100.0	9.7

1. Includes Bulgaria, Czechoslovakia, Hungary, Rumania, USSR, Albania, and German Democratic Republic.
Source: Department of Trade - London.

UNITED KINGDOM

NIGHTS SPENT BY FOREIGN TOURISTS IN TOURIST ACCOMMODATION [1]
(quarterly)

	Total number 1984	% Variation over 1983	% of 1984 total	From Germany	% Variation over 1983	From United States	% Variation over 1983
January February March	22 336 000	1.1	14.4	2 180 000	− 8.2	2 864 000	6.5
April May June	35 450 000	12.2	22.8	4 081 000	32.4	5 827 000	11.9
July August September	67 606 000	8.2	43.5	6 155 000	− 1.8	12 525 000	22.4
October November December	29 935 000	2.2	19.3	1 888 000	−20.7	5 468 000	9.1
Total	155 327 000	6.8	100.0	14 304 000	1.4	26 684 000	15.3

(by country of residence)

	1983	Relative share	1984	Relative share	% Variation over 1983
Austria	888 000	0.6	1 179 000	0.8	32.8
Belgium	2 203 000	1.5	2 196 000	1.4	−0.3
Denmark	1 785 000	1.2	1 480 000	1.0	−17.1
Finland	576 000	0.4	899 000	0.6	56.1
France	11 467 000	7.9	13 042 000	8.4	13.7
Germany (F.R.)	14 108 000	9.7	14 303 000	9.2	1.4
Greece	1 226 000	0.8	1 142 000	0.7	−6.9
Iceland	132 000	0.1	224 000	0.1	69.7
Ireland	7 625 000	5.2	8 004 000	5.2	5.0
Italy	6 372 000	4.4	6 211 000	4.0	−2.5
Luxembourg	69 000	0.0	111 000	0.1	60.9
Netherlands	4 794 000	3.3	4 562 000	2.9	−4.8
Norway	1 676 000	1.2	1 889 000	1.2	12.7
Portugal	733 000	0.5	588 000	0.4	−19.8
Spain [2]	4 984 000	3.4	4 257 000	2.7	−14.6
Sweden	2 346 000	1.6	3 930 000	2.5	67.5
Switzerland	3 891 000	2.7	3 249 000	2.1	−16.5
Turkey	576 000	0.4	357 000	0.2	−38.0
United Kingdom					
Other OECD-Europe					
Total Europe	65 451 000	45.0	67 623 000	43.5	3.3
Canada	8 064 000	5.5	8 434 000	5.4	4.6
United States	23 140 000	15.9	26 684 000	17.2	15.3
Total North America	31 204 000	21.5	35 118 000	22.6	12.5
Australia	8 934 000	6.1	10 398 000	6.7	16.4
New Zealand	2 634 000	1.8	3 525 000	2.3	33.8
Japan	987 000	0.7	1 533 000	1.0	55.3
Total Australasia and Japan	12 555 000	8.6	15 456 000	10.0	23.1
Total OECD Countries	109 210 000	75.1	118 197 000	76.1	8.2
Yugoslavia (S.F.R.)	659 000	0.5	496 000	0.3	−24.7
Other European countries	2 186 000	1.5	1 221 000	0.8	−44.1
of which: Bulgaria Czechoslovakia Hungary [3] Poland Rumania USSR	679 000	0.5	804 000	0.5	18.4
Latin America	1 562 000	1.1	1 544 000	1.0	−1.2
Asia-Oceania	18 573 000	12.8	20 455 000	13.2	10.1
Africa	12 192 000	8.4	11 506 000	7.4	−5.6
Origin country undetermined	1 050 000	0.7	1 909 000	1.2	81.8
Total Non-OECD Countries	36 222 000	24.9	37 131 000	23.9	2.5
TOTAL	145 432 000	100.0	155 328 000	100.0	6.8

1. Estimates of total number of nights, spent in all forms of accommodation, including stays with friends and relatives. Excluding: visitors in transit, visits of merchant seamen, airline personnel and military on duty.
2. Including Canary Islands.
3. Includes Bulgaria, Czechoslovakia, Hungary, Rumania, USSR, Albania and German Democratic Republic.
Source: Department of Trade - London.

UNITED STATES

ARRIVALS OF FOREIGN TOURISTS AT FRONTIERS
(quarterly)

	Total number 1984	% Variation over 1983	% of 1984 total	From Canada	% Variation over 1983	
January						
February						
March						
April						
May						
June						
July						
August						
September						
October						
November						
December						
Total	20 810 000	− 4.0	100.0	10 982 000	− 8.0	

(by country of residence)

	1983	Relative share	1984	Relative share	% Variation over 1983
Austria					
Belgium					
Denmark					
Finland					
France	309 000	1.4	334 000	1.6	8.1
Germany (F.R.)	563 000	2.6	540 000	2.6	−4.1
Greece					
Iceland					
Ireland					
Italy					
Luxembourg					
Netherlands					
Norway					
Portugal					
Spain					
Sweden					
Switzerland					
Turkey					
United Kingdom	1 013 000	4.7	922 000	4.4	−9.0
Other OECD-Europe					
Total Europe	1 885 000	8.7	1 796 000	8.6	−4.7
Canada	11 937 000	55.1	10 982 000	52.8	−8.0
United States					
Total North America	11 937 000	55.1	10 982 000	52.8	−8.0
Australia					
New Zealand					
Japan	1 279 000	5.9	1 407 000	6.8	10.0
Total Australasia and Japan	1 279 000	5.9	1 407 000	6.8	10.0
Total OECD Countries	15 101 000	69.7	14 185 000	68.2	−6.1
Yugoslavia (S.F.R.)					
Other European countries					
of which: Bulgaria					
Czechoslovakia					
Hungary					
Poland					
Rumania					
USSR					
Latin America [1]	1 900 000	8.8	2 300 000	11.1	21.1
Asia-Oceania					
Africa					
Origin country undetermined [2]	4 676 000	21.6	4 325 000	20.8	−7.5
Total Non-OECD Countries	6 576 000	30.3	6 625 000	31.8	0.7
TOTAL	21 677 000	100.0	20 810 000	100.0	−4.0

1. Mexico only.
2. Of which Other European countries (1 167 000 arrivals), Other Asian countries (701 000 arrivals), Oceania (335 000 arrivals), Caraibbean (703 000 arrivals), South America (773 000 arrivals), Central America (295 000 arrivals), Middle East (327 000 arrivals), and Africa (152 000 arrivals).
Source: United States Travel and Tourism Administration - Washington.

YUGOSLAVIA

ARRIVALS OF FOREIGN VISITORS AT FRONTIERS[1]
(by month)

	Total number 1984	% Variation over 1983	% of 1984 total		
January	649 504	35.5	3.3		
February	587 573	49.2	3.0		
March	778 003	25.5	3.9		
April	1 110 585	40.9	5.6		
May	1 228 045	9.2	6.2		
June	2 013 296	17.2	10.2		
July	3 801 838	−31.7	19.3		
August	4 115 300	15.9	20.9		
September	2 116 682	14.5	10.7		
October	1 279 528	14.7	6.5		
November	991 779	33.5	5.0		
December	1 044 441	33.5	5.3		
Total	19 716 574	5.3	100.0		

1. Number of foreign tourists and excursionists.

ARRIVALS OF FOREIGN TOURISTS IN HOTELS
(by month)

	Total number 1984	% Variation over 1983	% of 1984 total		
January	71 018	13.9	1.5		
February	89 230	39.0	1.9		
March	124 482	− 3.6	2.7		
April	366 099	65.9	8.0		
May	483 449	13.4	10.5		
June	633 776	29.7	13.8		
July	723 216	10.9	15.8		
August	872 262	18.9	19.0		
September	660 375	19.1	14.4		
October	313 686	15.2	6.8		
November	126 060	24.1	2.8		
December	119 473	27.3	2.6		
Total	4 583 126	20.6	100.0		

NIGHTS SPENT BY FOREIGN TOURISTS IN HOTELS
(by month)

	Total number 1984	% Variation over 1983	% of 1984 total		
January	232 818	12.8	1.0		
February	316 646	41.7	1.3		
March	402 682	− 8.6	1.7		
April	1 262 834	67.2	5.3		
May	2 245 724	6.8	9.4		
June	3 750 512	20.5	15.7		
July	4 442 345	10.9	18.6		
August	5 217 770	14.7	21.8		
September	3 791 741	16.9	15.9		
October	1 483 651	22.5	6.2		
November	390 145	31.9	1.6		
December	354 362	33.5	1.5		
Total	23 891 230	17.0	100.0		

Source: Federal Bureau of Statistics - Belgrade.

YUGOSLAVIA

ARRIVALS OF FOREIGN TOURISTS IN REGISTERED TOURIST ACCOMMODATION
(by month)

	Total number 1984	% Variation over 1983	% of 1984 total	From Germany	% Variation over 1983	From United States	% Variation over 1983
January	86 647	16.5	1.2	19 805	32.1	3 459	56.4
February	115 966	57.8	1.6	19 894	59.5	12 562	301.5
March	137 444	−10.0	1.9	25 751	−47.8	5 883	23.1
April	395 966	63.7	5.5	110 381	97.1	14 900	59.1
May	556 954	7.3	7.7	146 088	−19.3	25 425	39.4
June	942 013	31.3	13.0	312 396	23.3	27 968	42.0
July	1 605 671	17.0	22.2	464 730	0.1	37 447	22.6
August	1 849 423	22.3	25.6	588 244	14.1	28 407	21.3
September	902 716	19.0	12.5	303 172	19.8	35 196	27.9
October	349 347	14.9	4.8	100 891	15.6	24 394	25.4
November	144 789	27.2	2.0	31 563	31.4	6 115	− 1.8
December	136 868	28.6	1.9	22 520	13.6	5 000	63.3
Total	7 223 804	21.5	100.0	2 145 435	11.1	226 756	35.3

(by country of residence)

	1983	Relative share	1984	Relative share	% Variation over 1983
Austria	540 160	9.1	626 631	8.7	16.0
Belgium	90 524	1.5	117 121	1.6	29.4
Denmark	78 078	1.3	118 794	1.6	52.1
Finland	26 635	0.4	28 678	0.4	7.7
France	266 103	4.5	431 894	6.0	62.3
Germany (F.R.)	1 931 268	32.5	2 145 435	29.7	11.1
Greece	124 578	2.1	130 301	1.8	4.6
Iceland [1]					
Ireland [1]					
Italy	718 330	12.1	958 847	13.3	33.5
Luxembourg [1]					
Netherlands	241 139	4.1	356 808	4.9	48.0
Norway	36 840	0.6	43 724	0.6	18.7
Portugal [1]					
Spain [1]					
Sweden	59 453	1.0	79 520	1.1	33.8
Switzerland	111 618	1.9	123 624	1.7	10.8
Turkey	117 635	2.0	119 815	1.7	1.9
United Kingdom	354 225	6.0	445 076	6.2	25.6
Other OECD-Europe					
Total Europe	4 696 586	79.0	5 726 268	79.3	21.9
Canada	23 818	0.4	33 375	0.5	40.1
United States	167 624	2.8	226 756	3.1	35.3
Total North America	191 442	3.2	260 131	3.6	35.9
Australia [2]					
New Zealand [2]					
Japan	8 747	0.1	9 346	0.1	6.8
Total Australasia and Japan	8 747	0.1	9 346	0.1	6.8
Total OECD Countries	4 896 775	82.3	5 995 745	83.0	22.4
Yugoslavia (S.F.R.)					
Other European countries	865 395	14.6	1 013 393	14.0	17.1
of which: Bulgaria	22 969	0.4	26 019	0.4	13.3
Czechoslovakia	280 414	4.7	398 942	5.5	42.3
Hungary	144 205	2.4	175 084	2.4	21.4
Poland	21 258	0.4	50 035	0.7	135.4
Rumania	11 678	0.2	16 074	0.2	37.6
USSR	261 090	4.4	211 109	2.9	−19.1
Latin America [2]					
Asia-Oceania [2]					
Africa [2]					
Origin country undetermined	184 869	3.1	214 666	3.0	16.1
Total Non-OECD Countries	1 050 264	17.7	1 228 059	17.0	16.9
TOTAL	5 947 039	100.0	7 223 804	100.0	21.5

1. Included in "Other European countries".
2. Included in "Origin country undetermined".
Source: Federal Bureau of Statistics - Belgrade.

YUGOSLAVIA

NIGHTS SPENT BY FOREIGN TOURISTS IN REGISTERED TOURIST ACCOMMODATION
(by month)

	Total number 1984	% Variation over 1983	% of 1984 total	From Germany	% Variation over 1983	From United States	% Variation over 1983
January	264 032	14.4	0.6	55 838	21.0	12 624	85.9
February	490 784	99.7	1.2	66 296	56.2	74 840	494.6
March	441 901	− 9.2	1.0	109 797	−36.8	18 057	− 2.4
April	1 364 305	68.4	3.2	494 626	118.4	43 692	63.8
May	2 553 214	0.6	6.0	836 879	−25.1	57 708	33.7
June	5 721 799	23.8	13.5	2 443 455	16.2	62 938	27.4
July	11 016 273	16.3	26.1	3 964 986	− 0.2	92 794	19.9
August	12 551 668	19.7	29.7	5 004 968	10.2	74 295	9.1
September	5 401 802	19.3	12.8	2 304 364	21.6	78 186	22.7
October	1 629 820	23.3	3.9	562 486	20.4	59 200	20.0
November	442 775	34.8	1.0	115 987	51.9	17 648	−14.4
December	391 474	34.9	0.9	79 841	42.6	12 243	18.7
Total	42 269 847	19.6	100.0	16 039 523	8.9	604 225	35.3

(by country of residence)

	1983	Relative share	1984	Relative share	% Variation over 1983
Austria	3 779 073	10.7	4 282 854	10.1	13.3
Belgium	560 462	1.6	729 173	1.7	30.1
Denmark	460 275	1.3	690 176	1.6	49.9
Finland	155 931	0.4	185 690	0.4	19.1
France	1 047 290	3.0	1 499 969	3.5	43.2
Germany (F.R.)	14 722 598	41.6	16 039 523	37.9	8.9
Greece	173 498	0.5	181 742	0.4	4.8
Iceland [1]					
Ireland [1]					
Italy	3 230 533	9.1	4 160 557	9.8	28.8
Luxembourg [1]					
Netherlands	1 549 164	4.4	2 270 268	5.4	46.5
Norway	258 434	0.7	329 444	0.8	27.5
Portugal [1]					
Spain [1]					
Sweden	308 199	0.9	429 818	1.0	39.5
Switzerland	622 411	1.8	618 996	1.5	−0.5
Turkey	139 144	0.4	144 978	0.3	4.2
United Kingdom	2 754 970	7.8	3 570 724	8.4	29.6
Other OECD-Europe					
Total Europe	29 761 982	84.2	35 133 912	83.1	18.0
Canada	70 895	0.2	105 778	0.3	49.2
United States	446 632	1.3	604 225	1.4	35.3
Total North America	517 527	1.5	710 003	1.7	37.2
Australia [2]					
New Zealand [2]					
Japan	27 426	0.1	26 352	0.1	−3.9
Total Australasia and Japan	27 426	0.1	26 352	0.1	−3.9
Total OECD Countries	30 306 935	85.7	35 870 267	84.9	18.4
Yugoslavia (S.F.R.)					
Other European countries	4 316 221	12.2	5 641 817	13.3	30.7
of which: Bulgaria	73 038	0.2	72 524	0.2	−0.7
Czechoslovakia	2 413 216	6.8	3 439 638	8.1	42.5
Hungary	539 729	1.5	684 988	1.6	26.9
Poland	107 559	0.3	246 967	0.6	129.6
Rumania	71 318	0.2	139 575	0.3	95.7
USSR	662 337	1.9	556 237	1.3	−16.0
Latin America [2]					
Asia-Oceania [2]					
Africa [2]					
Origin country undetermined	731 758	2.1	757 763	1.8	3.6
Total Non-OECD Countries	5 047 979	14.3	6 399 580	15.1	26.8
TOTAL	35 354 914	100.0	42 269 847	100.0	19.6

1. Included in "Other European countries".
2. Included in "Origin country undetermined".
Source: Federal Bureau of Statistics - Belgrade.

A.II.2. FOREIGN TOURISM BY PURPOSE OF VISIT

	1983						1984					
	Business journeys (%)[1]	Private journeys (%)				Total number of foreign arrivals in thousands	Business journeys (%)[1]	Private journeys (%)				Total number of foreign arrivals in thousands
		Holiday	VFR[2]	Others	Total			Holiday	VFR[2]	Others	Total	
Greece[3]							7.0	83.0	1.0	9.0	93.0	6 027.3
Ireland[4]	20.1	40.5	31.8	7.6	79.9	1 778.0	17.1	37.4	38.7	6.8	82.9	1 866.0
Portugal[5]	3.2	87.2	1.1	8.5	96.8	8 875.0	3.3	86.3	1.1	9.3	96.7	9 811.0
Spain[6]	5.0	90.0		5.0	95.0	25 583.5						
United Kingdom[7]	20.6	46.6	20.4	12.4	79.4	12 499.0	21.0	46.6	19.3	13.1	79.0	13 713.0
Canada[8]	14.5	59.0	24.7	1.7	85.5	12 491.0						
Australia[9]	16.1	42.0	28.4	13.5	83.9	943.9						
New Zealand[10]	11.7	54.5	22.9	11.0	88.3	508.5	11.8	56.3	21.9	10.0	88.2	567.6
Japan[11]	20.8	61.5		17.7	79.2	1 968.5						

1. Includes : business, congresses, seminars, on mission, etc.
2. VFR : visits to friends and relatives.
3. Greece: number of tourists. "Others" includes journeys for visiting relatives and holiday (3% in 1984) or for business and holiday (2% in 1984).
4. Ireland: number of journeys. Excluding visitors from Northern Ireland.
5. Portugal: "Others" includes visits for cultural purposes and journeys for educational reasons (0.6% in 1983 and 0.2% in 1984).
6. Spain: "Others" includes journeys for educational reasons (1% in 1983).
7. United Kingdom: "Others" includes journeys for educational reasons (2.7% in 1983 and 3.6% in 1984).
8. Canada: number of tourists.
9. Australia: short-term visitors (less than one year). "Others" includes journeys for educational reasons (1.9% in 1983).
10. New Zealand: number of visitors. "Others" includes journeys for educational reasons (0.6% in 1983 and 0.6% in 1984).
11. Japan: number of visitors. "Others" includes journeys for educational reasons (1.7% in 1983).

A.II.3. AVERAGE LENGTH OF STAY OF FOREIGN TOURISTS

	Tourists from all foreign countries			Tourists from Europe (OECD)			Tourists from North America (OECD)			Tourists from Pacific (OECD)		
	1982	1983	1984	1982	1983	1984	1982	1983	1984	1982	1983	1984
	Average length of stay in tourist accommodation											
Austria	6.31	6.04	5.74	6.70	6.48	6.25	2.72	2.55	2.38	2.20	2.22	2.10
France[1]	2.63	2.72	2.75	2.55	2.64	2.73	2.60	2.75	2.67	2.44	2.55	2.46
Germany	2.21	2.20		2.19	2.21		1.95	1.93		1.83	1.84	
Greece	4.93			5.54			2.61			2.40		
Italy	5.46	5.26		6.25	6.11		2.86	2.69		2.55	2.53	
Luxembourg	2.07	3.75		2.22	3.97		1.70	1.76			1.58	
Netherlands	3.07	3.06		3.36	3.39		2.03	1.94		2.12	2.24	
Portugal	4.95	4.67	4.47	5.38	5.09	4.89	2.92	2.84	2.82	2.82	2.76	2.51
Spain[2]	7.35			8.24			2.54			2.28		
Switzerland	4.00	3.91	3.69	4.52	4.48	4.31	2.28	2.20	2.16	1.94	1.93	1.88
Turkey	2.52	2.59		2.55	2.66		3.01	2.67		2.35	2.06	
Japan[3]	2.09			2.76			2.23			2.11		
Yugoslavia	5.97	5.94	5.85	6.41	6.34	6.14	2.73	2.70	2.73	2.92	3.14	2.82

Average length of stay in tourist accommodation is obtained by dividing the number of nights recorded in particular means of accommodation by the number of arrivals of tourists at the same means of accommodation (see tables series II.1).
Covers all means of accommodatiom unless otherwise stated.
1. France: hotels only in Ile-de-France region.
2. Spain: hotels only.
3. Japan: hotels only.

	Tourists from all foreign countries			Tourists from Europe (OECD)			Tourists from North America (OECD)			Tourists from Pacific (OECD)		
	1982	1983	1984	1982	1983	1984	1982	1983	1984	1982	1983	1984
	Average length of stay in the country visited											
France	8.90	9.00		8.30	8.40		11.50	11.60		7.00	7.30	
Greece[1]			14.00									
Ireland	10.00	9.00	10.00		9.00	9.00		10.00	10.00		11.00	13.00
Portugal	9.40	8.60	8.90	8.90	8.50	8.80	16.90	15.80	12.50	5.60	5.20	4.80
Spain	6.90	6.80					2.50					
United Kingdom	12.00	12.00	11.00	9.00	9.00	9.00	12.00	11.00	11.00	19.00	22.00	21.00
Canada	6.00	5.60		14.70	14.40		4.50	4.40		9.80	8.60	
Australia		33.00			45.00			30.00			19.00	
Japan	12.20	11.60										

Average length of stay in the country visited expressed in number of nights spent unless otherwise stated:
1. Greece: number of days.

119

A.II.4.1. NIGHTS SPENT BY FOREIGN AND DOMESTIC TOURISTS IN ALL MEANS OF ACCOMMODATION[1]

(in thousands)

	Nights spent by foreign tourists			Nights spent by domestic tourists			Total nights			Proportion spent by foreign tourists (%)	
	1983	1984	% 84/83	1983	1984	% 84/83	1983	1984	% 84/83	1983	1984
Austria	87 444.5	86 713.3	–0.8	28 349.1	27 912.4	–1.5	115 793.5	114 625.6	–1.0	75.5	75.6
Belgium	8 938.9			21 396.6			30 335.5			29.5	
Denmark	9 528.9	9 112.3	–4.4	11 633.1	11 497.2	–1.2	21 162.0	20 609.5	–2.6	45.0	44.2
Finland	2 561.6	2 542.5	–0.7	7 668.2	7 805.3	1.8	10 229.8	10 347.8	1.2	25.0	24.6
France[2]	50 170.9	47 892.3	–4.5	87 173.6	79 000.4	–9.4	137 344.5	126 892.7	–7.6	36.5	37.7
Germany	26 428.8			195 321.1			221 749.9			11.9	
Italy	97 242.1	95 162.4	–2.1	235 391.7	236 278.0	0.4	332 633.8	331 440.3	–0.4	29.2	28.7
Netherlands	12 405.1										
Norway[3]	4 912.1	3 459.8	–29.6	10 646.5	7 474.0	–29.8	15 558.7	10 933.9	–29.7	31.6	31.6
Portugal[4]	11 932.7	12 532.2	5.0	13 230.5	12 094.0	–8.6	25 163.2	24 626.2	–2.1	47.4	50.9
Spain[5]	79 725.4			40 202.3			119 927.7			66.5	
Sweden	7 267.4	7 550.0	3.9	23 558.9	24 267.9	3.0	30 826.2	31 817.9	3.2	23.6	23.7
Switzwerland	35 977.3	34 958.0	–2.8	38 372.5	38 491.7	0.3	74 349.8	73 449.7	–1.2	48.4	47.6
Turkey[6]	2 942.5			4 097.4			7 039.9			41.8	
Canada[7]					229 280.0						
Australia[8]	14 328.4			114 684.0			129 012.4			11.1	
Yugoslavia	35 354.9	42 269.8	19.6	55 293.6	55 267.1	0.0	90 648.5	97 536.9	7.6	39.0	43.3

1. For "Types of accommodatiom covered by the statistics", see Table A.II.4.4.
2. France: see note to table A.II.4.2 .
3. Norway: see notes to tables A.II.4.2 et A.II.4.3 .
4. Portugal: see notes to table A.II.4.2 .
4. Spain: see note to table A.II.4.2 .
6. Turkey: figures based on a monthly sample survey carried out amoung establishments licenced by the Ministry of Tourism and Culture.
7. Canada: person-nights: covers all forms of accommodation, including homes of friends or relatives, and rented chalets.
8. Australia: see note to table A.II.4.3 .

A.II.4.2. NIGHTS SPENT BY FOREIGN AND DOMESTIC TOURISTS IN HOTELS AND SIMILAR ESTABLISHMENTS[1]

(in thousands)

	Nights spent by foreign tourists			Nights spent by domestic tourists			Total nights			Proportion spent by foreign tourists (%)	
	1983	1984	% 84/83	1983	1984	% 84/83	1983	1984	% 84/83	1983	1984
Austria	54 993.2	55 523.9	1.0	14 263.9	14 104.7	–1.1	69 257.1	69 628.6	0.5	79.4	79.7
Belgium	4 928.3			2 318.1			7 246.4			68.0	
Denmark	4 501.1	4 608.3	2.4	3 954.6	4 037.9	2.1	8 455.7	8 646.2	2.3	53.2	53.3
Finland	2 060.6	2 112.5	2.5	5 869.2	6 166.3	5.1	7 929.8	8 278.8	4.4	26.0	25.5
France[2]	17 942.4	16 651.2	–7.2								
Germany	19 149.4			108 918.3			128 067.7			15.0	
Italy	63 383.5	63 034.0	–0.6	105 050.8	105 233.2	0.2	168 434.3	168 267.2	–0.1	37.6	37.5
Netherlands	6 535.2										
Norway[3]	2 340.1	2 511.6	7.3	5 005.5	5 246.7	4.8	7 345.7	7 758.3	5.6	31.9	32.4
Portugal[4]	9 892.3	11 025.2	11.5	6 217.0	5 763.8	–7.3	16 109.3	16 789.0	4.2	61.4	65.7
Spain[5]	79 725.4			40 202.3			119 927.7			66.5	
Sweden	3 024.7	3 275.6	8.3	10 540.8	11 225.1	6.5	13 565.5	14 500.8	6.9	22.3	22.6
Switzwerland	19 849.9	20 178.3	1.7	12 728.0	12 785.7	0.5	32 577.9	32 964.0	1.2	60.9	61.2
Turkey	2 640.0			3 796.6			6 436.5			41.0	
Canada[6]					35 203.0						
Australia	6 011.7			45 150.0			51 161.7			11.8	
Yugoslavia	20 412.3	23 891.2	17.0	21 658.3	22 289.9	2.9	42 070.6	46 181.2	9.8	48.5	51.7

1. For "Types of accommodatiom covered by the statistics", see Table A.II.4.4.
2. France: Data concerns Ile-de-France region only.
3. Norway: approved hotels only. As from 1st July 1983 the system of approval of hotels was discontinued.
4. Portugal: hotels includes "studio-hotels", "holiday flats", and "holiday villages".
5. Spain: hotels includes "paradors" and boarding houses.
6. Canada: person-nights: covers also nights spent by Canadians travelling both in Canada and the United States.

A.II.4.3. NIGHTS SPENT BY FOREIGN AND DOMESTIC TOURISTS IN SUPPLEMENTARY MEANS OF ACCOMMODATION

(In thousands)

	Nights spent by foreign tourists			Nights spent by domestic tourists			Total nights			Proportion spent by foreign tourists (%)	
	1983	1984	% 84/83	1983	1984	% 84/83	1983	1984	% 84/83	1983	1984
	In supplementary means of accommodation[1]										
Austria	32 451.3	31 189.3	−3.9	14 085.1	13 807.7	−2.0	46 536.4	44 997.0	−3.3	69.7	69.3
Belgium	4 010.6			19 078.5			23 089.2			17.4	
Denmark	5 027.8	4 504.0	−10.4	7 678.5	7 459.3	−2.9	12 706.3	11 963.3	−5.8	39.6	37.6
Finland	501.0	430.0	−14.2	1 799.0	1 639.0	−8.9	2 300.0	2 069.0	−10.0	21.8	20.8
France	32 228.6	31 241.1	−3.1	87 173.6	79 000.4	−9.4	119 402.2	110 241.5	−7.7	27.0	28.3
Germany	7 279.5			86 402.8			93 682.2			7.8	
Italy	33 858.6	32 128.4	−5.1	130 340.9	131 044.7	0.5	164 199.6	163 173.1	−0.6	20.6	19.7
Netherlands	5 869.9										
Norway[2]	2 572.0	948.2		5 641.0	2 227.3		8 213.0	3 175.5		31.3	29.9
Portugal	2 040.5	1 507.0	−26.1	7 013.5	6 330.2	−9.7	9 053.9	7 837.2	−13.4	22.5	19.2
Sweden	4 242.7	4 274.3	0.7	13 018.1	13 042.8	0.2	17 260.8	17 317.2	0.3	24.6	24.7
Switzwerland	16 127.4	14 779.7	−8.4	25 644.5	25 706.0	0.2	41 771.9	40 485.7	−3.1	38.6	36.5
Turkey	302.5			300.9			603.4			50.1	
Canada[3]				194 077.0							
Australia	8 316.7			69 534.0			77 850.7			10.7	
Yugoslavia	14 942.6	18 378.6	23.0	33 635.4	32 977.2	−2.0	48 577.9	51 355.8	5.7	30.8	35.8
	Of which: on camping sites										
Austria	5 146.6	5 052.1	−1.8	1 235.6	1 177.8	−4.7	6 382.2	6 229.9	−2.4	80.6	81.1
Belgium	1 802.9			7 536.6			9 339.5			19.3	
Denmark	4 670.3	4 126.8	−11.6	7 274.0	7 040.5	−3.2	11 944.3	11 167.3	−6.5	39.1	37.0
Finland	501.0	430.0	−14.2	1 799.0	1 639.0	−8.9	2 300.0	2 069.0	−10.0	21.8	20.8
France	32 228.6	31 241.1	−3.1	87 173.6	79 000.4	−9.4	119 402.2	110 241.5	−7.7	27.0	28.3
Germany	4 161.9			14 725.9			18 887.9			22.0	
Italy	14 476.0			24 097.8			38 573.8			37.5	
Netherlands	5 520.8										
Portugal	1 972.0	1 430.5	−27.5	6 105.9	5 460.8	−10.6	8 077.9	6 891.4	−14.7	24.4	20.8
Sweden	3 278.6	3 296.4	0.5	8 965.9	9 482.7	5.8	12 244.5	12 779.2	4.4	26.8	25.8
Switzwerland	2 588.4	2 319.2	−10.4	4 768.4	4 805.8	0.8	7 356.8	7 125.0	−3.2	35.2	32.6
Turkey	72.9			45.5			118.4			61.6	
Canada[3]				24 569.0							
Australia	1 993.5			26 139.0			28 132.5			7.1	
Yugoslavia	8 802.6	10 571.7	20.1	6 792.4	6 480.0	−4.6	15 595.0	17 051.7	9.3	56.4	62.0
	Of which: in youth hostels										
Austria	496.2	441.0	−11.1	522.3	497.3	−4.8	1 018.5	938.3	−7.9	48.7	47.0
Denmark	357.5	377.2	5.5	404.5	418.8	3.5	762.0	796.0	4.5	46.9	47.4
Germany	658.9			8 607.9			9 266.9			7.1	
Italy	431.2			177.3			608.4			70.9	
Netherlands	349.1										
Sweden	210.5	244.5	16.2	569.5	705.1	23.8	780.0	949.6	21.8	27.0	25.7
Switzwerland	480.0	469.5	−2.2	323.5	323.0	−0.2	803.5	792.5	−1.4	59.7	59.2
Australia	1 183.7										
Yugoslavia	257.9	298.7	15.8	4 458.1	4 451.9	−0.1	4 716.0	4 750.6	0.7	5.5	6.3
	Of which: in private rooms, rented apartements and houses										
Austria	19 582.0	18 201.3	−7.1	5 153.6	4 880.1	−5.3	24 735.6	23 081.4	−6.7	79.2	78.9
Belgium	865.6			6 903.6			7 769.2			11.1	
Italy	17 504.6			93 949.1			111 453.7			15.7	
Sweden	305.5	195.8	−35.9	1 309.3	609.1	−53.5	1 614.8	804.9	−50.2	18.9	24.3
Switzwerland	10 560.0	9 730.0	−7.9	14 210.0	14 240.0	0.2	24 770.0	23 970.0	−3.2	42.6	40.6
Australia[4]	3 083.7			19 846.0			22 929.7			13.4	
Yugoslavia	5 101.9	6 388.0	25.2	9 948.2	9 610.2	−3.4	15 050.1	15 998.2	6.3	33.9	39.9

1. For "Types of accommodatiom covered by the statistics", see Table A.II.4.4.
2. Norway: nights spent on camping sites are not included for 1984.
3. Canada: person-nights; covers also nights spent by Canadians travelling both in Canada and the United States.
4. Australia: for foreign tourists, includes nights spent on rented farms, boats, house-boats, or rented camper-vans. For domestic tourists, includes nights spent on farms, on boats or cabin-cruisers, or on camping outside commercial grounds.

A.II.4.4. TYPES OF ACCOMMODATION COVERED BY THE STATISTICS IN TABLES OF SERIES A.II.4.

Countries	Hotels and similar establishments					Supplementary means of accommodation							
	Hotels	Motels	Boarding houses	Inns	Others[1]	Youth hostels	Camping and caravaning sites	Holiday villages	Mountain huts and shelters	Rented rooms, houses and flats	Sanatoria, health establishments	Recreation homes for children	Others[2]
Austria[3]	x					x	x	x	x	x	x	x	x
Belgium	x				x		x			x	x	x	x
Denmark[3]	x				x	x	x						x
Finland	x	x	x	x		x	x						
France	x						x	x					
Germany	x	x	x	x		x	x	x			x		x
Italy	x	x	x	x		x	x			x	x		x
Netherlands	x		x		x	x	x						
Norway[3, 4]	x						x						
Portugal	x	x	x	x	x		x						
Spain	x	x	x			x	x	x		x			
Sweden	x	x	x		x	x	x			x			
Switzerland	x	x	x	x		x	x	x		x	x		x
Turkey	x	x		x			x	x			x		
Canada	x	x	x			x	x			x			x
Australia	x	x	x		x	x	x						x
Yugoslavia	x	x	x	x		x	x	x	x	x	x		x

1. Other "Hotels and similar establishments" include :
   Belgium: non-licenced establishments;
   Netherlands: youth hostels in Amsterdam;
   Portugal: holiday flats and villages;
   Sweden: boarding houses, inns and resort hotels;
   Australia: hotels and motels without facilities in most rooms and not necessarily providing meals and liquor.
2. Other "supplementary means of accommodation" include :
   Belgium: youth hostels, holiday villages and social tourism establishments;
   Canada: homes of friends or relatives, private cottages, commercial cottages and others (universities, hostels);
   Germany: recreation and holiday homes;
   Italy: recreation homes for children, mountain huts and shelters, holiday homes and religious establishments;
   Switzerland: dormitories in: recreation homes for children, tourist camps, mountain huts and shelters;
   Australia: rented farms, house-boats, rented camper-vans, boats, cabin cruisers, camping outside commercial grounds;
   Yugoslavia: children and student homes, sleeping cars, cabins on ships.
3. Totals available without breakdown for "hotels and similar establishments";
4. Totals available without breakdown for "supplementary means of accommodation".

A.III.1. INTERNATIONAL TOURIST RECEIPTS (R) AND EXPENDITURE (E) IN NATIONAL CURRENCIES

(in millions)

	Currency	Receipts			Expenditure		
		1983	1984	%	1983	1984	%
Austria[1]	Schilling	94 385	100 606	6.6	52 055	52 160	0.2
Belgium-Luxembourg	Franc	87 507	96 800	10.6	107 171	112 900	5.3
Denmark	Krone	11 948	13 379	12.0	11 019	12 634	14.7
Finland	Markka	2 768	2 940	6.2	3 463	4 094	18.2
France	Franc	55 075	66 401	20.6	32 631	37 726	15.6
Germany	Deutsche Mark	13 934	15 595	11.9	38 661	39 594	2.4
Greece	Drachma	103 716	147 518	42.2	28 376	34 098	20.2
Iceland	Krona	682	1 087	59.4	1 218	2 166	77.8
Ireland[2]	Pound	390	442	13.3	363	379	4.4
Italy	Lira	13 721 000	15 099 000	10.0	2 767 000	3 686 000	33.2
Netherlands	Guilder	4 212	4 916	16.7	9 411	9 678	2.8
Norway	Krone	4 910	5 299	7.9	11 586	12 029	3.8
Portugal	Escudo	93 083	140 436	50.9	25 345	32 805	29.4
Spain	Peseta	990 023	1 247 798	26.0	128 601	135 029	5.0
Sweden	Krona	8 150	8 874	8.9	12 458	13 678	9.8
Switzerland	Franc	6 620	7 450	12.5	4 830	5 375	11.3
Turkey	Lira	92 719	204 185	120.2	28 628	100 519	251.1
United Kingdom[3]	Pound	3 651	4 168	14.2	4 047	4 617	14.1
Canada[4]	Dollar	3 182	3 663	15.1	4 825	5 029	4.2
United States	Dollar	11 408	11 426	0.2	13 977	15 805	13.1
Australia	Dollar	1 187	1 401	18.0	1 892	2 247	18.8
New Zealand	Dollar	353	545	54.4	678	843	24.4
Japan	Yen	195 985	231 127	17.9	1 052 314	1 102 057	4.7
Yugoslavia	Dinar	58 892	131 499	123.3			

1. Austria: including international fare payments.
2. Ireland: receipts from and expenditure to Northern Ireland excluded. Receipts excluding all passenger fares. Expnditure excluding passenger fares to Irish carriers only.
3. United Kingdom: including estimates for the Channel Islands receipts and expenditure, and cruise expenditure.
4. Canada: excluding international fare payments and crew spending.

A.III.2. INTERNATIONAL FARE PAYMENTS

RAIL, AIR, SEA AND ROAD TRANSPORT

(In million U.S. dollar)

	Receipts			Expenditure		
	1982	1983	1984	1982	1983	1984
Austria	260.7	267.9		88.5	81.6	
Finland	228.8	206.3	217.9	174.7	176.5	181.2
France[1]		2 411.6				
Germany	1 988.0	1 841.5	2 028.5	1 862.3	1 811.8	1 825.8
Greece	3.3	3.3	4.9	54.4	73.5	74.8
Ireland	171.8	161.6	161.5	126.4	123.0	110.5
Italy[2]	950.0	954.6	962.0	295.7	296.3	313.1
Spain	549.5	513.8		53.4	49.6	
Sweden	455.3	381.5	407.2	473.7	403.5	402.9
Switzwerland	965.7	957.4	915.0	571.5	528.7	517.1
Turkey[3]	185.9	200.1	170.5	172.7	183.8	129.0
United Kingdom[4]	1 482.7			1 681.8		
Canada	571.6	516.1	499.8	857.0	972.1	1 039.0
New Zealand	185.4	260.0	277.3			
Japan	556.7			1 715.7		

1. France: air transport.
2. Italy: air and sea transport.
3. Turkey: air transport, 1984 receipts includes also rail and sea transport.
4. United Kingdom: air and sea transport.

A.III.3. INTERNATIONAL TOURIST RECEIPTS (R) AND EXPENDITURE (E) IN US DOLLARS

REGIONAL BREAKDOWN

(Rounded figures in million dollars)

	R/E	Europe			North America			Australasia-Japan		
		1983	1984	% 84/83	1983	1984	% 84/83	1983	1984	% 84/8
Austria[1]	R	4 711.3	4 423.9	-6.1	431.0	491.2	14.0	12.6	18.4	46.6
	E	2 412.1	2 161.0	-10.4	280.8	271.9	-3.2	10.6	14.6	38.0
Belgium-Luxembourg	R									
	E									
Denmark	R	1 048.0	1 018.1	-2.9	189.7	198.0	4.3	3.9	4.2	5.5
	E	965.8	975.4	1.0	151.5	151.8	0.2	3.0	3.4	14.5
Finland	R	416.4	408.1	-2.0	65.1	65.5	0.6	2.7	3.5	29.8
	E	442.1	490.4	10.9	100.8	106.9	6.1	3.1	3.8	25.4
France	R	4 129.1	3 901.2	-5.5	2 051.4	2 442.6	19.1	148.9	300.7	101.9
	E	2 448.2	2 231.2	-8.9	992.9	1 080.5	8.8	33.1	158.9	380.7
Germany	R	4 158.1	4 033.5	-3.0	617.6	711.1	15.1	182.5	199.9	9.5
	E	12 735.2	11 622.4	-8.7	571.0	542.4	-5.0	100.7	90.6	-9.9
Greece	R	687.4	760.3	10.6	449.7	502.0	11.6	18.5	22.7	22.6
	E	202.0	188.9	-6.5	140.0	134.4	-4.0	2.1	2.1	-2.6
Iceland	R	12.6	15.2	21.0	14.9	18.8	26.6			
	E	30.3	34.9	15.1	18.7	33.3	78.2			
Ireland[2]	R	336.8	316.4	-6.0	129.2	142.0	9.8			
	E	408.9	364.1	-10.9	37.3	40.1	7.5			
Italy	R	6 232.0	5 962.9	-4.3	2 703.0	2 551.5	-5.6	12.0	15.5	29.7
	E	1 034.4	1 213.2	17.3	744.4	845.3	13.6	4.7	4.7	0.1
Netherlands	R	1 110.8	1 100.4	-0.9	296.8	351.5	18.4	11.2	17.1	52.9
	E	2 926.7	2 621.9	-10.4	277.9	280.8	1.0	11.2	12.5	11.2
Norway	R	512.9	473.8	-7.6	149.3	167.4	12.1	3.6	2.5	-31.2
	E	1 340.9	1 224.7	-8.7	215.9	211.8	-1.9	4.9	4.2	-15.6
Portugal	R	530.9	595.9	12.2	296.7	344.9	16.2	0.9	1.3	36.2
	E	142.3	132.0	-7.3	73.7	82.8	12.3	0.5	0.4	-15.2
Spain	R	4 915.2								
	E									
Sweden	R	812.6	783.0	-3.6	137.9	185.3	34.4	0.4	2.7	579.6
	E	1 142.9	1 212.0	6.0	255.1	286.8	12.4	5.3	6.6	24.3
Switzerland	R									
	E									
Turkey	R									
	E									
United Kingdom[3]	R	1 846.2	1 801.7	-2.4	1 418.7	1 579.5	11.3	357.7	435.1	21.6
	E	4 097.0	4 260.8	4.0	630.5	594.8	-5.7	154.6	183.6	18.8
Canada[4]	R	313.2			1 980.7			79.5		
	E	662.1			2 686.7			83.6		
United States	R									
	E									
Australia	R	296.7			225.4			276.8		
	E									
New Zealand	R									
	E									
Japan	R									
	E									
Yugoslavia	R									
	E									

Important notice: the amounts, excluding those concerning Canada, United States, Ireland, Italy, United Kingdom and Switzerland, refer to receipts and expenditure registered in foreign currency grouped regionally according to the denomination of the currency.
1. Austria: including international fare payments.

A.III.3. INTERNATIONAL TOURIST RECEIPTS (R) AND EXPENDITURE (E) IN US DOLLARS (Continued)

REGIONAL BREAKDOWN

Total OECD Countries			Non-Member countries			All countries			
1983	1984	% 84/83	1983	1984	% 84/83	1983	1984	% 84/83	
5 154.9	4 933.5	−4.3	98.0	95.1	−2.9	5 253.0	5 028.6	−4.3	Austria[1]
2 703.5	2 447.5	−9.5	193.6	159.6	−17.5	2 897.1	2 607.1	−10.0	
						1 711.5	1 675.8	−2.1	Belgium-Luxembourg
						2 096.0	1 954.6	−6.7	
1 241.7	1 220.3	−1.7	64.8	71.8	10.6	1 306.5	1 292.0	−1.1	Denmark
1 120.2	1 130.5	0.9	84.7	89.5	5.6	1 205.0	1 220.1	1.3	
484.1	477.1	−1.5	13.3	12.7	−4.8	497.4	489.7	−1.5	Finland
545.9	601.4	10.2	76.4	80.6	5.6	622.3	682.0	9.6	
6 329.4	6 644.5	5.0	897.1	953.4	6.3	7 226.5	7 597.9	5.1	France
3 474.1	3 470.6	−0.1	807.5	800.2	−0.9	4 281.6	4 270.8	−0.3	
4 958.3	4 944.5	−0.3	499.0	534.4	7.1	5 457.2	5 478.9	0.4	Germany
13 406.9	12 255.5	−8.6	1 734.6	1 654.7	−4.6	15 141.5	13 910.2	−8.1	
1 155.7	1 285.0	11.2	24.2	24.5	1.0	1 179.9	1 309.4	11.0	Greece
344.1	325.4	−5.5	20.9	15.1	−27.5	365.0	340.5	−6.7	
27.4	34.0	24.1		0.1		27.4	34.1	24.3	Iceland
49.0	68.2	39.2		0.1		49.0	68.3	39.3	
466.0	458.4	−1.6	18.6	20.6	10.5	484.7	479.0	−1.2	Ireland[2]
446.1	404.2	−9.4	5.0	6.5	30.8	451.1	410.7	−9.0	
8 947.0	8 529.9	−4.7	86.4	64.8	−25.0	9 033.4	8 594.8	−4.9	Italy
1 783.4	2 063.1	15.7	38.5	35.0	−9.0	1 822.0	2 098.2	15.2	
1 418.8	1 469.1	3.5	57.1	63.0	10.2	1 476.0	1 532.0	3.8	Netherlands
3 215.8	2 915.1	−9.4	82.0	101.0	23.1	3 297.8	3 016.1	−8.5	
665.7	643.6	−3.3	7.4	5.8	−22.2	673.1	649.4	−3.5	Norway
1 561.7	1 440.6	−7.8	26.2	33.5	27.8	1 587.9	1 474.1	−7.2	
829.0	942.4	13.7	11.2	17.0	51.5	840.2	959.4	14.2	Portugal
216.7	215.4	−0.6	12.1	8.8	−27.5	228.8	224.1	−2.0	
4 915.2			1 982.1			6 898.0	7 759.9	12.5	Spain
						896.0	839.7	−6.3	
950.9	971.0	2.1	112.0	101.7	−9.3	1 063.0	1 072.6	0.9	Sweden
1 403.8	1 505.5	7.2	221.1	147.8	−33.1	1 624.9	1 653.3	1.8	
						3 153.3	3 170.7	0.5	Switzerland
						2 300.7	2 287.6	−0.6	
						414.5	561.8	35.5	Turkey
						128.0	276.6	116.1	
3 625.6	3 819.0	5.3	1 908.3	1 727.2	−9.5	5 533.9	5 546.2	0.2	United Kingdom[3]
4 886.7	5 044.6	3.2	1 095.9	1 097.8	0.2	5 982.6	6 142.4	2.7	
2 373.5			208.5			2 582.0	2 828.6	9.5	Canada[4]
3 432.4			482.8			3 915.2	3 883.4	−0.8	
						11 408.0	11 426.0	0.2	United States
						13 977.0	15 805.0	13.1	
798.9			271.4			1 070.3	1 228.3	14.8	Australia
						1 706.0	1 969.9	15.5	
						236.1	308.7	30.7	New Zealand
						452.8	476.9	5.3	
						825.3	972.9	17.9	Japan
						4 431.2	4 639.2	4.7	
						928.9	1 053.7	13.4	Yugoslavia

Ireland: receipts from and expenditure to Northern Ireland excluded. Receipts excluding all passenger fares. Expenditure excluding passenger fares to Irish carriers only.
United Kingdom: including estimates for the Channel Islands receipts and expenditure, and cruise expenditure.
Canada: excluding international fare payments and crew spending.

A.III.4. NOMINAL EXCHANGE RATES OF NATIONAL CURRENCIES AGAINST THE US DOLLAR

	Exchange rates (units per U.S. dollar)			Per cent changes	
	1982	1983	1984	83/82	84/83
Austria	17.06	17.97	20.01	5.33	11.35
Belgium-Luxembourg	45.70	51.13	57.76	11.89	12.97
Denmark	8.33	9.14	10.36	9.74	13.24
Finland	4.81	5.56	6.00	15.62	7.88
France	6.57	7.62	8.74	15.97	14.67
Germany	2.43	2.55	2.85	5.22	11.48
Greece	66.65	87.90	112.66	31.88	28.16
Iceland	12.30	24.85	31.73	102.12	27.66
Ireland	0.70	0.80	0.92	14.25	14.67
Italy	1 352.66	1 518.94	1 756.73	12.29	15.65
Netherlands	2.67	2.85	3.21	6.87	12.44
Norway	6.45	7.30	8.16	13.10	11.85
Portugal	79.39	110.79	146.38	39.54	32.13
Spain	109.80	143.52	160.80	30.71	12.04
Sweden	6.28	7.67	8.27	22.04	7.90
Switzerland	2.04	2.10	2.35	2.91	11.92
Turkey	160.75	223.67	363.46	39.14	62.50
United Kingdom	0.57	0.66	0.75	15.22	13.91
Canada	1.23	1.23	1.30	−0.08	5.08
United States	1.00	1.00	1.00	0.00	0.00
Australia	0.99	1.11	1.14	12.48	2.85
New Zealand	1.33	1.50	1.77	12.29	18.09
Japan	249.08	237.48	237.55	−4.66	0.03
Yugoslavia	45.12	63.40	124.80	40.52	96.85

Source : Figures provided by the OECD Balance of Payments Division, except for Yugoslavia.

A.III.5. EXPENDITURE OF U.S. RESIDENTS TRAVELLING ABROAD

(In million U.S. dollars)

	1981	1982	1983
I. EXPENDITURE ABROAD(1)	11 252	12 205	13 797
Canada(2)	1 843	1 747	1 980
Mexico	2 862	3 324	3 576
- Persons visiting Mexican border only	1 648	2 089	1 996
Overseas areas	6 547	7 134	8 241
of which: . Europe and Mediterranean area(3)	3 587	3 787	4 412
of which: European Member countries	3 123	3 413	3 991
. West Indies and Central America	1 277	1 349	1 519
- Bermuda	192	230	220
- Bahamas	243	340	402
- Jamaica	127	153	183
- Other British West Indies	252	188	225
- Dutch West Indies	249	155	200
. South America	383	380	422
. Other overseas areas	1 300	1 618	1 888
- Japan	214	272	302
- Hong Kong	151	197	212
- Australia - New-Zealand	343	367	492
II. FARE PAYMENTS	..	..	
Foreign-flag carriers	4 487	4 772	5 532
U.S.-flag carriers	..	..	

1. Excludes travel by military personnel and other Government employees stationed abroad, their dependents and United States citizens residing abroad; includes shore expenditure of United States cruise travellers.
2. Excluding fare payments and crew spending.
3. For more data concerning Europe and Mediterranean area and individual Member countries in Europe, see Table III.6.
Source: U.S. Department of Commerce, Bureau of Economic Analysis.

A.III.6. NUMBER AND EXPENDITURE OF U.S. RESIDENTS TRAVELLING OVERSEAS

	Number of travellers (thousands)(1)			Total expenditure (millions of U.S. dollars) (2)			Average expenditure (U.S. dollars) (3)		
	1981	1982	1983	1981	1982	1983	1981	1982	1983
I. Europe and Mediterranean area	3 931	4 144	5 026	3 587	3 787	4 412	912	914	878
of which: European Member countries	..	..		3 123	3 413	3 991	..	..	
II. West Indies and Central America	2 453	2 637	3 107	1 277	1 349	1 519	483	476	459
III. South America	567	529	578	383	380	422	674	715	728
IV. Other overseas countries	1 089	1 200	1 443	1 300	1 618	1 888	1 191	1 346	1 307
TOTAL (I - IV)	8 040	8 510	10 154	6 547	7 134	8 241	802	827	802

1. Excludes travel by military personnel and other Government employees stationed abroad, their dependents and United States citizens residing abroad and cruise travellers.
2. Includes shore expenditure of cruise travellers; excludes fares.
3. Excludes shore expenditure of cruise travellers.
Source: U.S. Department of Commerce, Bureau of Economic Analysis, based on data of the U.S. Department of Justice, Immigration and Naturalization Service.

A. III.7. NUMBER AND EXPENDITURE OF U.S. RESIDENTS TRAVELLING IN EUROPE AND THE MEDITERRANEAN AREA

		1981	1982	1983
Europe and Mediterranean area	A	3 931	4 144	5 026
	B	3 587	3 787	4 412
	C	912	914	878
European Member countries	A	..	..	
	B	3 123	3 413	3 991
	C	..	..	
of which: Austria	A	306	533	551
	B	74	145	150
	C	242	272	272
Belgium-Luxembourg	A	252	280	378
	B	45	57	65
	C	179	204	172
Denmark	A	208	206	265
	B	65	48	73
	C	313	233	275
France	A	863	1 005	1 270
	B	375	464	596
	C	435	462	469
Germany	A	834	1 061	1 118
	B	361	411	416
	C	433	387	372
Greece	A	350	242	384
	B	171	145	225
	C	489	599	586
Ireland	A	167	209	178
	B	84	104	84
	C	503	498	472
Italy	A	726	876	877
	B	301	490	485
	C	415	559	553
Netherlands	A	330	383	521
	B	75	97	128
	C	227	253	246
Norway	A	167	121	175
	B	89	55	60
	C	533	455	343
Portugal	A	138	117	98
	B	41	45	27
	C	297	385	276
Spain	A	397	290	385
	B	208	153	208
	C	524	528	540
Sweden	A	173	133	249
	B	65	45	71
	C	376	338	285
Switzerland	A	502	655	791
	B	127	206	294
	C	253	317	372
United Kingdom	A	1 281	1 489	1 918
	B	952	895	1 061
	C	743	601	553

A: Number of U.S. travellers (in thousands): excludes travel by military personnel and other Goverment employees stationed abroad, their dependants and United States citizens residing abroad and cruise travellers. Since some travellers visit more than one country, the total of estimated visits to specific countries is greater than the number of travellers .
B: Total expenditure (in million U.S. dollars): includes shore expenditure of cruise travellers but not their transportation fares.
C: Average expenditure for U.S. travellers (in U.S. dollars).
Source: U.S. Department of Commerce, Bureau of Economic Analysis, based on data of the U.S. Department of Justice, Immigration and Naturalization Service.

A.IV.FOREIGN TOURISM BY MODE OF TRANSPORT

	1983					1984				
	Breakdown of arrivals (%)				Total number of arrivals in thousands	Breakdown of arrivals (%)				Total number of arrivals in thousands
	Air	Sea	Rail	Road		Air	Sea	Rail	Road	
Belgium[1]	15.6	13.5	70.9		34 564.8	55.2	44.8			10 310.4
Greece[2]	73.3	13.0	2.5	11.2	4 778.5	73.8	11.2	2.5	12.5	5 523.2
Iceland	91.5	8.5			77.6					
Ireland[3]	8.6	9.6	0.9	81.0	9 797.0	8.8	10.1	0.9	80.2	9 891.0
Italy[4]	10.4	2.2	12.2	75.2	46 576.8	9.9	2.0	10.4	77.8	49 150.7
Portugal[5]	15.2	2.4	1.0	81.4	8 875.0	15.5	1.9	1.1	81.5	9 811.0
Spain[6]	28.3	3.5	5.9	62.3	41 263.3	31.3	3.3	6.1	59.4	42 931.7
Turkey[7]	33.4	27.3	4.7	34.6	1 625.1	32.3	23.9	2.0	41.7	2 117.1
United Kingdom[8]	61.5	38.5			12 464.0	62.2	37.8			13 712.0
Canada[9]	22.1	1.9	0.6	75.4	12 490.7	23.7	7.8	0.5	68.0	13 416.6
Australia[10]	99.4	0.6			943.9					
Japan[11]	97.8	2.2			2 112.8					
Yugoslavia[12]	5.1	3.1	5.1	86.7	18 731.9	5.5	3.0	5.6	85.8	19 716.6

1. Belgium: air and sea include both arrivals and departures of foreign and domestic visitors. Rail refers to international traffic only.
2. Greece: visitors arrivals.
3. Ireland: visitors arrivals, including those from Northern Ireland.
4. Italy: visitor arrivals.
5. Portugal: visitor arrivals.
6. Spain: visitor arrivals.
7. Turkey: traveller arrivals.
8. United Kingdom: visitor arrivals.
9. Canada: tourist arrivals.
10. Australia: arrivals of short-term visitors (less than one year).
11. Japan: visitor arrivals including those of returning residents and excluding crew members.
12. Yougoslavia: visitor arrivals.

A.V.1. CAPACITY IN HOTELS AND SIMILAR ESTABLISHMENTS

(In thousands)

Country	Year	Hotels	%	Motels	%	Boarding houses	%	Inns	%	Others	%	Total	%
Austria(1)	1983	..	..	..	..	..	..	..	..	..	..	655.6	0.7
	1984	..	..	..	..	..	..	..	..	..	..	662.9	1.1
Belgium(2)	1983	66.5	4.5	..	..	..	..	..	..	18.6	0.2	85.1	3.6
	1984	65.2	*	..	..	..	..	..	..	18.0	*	83.2	*
Denmark(3)	1983	..	..	..	..	..	..	..	..	..	..	71.4	2.7
	1984	..	..	..	..	..	..	..	..	..	..	71.3	-0.1
Finland(4)	1983	55.9	8.2	..	..	..	..	7.9	-25.4	5.0	42.4	68.7	4.6
	1984	58.7	5.1	..	..	..	..	7.5	-4.7	6.9	38.5	73.1	6.3
France(5)	1983	481.0	1.3	..	..	..	..	..	..	..	..	481.0	1.3
	1984	..	..	..	..	..	..	..	..	..	..	..	..
Germany(6)	1983	..	..	..	..	..	..	..	..	..	..	..	..
	1984	668.0	..	..	..	152.7	..	255.2	..	..	..	1 075.9	..
Greece(7)	1983	297.5	4.7	6.1	2.4	11.6	7.2	5.2	6.5	..	..	320.5	4.8
	1984	297.6	0.0	7.3	19.8	12.6	8.3	5.1	-1.1	..	..	322.7	0.7
Iceland	1983	2.2	0.0	..	..	..	..	..	..	2.2	0.0	4.4	0.0
	1984	..	..	..	..	..	..	..	..	..	..	..	..
Ireland(8)	1983	40.2	-4.7	..	..	4.6	-8.0	..	..	..	..	44.8	-5.1
	1984	40.1	-0.2	..	..	4.3	-5.2	..	..	..	..	44.4	-0.7
Italy(9)	1983	1 303.8	8.5	..	..	195.3	-24.2	99.2	-21.6	..	..	1 598.4	0.8
	1984	..	..	..	..	..	..	..	..	..	..	..	..
Netherlands	1983	91.6	1.8	..	..	10.5	-1.4	..	..	2.8	16.3	104.9	1.8
	1984	..	..	..	..	..	..	..	..	..	..	..	..
Norway(10)	1983	54.6	-4.7	..	..	..	..	47.0	0.0	..	..	101.6	-2.6
	1984	55.2	1.0	..	..	..	..	40.8	-13.1	..	..	96.0	-5.5
Portugal(11)	1983	62.3	2.4	0.7	-5.7	36.6	0.3	3.3	-5.9	23.8	6.0	126.8	2.2
	1984	63.6	2.0	1.0	30.0	38.1	4.1	3.5	4.0	24.9	4.7	131.0	3.3
Spain(12)	1983	834.5	0.5	..	..	170.7	-0.2	..	..	..	..	1 005.2	0.3
	1984	..	..	..	..	..	..	..	..	..	..	..	..
Sweden(13)	1983	66.2	2.5	18.2	0.8	37.4	0.8	..	..	..	..	121.8	1.7
	1984	76.3	15.2	19.1	4.6	41.4	10.8	..	..	..	..	136.8	12.3
Switzerland(14)	1983	234.6	0.6	6.8	1.1	..	..	33.1	-1.0	..	..	274.6	0.4
	1984	235.3	0.3	7.0	4.3	..	..	33.1	-0.3	..	..	275.4	0.3
Turkey(15)	1983	44.1	8.1	10.6	-3.3	2.0	0.3	1.6	-8.2	..	..	58.2	5.0
	1984	46.1	4.5	10.1	-4.5	2.2	13.6	2.0	22.0	..	..	60.4	3.7
Canada(16)	1983	211.4	3.3	79.2	0.9	..	..	..	..	0.6	0.9	291.3	2.7
	1984	..	..	..	..	..	..	..	..	..	..	..	..
Australia(17)	1983	..	..	..	..	..	..	..	..	..	..	102.9	3.3
	1984	33.9	..	73.5	..	..	..	..	..	..	..	107.4	4.3
Japan(18)	1983	85.6	..	..	..	..	..	86.3	..	..	..	171.9	..
	1984	..	..	..	..	..	..	..	..	..	..	..	..
Yugoslavia(19)	1983	277.9	4.9	10.3	-1.2	5.0	-2.6	1.3	5.0	8.1	-2.7	302.6	4.4
	1984	294.6	6.0	10.5	1.3	4.7	-4.8	1.2	-8.8	7.8	-3.9	318.8	5.3

Notice: this table contains data on available bed capacity unless otherwise stated in the following notes by country.
%:   percentage variation over the preceding year.
*:   not comparable over the preceding year.
 1. Austria: position at 31st August 1983 and 1984.
 2. Belgium: hotels includes motels, inns and boarding houses. Others includes non-licenced establishments.
 3. Denmark: position at 31st July 1983 and 1984.
 4. Finland: position at 31st December 1982 and 1983. Hotels includes motels. Boarding houses includes inns. Others includes some youth hostels and holiday villages.
 5. France: number of rooms. Hotels includes motels.
 6. Germany: position at April 1984.
 7. Greece: motels includes bungalows.
 8. Ireland: hotels includes motels. Boarding houses includes inns.
 9. Italy: position at 31st December 1983. Hotels includes motels.
10. Norway: position at 31st December 1983 and 1984. Hotels includes approved hotels only. Inns includes boarding houses.
11. Portugal: position at 31st July 1983 and 1984. Hotels includes studio-hotels. Inns includes private and state-owned inns. Others includes holiday flats and villages.
12. Spain: position at 31st December 1983. Boarding houses = "fondas" and "casas de huespedes".
13. Sweden: inns includes resort hotels.
14. Switzerland: position at 31st December 1983 and 1984. Hotels includes boarding houses.
15. Turkey: position at 31st December 1983 and 1984 of establishments approved by Ministry of Culture and Tourism.
16. Canada: number of rooms. Others includes tourist courts and cabins.
17. Australia: position at December 1984. Number of rooms.
18. Japan: number of rooms.
19. Yugoslavia: position at 31st August 1983 and 1984.

A.V.2. CAPACITY IN SUPPLEMENTARY MEANS OF ACCOMMODATION

(In thousands)

Country	Year	Youth Hostels	%	Camping sites Number	Places	%	Holiday villages	%	Rented rooms, Houses and flats	%	Sanatoria and Health establish-ments	%	Recreation homes for children	%	Others	%	Total	%
Austria	1983	9.1	-5.7	474	..	..	75.5	5.2	392.2	-2.7	16.1	-1.5	30.2	3.3	19.8	18.4	550.9	-0.6
	1984	9.6	5.5	491	..	..	82.0	8.6	377.3	-3.8	16.6	2.8	30.1	-0.4	18.2	-0.8	541.8	-1.7
Belgium(1)	1983	..	..	..	..	0.8	..	..	..	..	3.6	-1.8	27.5	0.8	49.2	8.3	412.7	1.6
	1984	..	..	..	..	..	..	..	..	..	2.8	*	26.2	*	46.8	*	409.1	*
Denmark	1983	9.3	3.3	524	..	..	..	..	..	..	..	..	..	..	..	..	9.3	3.3
	1984	9.4	1.1	519	..	..	..	..	..	..	..	..	..	..	..	..	9.4	1.1
France	1983	..	..	8373	2340.9	4.4	..	..	..	..	..	..	..	..	..	..	2340.9	4.4
	1984	..	..	..	..	..	..	..	..	..	..	..	..	..	..	..	..	..
Germany(2)	1983	..	..	..	..	..	..	..	..	..	..	..	..	..	..	..	..	..
	1984	92.8	..	..	..	..	167.6	..	..	..	113.0	..	..	..	117.2	..	490.6	..
Greece(3)	1983	..	..	196	..	21.0	..	..	8.0	53.4	..	..	..	..	8.9	0.0	74.0	20.7
	1984	..	..	234	..	15.0	..	..	11.1	38.4	..	..	..	..	8.9	0.0	85.6	15.8
Iceland(4)	1983	0.4	..	..	..	..	..	..	..	..	..	..	..	..	0.9	..	1.3	..
	1984	..	..	..	..	..	..	..	..	..	..	..	..	..	..	..	..	..
Ireland(5)	1983	..	..	..	..	..	..	..	..	..	..	..	..	..	8.4	1.2	8.4	1.2
	1984	..	..	..	..	..	..	..	..	..	..	..	..	..	..	..	..	..
Italy(6)	1983	9.4	15.8	1976	960.0	-2.9	..	..	1958.3	-0.2	..	..	..	..	238.1	-0.8	3165.9	-1.1
	1984	..	..	..	..	..	..	..	..	..	..	..	..	..	..	..	..	..
Netherlands(7)	1983	8.2	32.2	2505	1469.0	3.1	..	..	..	..	..	..	..	..	..	..	1477.2	3.2
	1984	..	..	..	..	..	..	..	..	..	..	..	..	..	..	..	..	..
Norway	1983	7.1	0.0	1429	239.0	0.0	..	..	..	..	..	..	..	..	..	..	246.1	0.0
	1984	7.1	1.2	1479	238.0	-0.4	..	..	..	..	..	..	..	..	..	..	245.2	-0.3
Portugal(8)	1983	..	..	104	213.1	14.4	..	..	..	..	..	..	8.9	-5.9	..	..	222.0	13.5
	1984	..	..	105	206.2	-3.2	..	..	..	..	..	..	8.7	-2.8	..	..	214.9	-3.2
Spain	1983	..	..	..	..	..	..	..	297.7	5.3	..	..	..	..	..	..	297.7	5.3
	1984	..	..	..	..	..	..	..	..	..	..	..	..	..	..	..	..	..
Sweden	1983	13.1	4.0	632	250.0	0.0	29.2	2.2	..	..	..	..	..	..	..	..	292.3	0.4
	1984	14.5	10.8	632	250.0	0.0	33.9	16.0	..	..	..	..	..	..	..	..	298.4	2.0
Switzerland(9)	1983	8.2	0.7	697	264.0	0.4	..	..	360.0	0.0	6.6	1.9	..	..	214.0	4.9	852.8	1.3
	1984	8.1	-1.0	694	271.0	2.7	..	..	370.0	2.8	6.7	2.0	..	..	212.5	-0.7	868.3	1.8
Turkey(10)	1983	..	..	27	0.3	0.0	6.0	3.1	..	..	0.3	0.0	..	..	1.0	118.7	7.7	10.8
	1984	..	..	29	0.3	0.0	6.2	3.1	..	..	0.3	0.0	..	..	1.0	0.0	7.9	2.4
Canada(11)	1983	2.7	30.3	2962	0.5	-11.0	..	..	..	..	..	..	..	..	1.1	6.8	1.6	0.0
	1984	..	..	..	..	..	..	..	..	..	..	..	..	..	..	..	..	..
Australia(12)	1983	..	..	1875	205.4	-0.2	..	..	..	..	..	..	..	..	..	..	205.4	-0.2
	1984	..	..	1873	207.7	1.1	..	..	..	..	..	..	..	..	..	..	207.7	1.1
Japan	1983	33.3	-0.9	..	..	..	..	..	..	..	..	..	..	..	..	..	33.3	-0.9
	1984	..	..	..	..	..	..	..	..	..	..	..	..	..	..	..	..	..
Yugoslavia(13)	1983	58.1	0.7	356	328.0	-1.0	107.8	2.4	358.7	1.8	13.4	0.4	..	..	20.3	-3.8	893.7	0.6
	1984	56.5	-2.8	319	342.3	4.4	106.8	-0.9	364.5	1.6	13.4	-0.2	..	..	25.3	24.3	916.3	2.5

Notice: this table contains data on available bed capacity unless otherwise stated in the following notes by country.
% percentage variation over the preceding year.
* not comparable to preceding year.

1. Belgium: others includes youth hostels, holiday villages and social tourism establishments.
2. Germany: youth hostels includes mountain huts and shelters. Others includes recreation homes for children.
3. Greece: others includes holiday centres.
4. Iceland: others includes mountain huts and shelters.
5. Ireland: Others includes town and country homes and farmhouses.
6. Italy: camping includes holiday villages. Others includes recreation homes for children, holiday homes and religious establishments.
7. Netherlands: camping includes holiday villages.
8. Portugal: recreation homes for children includes youth hostels.
9. Switzerland: others includes dormitories in: recreation homes for children, tourist camps, mountain huts and shelters.
10. Turkey: others includes non-licensed establishments.
11. Canada: number of rooms except for youth hostels (number of beds). Others includes "outfitters".
12. Australia: number of rooms. Camping sites includes all sites (with and without facilities), cabins and flats.
13. Yugoslavia: others includes mountain huts and shelters, 7.4 % thousand beds in 1984 (+1.6 % compared with 1983) and 7.3 thousand beds in 1983 (+9.3 % compared with 1982).

A.V.3. ANNUAL HOTEL OCCUPANCY RATES

Country			Annual rates (in per cent)		
			1982	1983	1984
Austria		B	27.6	26.8	26.7
Denmark		R	43.2	43.6	44.6
Finland		R	57.3	52.6	53.2
Germany		B	35.8	34.3	..
Greece		B	45.9	..	..
Italy		B	37.6	36.3	..
Norway		B	41.3	41.1	41.7
Portugal		B	51.0	..	..
Spain		B	52.2	..	..
Sweden		B	32.9	35.5	35.5
Switzerland		B	34.2	33.7	34.0
Turkey		B	43.3	43.6	..
United Kingdom		B	37.3	41.5	43.7
Australia		B	11.6	11.0	11.5
Japan		B	71.7	73.5	..
Yugoslavia		B	46.8	..	..

Concerning the coverage see notes to Tables V.4 and V.4 (continued).

B = Beds
R = Rooms

A.V.4. MONTHLY HOTEL OCCUPANCY RATES

Month	Austria (1) (B)			Denmark (R)			Finland (2) (R)		
	1982	1983	1984	1982	1983	1984	1982	1983	1984
January	32.8	30.5	31.6	26.3	26.1	27.4	48.0	44.0	45.7
February	39.8	39.7	38.7	28.9	28.1	30.2	60.0	55.0	54.7
March	28.2	32.0	32.0	38.2	37.9	37.6	65.0	59.0	57.5
April	20.7	16.4	18.5	36.3	36.6	36.7	58.0	54.0	50.9
May	13.9	14.4	12.4	46.2	48.8	49.3	58.0	51.0	54.2
June	26.4	25.5	25.6	55.0	57.3	54.7	59.0	53.0	54.0
July	51.7	49.3	46.1	67.4	68.1	67.4	61.0	57.0	57.0
August	55.6	51.9	51.3	64.4	65.1	66.8	58.0	56.0	56.8
September	28.9	28.2	27.4	51.3	51.3	53.2	62.0	58.0	58.6
October	10.1	10.2	10.2	41.9	42.4	45.1	58.0	54.0	55.9
November	5.1	5.3	6.0	37.5	37.1	40.7	58.0	55.0	54.6
December	18.8	18.6	20.2	24.4	24.1	26.5	43.0	36.0	38.3

Month	Germany (B)			Greece (3) (B)			Italy (B)		
	1982	1983	1984	1982	1983	1984	1982	1983	1984
January	22.8	20.2	24.1	27.0	..	..	26.7	25.5	..
February	26.1	24.4	27.9	26.9	..	..	31.6	30.3	..
March	26.7	26.3	28.8	30.9	..	..	30.1	30.3	..
April	33.2	29.1	33.7	45.0	..	..	34.2	31.9	..
May	40.8	38.5	39.4	51.7	..	..	32.6	31.8	..
June	47.4	45.0	..	57.6	..	..	43.6	40.0	..
July	53.6	51.9	..	73.1	..	..	58.9	56.2	..
August	53.7	51.7	..	79.3	..	..	72.8	70.1	..
September	49.1	48.6	..	63.1	..	..	45.5	44.5	..
October	36.6	36.6	..	43.5	..	..	32.8	31.8	..
November	20.6	20.8	..	27.1	..	..	21.1	21.6	..
December	18.5	18.7	..	26.0	..	..	22.1	21.4	..

Month	Norway (B)			Portugal (4) (B)			Spain (B)		
	1982	1983	1984	1982	1983	1984	1982	1983	1984
January	33.1	29.9	31.1	32.4	..	..	39.5	..	..
February	44.0	43.2	42.5	38.9	..	..	43.8	..	..
March	47.8	43.4	46.2	46.2	..	..	45.9	..	..
April	36.8	40.8	35.9	53.1	..	..	49.0	..	..
May	35.4	31.9	33.3	54.9	..	..	50.8	..	..
June	49.4	50.8	49.3	55.5	..	..	56.0	..	..
July	53.9	55.1	57.4	62.6	..	..	66.2	..	..
August	50.9	51.5	53.6	77.6	..	..	75.7	..	..
September	44.0	43.0	44.7	67.0	..	..	66.2	..	..
October	38.9	38.4	39.1	54.0	..	..	52.6	..	..
November	35.4	36.0	36.2	38.0	..	..	42.3	..	..
December	25.4	29.3	31.5	31.2	..	..	37.9	..	..

B = Beds
R = Rooms
Occupancy rates registered in hotels only, unless otherwise stated.
1. Austria: bed occupancy rates based on all forms of accommodation.
2. Finland: room occupancy rates in hotels and motels. Alterations in the method of calculation show lower occupancy rates in 1983.
3. Greece: available bed occupancy rate registered in hotels, furnished apartments and holiday centres.
4. Portugal: bed occupancy rates in hotels, studio-hotels, motels and state-owned inns. Figures based on sample surveys.

A.V.4. **MONTHLY HOTEL OCCUPANCY RATES** (Continued)

Month	Sweden (1)(B)			Switzerland (B)			Turkey (2) (B)		
	1982	1983	1984	1982	1983	1984	1982	1983	1984
January	25.3	24.7	26.1	30.9	29.6	30.4	32.6	29.4	..
February	36.4	35.1	35.8	39.8	38.9	35.8	38.2	34.0	..
March	40.4	37.5	36.8	35.9	37.1	37.6	37.0	35.8	..
April	35.5	35.4	34.0	31.3	28.5	30.4	42.7	40.0	..
May	33.5	33.0	34.2	28.1	27.1	26.6	43.4	43.9	..
June	41.1	40.2	38.7	34.9	35.7	37.9	44.7	46.8	..
July	53.6	55.9	55.0	48.1	47.7	48.3	51.8	55.0	..
August	41.3	42.8	42.0	52.4	50.5	50.2	58.2	62.8	..
September	34.4	34.9	35.1	43.8	43.9	43.3	54.6	54.5	..
October	32.7	31.9	32.9	27.7	29.4	27.9	45.3	44.6	..
November	30.6	30.6	30.8	15.6	15.0	16.0	35.9	40.5	..
Décember	24.0	23.5	24.4	22.0	21.3	22.9	34.7	35.8	..

Month	United Kingdom(3)(B)			Australia (4)(B)			Japan (5) (B)		
	1982	1983	1984	1982	1983	1984	1982	1983	1984
January	22.0	24.0	26.0				64.7	63.1	..
February	27.0	28.0	32.0				73.3	75.9	..
March	31.0	34.0	36.0	37.7	33.8	34.8	78.2	77.9	..
April	33.0	37.0	41.0				72.6	72.8	..
May	38.0	41.0	45.0				74.3	77.8	..
June	45.0	48.0	53.0	34.8	31.3	35.6	66.8	69.8	..
July	51.0	57.0	57.0				69.0	72.5	..
August	56.0	60.0	60.0				77.2	79.5	..
September	51.0	55.0	57.0	35.2	35.0	35.3	68.8	73.1	..
October	40.0	47.0	48.0				81.2	82.8	..
November	30.0	37.0	38.0				76.5	78.7	..
Décember	23.0	30.0	31.0	31.4	32.2	32.7	57.2	57.9	..

Month	Yugoslavia (B)		
	1982	1983	1984
January	28.5	..	..
February	27.0	..	..
March	27.8	..	..
April	37.6	..	..
May	57.1	..	..
June	70.0	..	..
July	79.2	..	..
August	81.0	..	..
September	69.0	..	..
October	40.4	..	..
November	23.2	..	..
Décember	20.9	..	..

B = Beds
R = Rooms
Occupancy rates registered in hotels only, unless otherwise stated.
1. Sweden: occupancy rates in hotels, motels, resort hotels, holiday villages and youth hostels.
2. Turkey: number of establishments which answered the questionnaire:
        - 525 in 1982 i.e. 59 609 beds.
        - 531 in 1983 i.e. 60 851 beds.
3. United Kingdom: figures apply to England only.
4. Australia: in bed-spaces in hotels and motels with facilities in most rooms.
5. Japan: rates concerning hotels which are members of the "Japan Hotel Association".

A.V.5. STAFF EMPLOYED IN THE TOURISM SECTOR

Country			Date of Census	1982	1983	1984
Austria	- men - women Total	HR	August	44 357 85 114 129 471	46 661 87 510 134 171	47 552 86 836 134 388
	- men - women Total	HR	November	32 537 60 094 92 631	33 311 59 595 92 906	37 959 69 378 107 337
	- men - women Total	HR	average	39 346 73 831 113 177	40 647 75 051 115 698	41 443 74 538 115 981
Belgium (1)	- men - women - total	HR	30th June	.. .. ..	28 073 28 777 56 850	.. .. ..
Finland	- men - women Total	HR	July	10 000 51 000 61 000	17 000 59 000 77 000	15 000 58 000 73 000
	- men - women Total	HR	January	6 000 49 000 55 000	14 000 47 000 61 000	15 000 46 000 60 000
	- men - women Total	HR	average	9 000 47 000 56 000	14 000 50 000 64 000	14 000 52 000 65 000
France (2)	- men - women Total	H	average	62 896 64 808 1127 704	63 063 65 714 128 777	.. .. ..
	- men - women Total	R	average	84 166 56 844 141 010	89 331 60 644 149 975	.. .. ..
	- men - women Total	V	average	7 318 10 735 18 053	7 111 10 803 17 914	.. .. ..
	- men - women - total	A	average	250 150 400	250 150 400	.. .. ..
	- men - women - total	O	average	111 359 133 925 245 284	108 872 130 885 239 757	.. .. ..
Germany - of which foreigners	- men - women Total	HR	average		268 200 389 800 658 000 155 400	.. ..
Greece (3)	Total	H	average	35 000	35 000	50 000
Iceland	Total	H V O VO	average	830 250 3 120 4 200	.. ..	.. ..
Norway	- men - women Total	HR	1st and 4th quarter average	11 000 29 000 40 000	13 000 29 000 42 000	13 000 32 000 45 000
Netherlands (4)	- men - women Total	H	31st March	9 800 7 200 17 000	9 000 7 200 16 200	9 600 8 100 17 700
	- men - women Total	R	31st March	17 100 12 400 29 500	18 800 12 600 31 400	18 700 13 200 31 900
	- men - women Total	V	31st March	1 900 2 600 4 500	2 300 3 200 5 500	2 300 3 400 5 700
Portugal	- men - women Total	HR	31st July	18 006 15 513 33 519	17 202 15 415 32 617	17 335 15 564 32 899
	- men - women Total	HR	31st January	15 751 12 104 27 855	15 255 12 489 27 744	15 076 12 118 27 194

Country			Date of census	1982	1983	1984
Sweden	- men	HR	2nd and 3rd quarter average	26 400	24 800	28 500
	- women			47 100	45 400	54 000
	Total			73 500	70 200	82 000
- of which foreigners				13 800	13 800	15 000
	- men	HR	1st and 4th quarter average	27 000	26 600	29 500
	- women			49 800	46 800	49 000
	Total			76 800	73 400	78 500
- of which foreigners				13 200	13 400	15 000
Switzerland	Total	HR	average	177 100	175 100	..
- of which foreigners				64 700	66 300	..
Turkey (5)	Total	HR	31st December	..	63 681	76 082
	Total	V	31st December	1 032	1 251	1 275
	- men	A	31st December	691	758	724
	- women			534	583	562
	Total			1 225	1 341	1 286
- of which foreigners				2	4	4
	Total	O	31st March	724	995	1 150
United Kingdom (6)	- men	H	September	108 900	110 400	114 700
	- women			173 500	182 400	188 200
	Total			282 400	292 800	302 900
	- men	H	March	85 300	87 100	89 500
	- women			141 300	136 700	146 500
	Total			226 600	223 800	236 000
	- men	R	September	69 600	69 400	71 600
	- women			116 600	116 900	118 400
	Total			186 200	186 300	190 000
	- men	R	March	64 700	61 700	65 800
	- women			111 400	99 500	113 000
	Total			176 100	161 200	178 800
	- men	O	September	266 700	284 200	273 800
	- women			426 100	425 800	443 600
	Total			692 800	710 000	717 400
	- men	O	March	258 100	256 600	262 400
	- women			411 900	404 700	417 700
	Total			670 000	661 300	680 100
Canada (7)	- men	HR	last week in September	135 800	132 666	..
	- women			367 000	141 900	..
	Total			277 700	499 666	..
	- men	HR	last week in January	128 300	..	..
	- women			136 200	..	..
	Total			264 500	249 200	..
	Total	A	average	5 725	..	..
Australia	- men	H	December	26 780	31 540	29 500
	- women			42 540	42 330	44 500
	Total			69 320	73 870	74 000
	- men	A	December	45	55	55
	- women			30	45	45
	Total			75	90	90
	Total	O	December	268 605	..	..

Staff employed in: H = hotels   V = travel agencies
                         R = restaurants   A = national tourism administrations
                         HR = hotels and restaurants   O = other sectors of tourist industry

1. Belgium: workers subject to social security contributions.
2. France: concern only permanent jobs. A = représentations abroad and regional tourist offices.
3. Greece: statistics from Hotel Employees Insurance Fund. Total persons employed in the tourism branch amounted to 310 000 in 1983 (of which 65 000 directly employed).
4. Netherlands: according to the new definition of employed persons: 1984 includes jobs of less than 15 hours a week.
5. Turkey: V = minimum number of persons which travel agencies (central and local offices) have to employ. A includes regional (637) and foreign (39) tourism administrations. Foreigners represent staff employed with a special contract. O = tourist guides whose licences have been renewed.
6. United Kingdom: O = "pubs", bars, night clubs, licensed clubs, librairies, museums, art galleries, sports and other recreational services.
7. Canada : HR = hotels, restaurants, taverns employing 20 persons or more; change in the coverage since April 1983. A = National Parks staff (provincial and federal).

A.V.6. TRENDS IN TOURISM PRICES

Per cent

Country		1979/78	1980/79	1981/80	1982/81	1983/82	1984/83
Austria	H	..	..	7.0	7.7	6.3	3.7
	R	..	..	5.8	5.8	4.3	6.1
	T	..	..	7.9	6.1	4.2	5.1
	C	..	..	6.8	5.4	3.3	5.6
Finland (1)	H	12.0	13.0	15.0	16.0	15.0	7.0
	R	6.0	14.0	14.0	11.0	12.0	7.0
	T	8.0	13.0	9.0	7.0	10.0	7.0
	C	8.0	12.0	12.0	9.0	9.0	7.1
France	H	13.4	15.6	18.1	14.5	..	..
	R	12.7	14.2	14.6	13.1	..	..
	T	..	..	..	..	..	..
	C	10.8	13.6	13.4	11.8	9.6	7.3
Germany	H	7.1	7.7	8.4	7.5	4.7	2.7
	R	5.1	5.1	6.0	5.2	3.3	2.5
	T	5.3	8.6	9.0	6.1	4.8	2.9
	C	4.1	5.5	5.9	5.3	3.3	2.4
Greece	H	15.0	19.0	19.0	20.0	20.0	12.0
	R	..	..	..	..	..	..
	T	..	..	..	..	..	..
	C	19.0	24.9	24.5	20.9	20.5	17.6
Iceland	H	..	..	..	..	..	..
	R	..	..	..	..	..	..
	T	..	..	..	..	..	..
	C	45.5	58.5	50.5	54.0	81.4	29.1
Ireland	H	17.3	..	15.0	..	..	..
	R	16.2	..	..	..	..	..
	T	..	..	..	..	..	..
	C	13.3	18.2	20.4	17.5	9.7	8.5
Italy (2)	H	19.0	26.6	26.3	18.3	19.3	15.8
	R	17.3	23.7	20.2	18.2	16.0	11.8
	T	15.2	23.3	21.7	18.8	16.5	10.8
	C	14.8	21.2	17.8	16.5	14.9	10.9
Netherlands (3)	H	..	..	8.0	6.0	3.0	1.0
	R	..	..	5.0	6.0	4.0	4.0
	T	..	..	..	..	..	..
	C	..	..	6.7	5.9	2.8	3.3
Norway (4)	H	4.0	10.4	15.0	19.5	15.6	9.4
	R	8.4	10.0	22.2	20.5	10.7	5.1
	T	5.3	12.0	..	..	..	..
	C	6.4	8.0	13.6	11.3	8.4	6.2
Portugal (5)	H	..	33.0	29.0	15.0	22.0	..
	R	..	20.0	27.0	27.0	57.0	13.0
	T	..	..	..	..	..	..
	C	23.9	16.6	20.0	22.4	25.5	29.3
Spain (6)	H	28.7	28.8	16.7	24.7	13.0	..
	R	..	..	..	..	..	..
	T	20.2	17.2	15.6	17.7	15.6	..
	C	15.6	15.4	14.6	14.4	12.1	11.3

A.V.6. TRENDS IN TOURISM PRICES *(Continued)*

Country		1979/78	1980/79	1981/80	1982/81	1983/82	Per cent 1984/83
Sweden (7)	H	14.2	22.4	18.2	11.3	16.8	12.4
	R	8.8	13.3	11.6	12.9	13.2	11.8
	T	..	..	..	..	..	..
	C	9.8	14.3	9.7	10.0	9.3	8.0
Switzerland (8)	H	2.9	4.5	7.3	8.3	5.1	6.2
	R	2.0	3.5	6.0	6.6	3.8	2.8
	T	..	..	..	..	..	..
	C	3.6	4.0	6.5	5.7	2.9	2.9
Turkey (9)	H	25.0	88.0	70.0	61.0	50.0	50.0
	R	..	10.0	25.0		50.0	55.0
	T	..	..	..	..	50.0	..
	C	56.7	116.5	35.9	27.1	28.0	52.8
United Kingdom (10)	H	21.0	25.0	26.0	15.0	8.9	13.4
	R	17.0	20.0	8.0	8.0	6.5	7.5
	T	12.0	26.0	13.0	9.0	6.4	6.4
	C	13.0	18.0	12.0	9.0	4.6	5.0
Canada (11)	H	8.1	13.2	16.3	16.3	5.7	4.2
	R	12.1	8.8	9.6	10.2	5.7	4.1
	T	9.3	12.7	15.9	14.0	5.5	5.0
	C	9.1	10.1	12.5	10.8	5.7	4.4
Australia (12)	H	11.3	11.3	12.0	10.3	5.9	8.4
	R	..	..	9.6	10.8	8.4	0.1
	T	..	..	..	..	9.1	3.5
	C	9.2	10.2	11.3	11.0	8.6	2.6
Yugoslavia (13)	H	19.2	22.8	29.8	44.4	27.3	48.6
	R	..	..	..	..	..	..
	T	..	..	..	..	..	..
	C	20.4	30.3	40.7	31.7	40.9	53.2

Average increase of: H: hotel prices T: travel price index
R: restaurant prices C: consummer price index (CPI)

1. Finland: H = hotels, R = food, T = transportation and communications.
2. Italy: T = hotels, restaurants and public establishments (bars, night clubs, sea-side resorts....).
3. Netherlands: H = Price of a night spent in an hotel, R = Price of a certain number of typical expenses made in bars and restaurants (cup of coffee, fruit drinks, beer, jenever, croquette, fried potatoes, several hot meals, ham roll, ice cream).
4. Norway: H = approved hotels and boarding houses, R = restaurants and cafés.
5. Portugal: H = hotels of from 1 to 5 stars, R concerns Lisbon only.
6. Spain: H takes into account the types of accommodation presented in the official guide.
7. Sweden: position at December every year. H = hotel room, R = meals not taken at home (lunch, dinner, coffee with bread, hot sausage with bread).
8. Switzerland: H = hotels and similar establishments. R is estimated.
9. Turkey: H = hotels, motels, inns, boarding houses, holiday villages, thermal resorts. R = first and second class restaurants. In 1983 H and R = freely determined prices approved by the Ministry of Culture and Tourism. C concerns the city of Ankara only.
10. United Kingdom: H = all holiday accommodation in the United Kingdom. R = meals and snacks including take-away. T = accommodation, meals, snacks, food, alcohol, tobacco, durable household goods, clothes, footwear, motoring and cycling fares, entertainment and other services.
11. Canada: H = hotels and motels. R = food purchases for restaurants, T calculated from domestic tourist spending patterns only.
12. Australia: position, every fourth quarter of each year. H = change in the price of a room in hotels, motels and similar establishments. R = change in the price of meals taken outside home and take-away food (one component of the CPI). C = weighted average of eight State capital cities. T = air, bus and rail fares, hotel, motel and caravan park charges, package tours.
13. Yugoslavia: H = all categories of hotel charges on a full pension basis.

OECD SALES AGENTS
DÉPOSITAIRES DES PUBLICATIONS DE L'OCDE

ARGENTINA – ARGENTINE
Carlos Hirsch S.R.L., Florida 165, 4° Piso (Galería Guemes)
1333 BUENOS AIRES. Tel. 33.1787.2391 y 30.7122

AUSTRIA – AUTRICHE
OECD Publications and Information Center
4 Simrockstrasse 5300 Bonn (Germany). Tel. (0228) 21.60.45
Local Agent/Agent local :
Gerold and Co., Graben 31, WIEN 1. Tel. 52.22.35

BELGIUM – BELGIQUE
Jean De Lannoy, Service Publications OCDE
avenue du Roi 202, B-1060 BRUXELLES. Tel. 02/538.51.69

CANADA
Renouf Publishing Company Limited/
Editions Renouf LimitéeHead Office/Siège social – Store/Magasin :
61, rue Sparks Street,
OTTAWA, Ontario KIP 5A6
Tel. (613)238-8985. 1-800-267-4164
Store/Magasin: 211, rue Yonge Street,
TORONTO, Ontario M5B 1M4
Tel. (416)363-3171
Regional Sales Office/
Bureau des Ventes régional :
7575 Trans-Canada Hwy., Suite 305,
SAINT-LAURENT, Québec H4T 1V6
Tél. (514)335-9274

DENMARK – DANEMARK
Munksgaard Export and Subscription Service
35, Nørre Søgade
DK 1370 KØBENHAVN K. Tel. +45.1.12.85.70

FINLAND – FINLANDE
Akateeminen Kirjakauppa
Keskuskatu 1, 00100 HELSINKI 10. Tel. 65.11.22

FRANCE
Bureau des Publications de l'OCDE,
2 rue André-Pascal, 75775 PARIS CEDEX 16. Tel. (1) 524.81.67
Principal correspondant :
13602 AIX-EN-PROVENCE : Librairie de l'Université.
Tel. 26.18.08

GERMANY – ALLEMAGNE
OECD Publications and Information Center
4 Simrockstrasse 5300 BONN Tel. (0228) 21.60.45

GREECE – GRÈCE
Librairie Kauffmann, 28 rue du Stade,
ATHÈNES 132. Tel. 322.21.60

HONG-KONG
Government Information Services,
Publications (Sales) Office,
Beaconsfield House, 4/F.,
Queen's Road Central

ICELAND – ISLANDE
Snaebjörn Jönsson and Co., h.f.,
Hafnarstraeti 4 and 9, P.O.B. 1131, REYKJAVIK.
Tel. 13133/14281/11936

INDIA – INDE
Oxford Book and Stationery Co. :
NEW DELHI-1, Scindia House. Tel. 45896
CALCUTTA 700016, 17 Park Street. Tel. 240832

INDONESIA – INDONÉSIE
PDIN-LIPI, P.O. Box 3065/JKT., JAKARTA, Tel. 583467

IRELAND – IRLANDE
TDC Publishers – Library Suppliers
12 North Frederick Street, DUBLIN 1 Tel. 744835-749677

ITALY – ITALIE
Libreria Commissionaria Sansoni :
Via Lamarmora 45, 50121 FIRENZE. Tel. 579751/584468
Via Bartolini 29, 20155 MILANO. Tel. 365083
Sub-depositari :
Ugo Tassi
Via A. Farnese 28, 00192 ROMA. Tel. 310590
Editrice e Libreria Herder,
Piazza Montecitorio 120, 00186 ROMA. Tel. 6794628
Costantino Ercolano, Via Generale Orsini 46, 80132 NAPOLI. Tel. 405210
Libreria Hoepli, Via Hoepli 5, 20121 MILANO. Tel. 865446
Libreria Scientifica, Dott. Lucio de Biasio "Aeiou"
Via Meravigli 16, 20123 MILANO Tel. 807679
Libreria Zanichelli
Piazza Galvani 1/A, 40124 Bologna Tel. 237389
Libreria Lattes, Via Garibaldi 3, 10122 TORINO. Tel. 519274
La diffusione delle edizioni OCSE è inoltre assicurata dalle migliori librerie nelle
città più importanti.

JAPAN – JAPON
OECD Publications and Information Center,
Landic Akasaka Bldg., 2-3-4 Akasaka,
Minato-ku, TOKYO 107 Tel. 586.2016

KOREA – CORÉE
Pan Korea Book Corporation,
P.O. Box n° 101 Kwangwhamun, SÉOUL. Tel. 72.7369

LEBANON – LIBAN
Documenta Scientifica/Redico,
Edison Building, Bliss Street, P.O. Box 5641, BEIRUT.
Tel. 354429 – 344425

MALAYSIA – MALAISIE
University of Malaya Co-operative Bookshop Ltd.
P.O. Box 1127, Jalan Pantai Baru
KUALA LUMPUR. Tel. 577701/577072

THE NETHERLANDS – PAYS-BAS
Staatsuitgeverij, Verzendboekhandel,
Chr. Plantijnstraat 1 Postbus 20014
2500 EA S-GRAVENHAGE. Tel. nr. 070.789911
Voor bestellingen: Tel. 070.789208

NEW ZEALAND – NOUVELLE-ZÉLANDE
Publications Section,
Government Printing Office Bookshops:
AUCKLAND: Retail Bookshop: 25 Rutland Street,
Mail Orders: 85 Beach Road, Private Bag C.P.O.
HAMILTON: Retail: Ward Street,
Mail Orders, P.O. Box 857
WELLINGTON: Retail: Mulgrave Street (Head Office),
Cubacade World Trade Centre
Mail Orders: Private Bag
CHRISTCHURCH: Retail: 159 Hereford Street,
Mail Orders: Private Bag
DUNEDIN: Retail: Princes Street
Mail Order: P.O. Box 1104

NORWAY – NORVÈGE
J.G. TANUM A/S
P.O. Box 1177 Sentrum OSLO 1. Tel. (02) 80.12.60

PAKISTAN
Mirza Book Agency, 65 Shahrah Quaid-E-Azam, LAHORE 3.
Tel. 66839

PORTUGAL
Livraria Portugal, Rua do Carmo 70-74,
1117 LISBOA CODEX. Tel. 360582/3

SINGAPORE – SINGAPOUR
Information Publications Pte Ltd,
Pei-Fu Industrial Building,
24 New Industrial Road N° 02-06
SINGAPORE 1953, Tel. 2831786, 2831798

SPAIN – ESPAGNE
Mundi-Prensa Libros, S.A.
Castelló 37, Apartado 1223, MADRID-28001, Tel. 275.46.55
Libreria Bosch, Ronda Universidad 11, BARCELONA 7.
Tel. 317.53.08, 317.53.58

SWEDEN – SUÈDE
AB CE Fritzes Kungl Hovbokhandel,
Box 16 356, S 103 27 STH, Regeringsgatan 12,
DS STOCKHOLM. Tel. 08/23.89.00
Subscription Agency/Abonnements:
Wennergren-Williams AB,
Box 30004, S104 25 STOCKHOLM.
Tel. 08/54.12.00

SWITZERLAND – SUISSE
OECD Publications and Information Center
4 Simrockstrasse 5300 BONN (Germany). Tel. (0228) 21.60.45
Local Agents/Agents locaux
Librairie Payot, 6 rue Grenus, 1211 GENÈVE 11. Tel. 022.31.89.50

TAIWAN – FORMOSE
Good Faith Worldwide Int'l Co., Ltd.
9th floor, No. 118, Sec. 2,
Chung Hsiao E. Road
TAIPEI. Tel. 391.7396/391.7397

THAILAND – THAILANDE
Suksit Siam Co., Ltd., 1715 Rama IV Rd.,
Samyan, BANGKOK 5. Tel. 2511630

TURKEY – TURQUIE
Kültur Yayinlari Is-Türk Ltd. Sti.
Atatürk Bulvari No : 191/Kat. 21
Kavaklidere/ANKARA. Tel. 17 02 66
Dolmabahce Cad. No : 29
BESIKTAS/ISTANBUL. Tel. 60 71 88

UNITED KINGDOM – ROYAUME-UNI
H.M. Stationery Office,
P.O.B. 276, LONDON SW8 5DT.
(postal orders only)
Telephone orders: (01) 622.3316, or
49 High Holborn, LONDON WC1V 6 HB (personal callers)
Branches at: EDINBURGH, BIRMINGHAM, BRISTOL,
MANCHESTER, BELFAST.

UNITED STATES OF AMERICA – ÉTATS-UNIS
OECD Publications and Information Center, Suite 1207,
1750 Pennsylvania Ave., N.W. WASHINGTON, D.C.20006 – 4582
Tel. (202) 724.1857

VENEZUELA
Libreria del Este, Avda. F. Miranda 52, Edificio Galipan,
CARACAS 106. Tel. 32.23.01/33.26.04/31.58.38

YUGOSLAVIA – YOUGOSLAVIE
Jugoslovenska Knjiga, Knez Mihajlova 2, P.O.B. 36, BEOGRAD.
Tel. 621.992

Les commandes provenant de pays où l'OCDE n'a pas encore désigné de dépositaire peuvent être adressées à :
OCDE, Bureau des Publications, 2, rue André-Pascal, 75775 PARIS CEDEX 16.

Orders and inquiries from countries where sales agents have not yet been appointed may be sent to:
OECD, Publications Office, 2, rue André-Pascal, 75775 PARIS CEDEX 16.

68837-08-1985

OECD PUBLICATIONS, 2, rue André-Pascal, 75775 PARIS CEDEX 16 - No. 43367 1985
PRINTED IN FRANCE
(78 85 01 1) ISBN 92-64-12760-7